Our Landless Patria

*Marginal Citizenship and Race
in Caguas, Puerto Rico, 1880–1910*

Rosa E. Carrasquillo

UNIVERSITY OF NEBRASKA

LINCOLN AND LONDON

Library of Congress Cataloging-in-Publication Data
Carrasquillo, Rosa E.
Our landless patria : marginal citizenship and race in
Caguas, Puerto Rico, 1880–1910 / Rosa E. Carrasquillo.
p. cm.
Includes bibliographical references and index.
ISBN-13: 978-0-8032-1537-5 (cloth : alk. paper)
ISBN-10: 0-8032-1537-1 (cloth : alk. paper)
ISBN-13:978-0-8032-2070-6 (paper : alk. paper)
1. Social stratification—Puerto Rico—Caguas.
2. Land tenure—Government policy–Puerto
Rico—Caguas. 3. Privatization—Puerto Rico—
Caguas. 4 Peasantry—Puerto Rico—Caguas—
Social conditions. 5. Citizenship—Puerto
Rico—Caguas. 6. Caguas (P.R.)—
Race relations. I. Title.
HN240.Z9S63 2006
306.2'097295–dc22
2005021555

Set in Sabon by Kim Essman.
Designed by R. W. Boeche.

Our Landless Patria

A Papi y Mami por su amor incondicional y por enseñarme el valor del trabajo . . .

A mis hermanas y hermanos por su hermosa humanidad . . .

Contents

Illustrations

Acknowledgments

The beauty of history and of writing history is partaking in the human collective experience. I am very fortunate and thankful to engage in these enterprises with the support, help, and encouragement of many wonderful human beings. It is impossible to appropriately thank and name all of them here, but hopefully they will find their positive imprints in this book. Most conspicuously, Karen Spalding, my graduate advisor and friend, has been inspirational, encouraging quality work and high standards. Other professors at the University of Connecticut also read earlier versions of the manuscript, among them, Blanca Silvestrini, Paul Goodwin, Susan Porter-Benson, and Sam Martínez. Elizabeth Mahan read various versions of the manuscript and offered valuable suggestions and insights. Her willingness and enthusiasm for my work have given me new strength and confidence. While in graduate school, my life was greatly enriched by good conversations, lively intellectual debates, and generous humor shared with fellow graduate students and friends, especially Hilda Lloréns, Ricardo Pérez, Luis Gabriel Villaronga, Adam Pagán, José Solá, and Onek Adyanga.

At the Archivo Histórico Municipal de Caguas, I found not only a huge amount of information but also a terrific group of people who made my work there so much easier. Marta Villaizán and Karín Cardona, former directors, facilitated my task enormously. The current director, Juan Acevedo, always goes the extra mile to accommodate my multiple petitions and needs. He shares a professional commitment to the completion of this work. I could not have written this book without his help and that of the invaluable workers and friends in the Archivo: Raquel, Juan David Hernández, and Millita (her fascinating stories must be amusing people in heaven). Father John Gauci, former director of the Redemptorist Archives of San Juan, facilitated my research with his guidance and friendship. Father Gauci welcomed me and treated me like family.

I am also thankful for the opportunity that Trinity College in Hartford, Connecticut, extended me with the Ann Plato Fellowship. That year gave me precious time to dedicate myself to write in the most convenient, intellectual environment. I also had the privilege to discuss my work with professors Luis Figueroa, Dario Euraque, and others. I found a similar setting at Assumption College. The Departments of History and Foreign Languages warmly welcomed me, supporting my research project in various ways. My colleagues at the history department at Assumption College have shown me a new level of commitment to research and academic excellence. Their support is priceless.

Finally, my family has always encouraged me with their love and unconditional support. My sisters Ceci and Blanca and my niece Laurita Zayas corroborated various details in the archives for me. My husband, Phil, read various versions of the manuscript, and his love, patience, and humor sustained me in the hardest moments. To all of you, my love.

Introduction
No Ground to Rest

For years Felipe Tirado and his family lived in Barrio Borinquen, working the land that was the base of their daily sustenance. They knew the color and smell of the soil as they walked, harvested, tilled, and ploughed every inch of their sharecropped farm. But in 1880 the owner of the farm, Pantaleón María Colón, asked Tirado to gather his things and depart with his family. Tirado refused to leave, for he had poured into that soil not only his and his family's sweat but also his emotions and a part of himself. Colón put the whole value of the soil on his title of ownership and, in August 1881, contacted the police to evict Tirado and his family from the farm. When Tirado still refused to leave, Colón asked the police a second time to evict Tirado from his property.[1] There is no other mention of this case in the archives, but it seems that Tirado was, in fact, thrown off his farm. According to the 1882 census, Tirado remained in the barrio but was no longer a sharecropper. He was forced to look for another way to make a living and became a day laborer.[2]

This case is representative of land privatization in late-nineteenth-century Puerto Rico. Both parties justified their position with legal principles—Colón citing his title of ownership and Tirado citing his right of use. Tirado's refusal to leave the farm was more an assertion of long-standing legal principles than a challenge to authorities, and although the authorities in Puerto Rico eventually reinstituted use as a legitimate, albeit limited, claim to land, in this case the system favored Colón because of his title of ownership.

By examining the process of land privatization in Caguas, Puerto Rico, in the last decades of the nineteenth century and the early twentieth century, this book discusses how the rural poor compelled the government to recognize and protect what they considered to be their basic rights. "Land privatization" refers to the process by which land titles were formalized, which was manifested at every social level in the countryside, and to the

resulting loss of access to land by those who were unable to formalize titles
of ownership, as happened to Felipe Tirado. Beginning with the Mortgage
Law of 1880, the process of land privatization unleashed a series of nego-
tiations for natural resources between the poorest sectors of society and
the landed elite, who greatly influenced the municipal government. After
1880 people from the upper class, large landowners in particular, organized their lives and government according to land access and agrarian
wealth. Even though agrarian wealth had been part of large landowners'
lives before that time, it acquired an unprecedented significance because
the new law of land privatization reinforced its relevance.

In Puerto Rico land ownership traditionally had guaranteed citizenship
and had been the most common indicator of status. Land accumulation
epitomized elites' desires for social control and political power.[3] There
was not enough land to satisfy the needs of all, not to mention the greed
of the landed elite, and the geographic limitations of the small island first
affected those in the poorest sectors of society, as they were forced to seek
a respectable livelihood apart from land ownership.[4] Seeking to establish
a person's capacity to work as an alternative source of legal identity, they
put in motion a series of civil claims that protected people's mobility rights
and access to land. In the end, these civil claims broke the constraining
bubble of the landed elite, and though the process of land privatization
affected the poor negatively, their claims to mobility rights and access
to land popularized a mechanism to fight for a more egalitarian society
in which land was not the only determining factor for social well-being.
They sought a *patria* (nation or fatherland) for the landless, or a landless
patria for all.

A landless patria for all also meant breaking with racial barriers and
color lines. The Mortgage Law of 1880, which officially ignited the process of land privatization, was issued seven years after the abolition of slavery (1873). Not coincidentally, land privatization targeted former slaves,
their descendants, and, in general, people of color. Specifically, the law
was intended to bar former slaves and their descendants from obtaining
a formal title to a piece of land. Thus, the accumulation of land in private
hands had the twofold effect of enriching the elite and asserting white
privileges over the colored population. In this sense land ownership was
not only a symbol of status and a requisite of citizenship but also the
basis of elites' ideological and political power. Controlling the land and
its accumulation was, in part, an ideological and practical extension of the
world of slavery and its racial divisions. Elites' worldview became very
narrow as people of color asserted their mobility rights and developed

alternatives to access land. The U.S. invasion of the island also challenged elites' social and political control, giving some civil liberties to people of color.

The scope of this book extends to the early 1900s and the inception of U.S. colonialism on the island. After 1898 many of the popular demands for equality found their way into the legal system as the U.S. colonial government put new pressures on local elites and restructured the government and economy. Although literacy and property holding were required for voting, the rural poor continued to demand social equality through labor organization. They joined labor organizations and political parties and expected social justice from a democratic nation like the United States. These labor organizations voiced some of their concerns and advocated for greater political representation. In part because of such tactics, the U.S. government granted universal male suffrage in 1904.

The Country, Its Space, and Its Peoples

Reviewing the vast literature on Latin American peasantry is beyond the scope of this discussion. I will turn instead to a brief discussion of recent works that link peasants, politics, and issues of citizenship, focusing on peasant political culture.[5]

Recent studies attempt to reconstruct peasant political culture by examining peasant consciousness of social conflict and interchange with elites and non-peasant groups in the context of the larger society—even the international arena—and within specific historical periods.[6] Most of these studies define peasant political culture through analysis of gender, generation, race, class, and ethnicity. They demonstrate that peasant political culture was not merely informed by and forged in reaction to elite political culture, but rather it actually contributed to the creation of elite and "formal" political culture.[7] For example, the emergence of popular liberalism in some Latin American countries illustrates how elites achieved political power only after negotiating with popular sectors and incorporating multiple popular demands.[8] The discussion also examines the process of nation formation and its outcome and focuses on political discourses of class, gender, and race that were fought over and negotiated among rural populations, the state, and upper classes.[9] This literature describes nationalism as a conglomerate of different political projects that were elaborated by peasants and non-peasants or as a language recognized and shared by all social sectors within a specific society and manipulated in various ways by local and national interests.[10] These studies analyze the nation-state as the product of the struggles over such nationalism(s) or manipulations of national discourses.[11]

In *Our Landless Patria*, I apply recent theoretical and methodological studies of peasant political culture developed in Latin American scholarship to the agrarian history of Puerto Rico and the Caribbean. For the most part, studies of Caribbean peasants have focused strictly on economic and family issues.[12] Peasant studies in Puerto Rico have linked agrarian history with modernization projects from the late nineteenth century to the 1960s. In the first half of the twentieth century, such studies emphasized modernization as modeled on the economic growth and industrialization of the United States. These scholars, mostly North Americans, conceptualized the Puerto Rican countryside as an obstacle to modernization in economic, cultural, and social terms. They viewed rural areas as being in need of major intervention in order to achieve a healthy development and believed poverty justified any intellectual or state intervention into the lives of rural peoples in Puerto Rico.[13] The eradication of poverty became a civil and legal concern for intellectual and colonial authorities, who associated poverty with earlier forms of agrarian production.[14]

As part of the revisionist attempts to understand agrarian unrest in Latin America in the 1970s and the 1980s, intellectuals, mostly from Puerto Rico, produced a new series of studies of rural peoples on the island. Highly influenced by the Annales School, these studies focused mostly on the nineteenth century and on the rural populations of the western Puerto Rican countryside and the coast—areas dominated by the production of coffee and sugar. However, this scholarship stressed only some aspects of the socio-economic structures of rural societies, specifically class formation and the processes of peonization and proletarianization.[15] Moreover, the few studies of the twentieth century consider only landholders.[16] Additionally, while this literature did attempt to recognize women as part of history, it focused on the urban population.[17]

Since the 1990s practitioners of the new cultural history have examined important elements of the mentalities of rural Puerto Ricans. Francisco Scarano analyzes the ways in which Puerto Rican Creole writers in the late eighteenth and early nineteenth centuries defined national identity and defied colonial policies by using the trope and the language of the rural poor (the *jíbaro*, or peasant).[18] Lillian Guerra echoes Scarano's analysis for a later period. She proposes that Puerto Rican intellectuals of the late nineteenth and early twentieth centuries imagined a nation whose membership was defined by both whiteness and Hispanism. Elites used the jíbaro as a symbol of this imagined nation and as a myth to protest their oppression under U.S. colonialism. Guerra maintains that popular masses concomitantly developed discourses of national and communal identity that expressed a more egalitarian worldview than the one imagined by the elites. Women, coloreds, and outlaws were accepted members within this community of the masses.[19]

While these studies are fascinating and innovative, they focus on literary works.[20] I will follow their lead but emphasize instead real people and their actions as a source of meaning and interpretation. As Mary Kay Vaughan suggests, the study of local history might be one of the soundest methods to write cultural history: "As a method, local history may be more effective than trying to read popular consciousness and culture across regions because it contextualizes meaning and action. Specificity becomes the vehicle for comparison."[21] As Paul E. Lovejoy puts it, "transformations always occur in context, which is inevitably local."[22]

Local history provides a basis for analyzing not only the cultural images of and about rural populations but also the specific material and political contexts that contain those images. By analyzing culture, politics, and material conditions at the local level, my study of the rural populations of Caguas, a town south of San Juan (see map 1), tries to avoid what Michael Kearny calls "bipolar structures" through which peasants have been studied. Kearny argues that the concept of the peasantry emerged as a category of analysis in the mid-twentieth century in an attempt to prolong the life of a threatened bipolar thought—classic anthropology's binary notion of primitive versus civilized. The peasant concept served to maintain that line of thinking by simply changing the equation to peasant versus modern. Bipolar structure still informs studies of the countryside today, but I think that we cannot simply discard such binaries because they were recreated and incorporated into the political agendas of nation-states and colonies and their projects of controlling and containing rural populations.[23] By representing peasants in a category of their own, state official policies often denied them basic civil rights. But as more and more people claimed individual rights, country people ascertained their status as citizens. Their claims to citizenship in the local context constituted a new understanding of civil rights based on a combination of old principles and new circumstances.

Marginal Citizenship: A New Perspective

Recreating any aspect of daily life in the past is difficult, but the task is especially daunting when examining citizenship issues. It is very hard to find historical data on autonomous legal identities because in day-to-

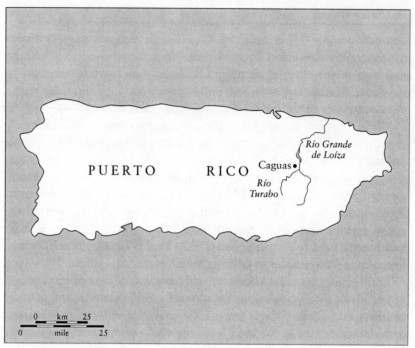

Valley of Caguas, Puerto Rico

day life, as Elizabeth Jelin explains, "subordinated social sectors tend to consider their subordination as 'normal,'" and "a naturalizing view of social hierarchy predominates."[24] However, many people's actions contradicted what was thought of as normal behavior, challenging both social hierarchies and social subordination. Thus, people's actions within the legal system represent the best window available to study perceptions of what was right and what was unacceptable because in Puerto Rico, as in colonial Latin America, the judiciary and the administrative branches were not clearly separated under Spanish rule; therefore, the legal system was central in administration. As Charles Cutter concludes for colonial Mexico, "Spanish subjects from all stations sought to articulate their identities in juridical terms; that is, they sought to construct plausible legal identities."[25] In Caguas, people also sought resolution to conflicts within the legal system, building their identities in legal terms because the local courts were readily accessible to the majority of the population, including marginalized sectors such as free people of color.[26] Also, voting and holding political office were the prerogative of a wealthy few, as discussed in chapter 2, leaving local courts as the only viable alternative for the majority of the population. Local courts became true forums of claims for popular justice because in them the landed elite's influence was limited. Judges responded directly to the mayor and the governor, as they did in other areas of Latin America, rather than to local elites.[27] Since the late eighteenth century, the Spanish Empire in the Americas gave priority to restricting the power of local elites in the judicial system and named Spanish judges who were mostly foreigners to the locality.[28] This was the case in Caguas, where judges were outsiders to the town and had little connection with the local elites. Therefore, the law and the court were central to claims of citizenship. This trend continued after 1898 and was solidified by U.S. authorities in an effort to democratize justice on the island. In 1908 the governor of Puerto Rico, Regis H. Post, emphasized the significance of municipal courts because they were "essentially the courts of the poor people, where the great mass of small cases involving their property and social relations are disposed of."[29]

Because citizenship's definitions and uses in the Western tradition have been analyzed elsewhere, I refer only briefly to those elements that directly apply to the case of Puerto Rico.[30] Generally, modern citizenship entails a system of rights, mainly civic, political, and social. Civic rights refer to individual freedom and are usually related to a court system. The political aspect of citizenship entails participation in the exercise of political power. The social part of citizenship "is made up of a right to the prevailing standard of life and the social heritage of the society."[31] Citizenship also "presupposes authority," because it implies a relationship between rulers and those who are ruled.[32] In this sense, rulers and ruled are bound by the recognition of authority, either by representing authority itself (i.e., holding office) or by accepting it. This link is usually described in political theory as high and low citizenship. High citizenship refers to an ideal relationship in which each citizen has equal opportunity to rule, as the political community is an aggregate of equals. Low citizenship accepts inequality among the members of the political community, crystallizing empirical forms of citizenship; it is also described as "chastened" or second-class citizenship.[33] In its empirical interpretation, low citizenship offers an opportunity to analyze the ways laws and government work in practice, but because of its different meanings and uses, I introduce the phrase "marginal citizenship" to describe the concrete, historical example of citizenship in late-nineteenth- and early-twentieth-century Caguas.

My phrase borrows from low citizenship its efforts to measure citizenship as it takes shape in reality but is distinguished from low citizenship because marginal citizenship does not connote negative or victimized aspects of marginality. Rather, it entails action and inaction from the margins of society to fully participate in the social and, by extension, the political arenas, searching for access to resources and power. But because, by definition, margins imply limits or borders, I will focus on a smaller geographic sphere rather than view marginality in the whole island of Puerto Rico. I chose Caguas because its location south of the capital, San Juan, is literally at the margins of the center of power and because of its multiple similarities with many other areas of Puerto Rico. Partially influenced by its diverse geography, Caguas encapsulates a number of historical processes that occurred throughout Puerto Rico on a smaller scale. For this reason, some historians have called Caguas a mini-Puerto Rico.[34] More important, most people on a day-to-day basis live localized lives so that Caguas and its inhabitants, Cagüeños, offer a perfect setting to study marginal citizenship. To avoid repetitions, this book discusses mainly the case of Caguas, referring occasionally to Puerto Rico when clearly specified.

Marginal citizenship did not form part of written law or mainstream culture but depended completely on individuals who used the courts to challenge powerful opponents. It did not focus on attaining political representation either through office holding or voting but rather sought social and economic ends. Public office was out of reach for the majority of the population because of money—holding office did not pay a salary—and because the majority of Puerto Ricans were poor and illiterate, disqualifying them as voters. The most common way to guarantee voting rights and office holding was landownership, which proved difficult for the majority to obtain. Therefore, most Cagüeños sought to achieve immediate gains, such as informal access to land and the right to move around in order to maintain a livelihood.

The main strategy of marginal citizenship was evasion, even though this represents the antithesis of citizenship in traditional studies. "Evasion" here refers to "avoidance protest," coined by Michael Adas to express the ways in which "dissatisfied groups seek to attenuate their hardships and express their discontent through flight, sectarian withdrawal, or other activities that minimize challenges to or clashes with those whom they view as their oppressors."[35] This form of protest has been either ignored or condemned by modern governments in Latin America, although in recent decades the development of civil society has been a major concern for governments, political organizations, and intellectuals of Latin American countries.[36] Most of their efforts deal with the active participation of citizens, and they regard inaction or apathy as an obstacle to civil society.[37] Cagüeños demonstrated, however, the possibility of developing a civic culture based on avoidance of government laws that were regarded unfair by the majority of the population. Because Puerto Rico was a densely populated colony by the late nineteenth century, evasion of authorities en masse represented an effective strategy to challenge Spanish and U.S. authorities. If the majority of the population did not obey a legal order, it became practically ineffective. Evasion of legal ordinances that were regarded as unfair by the majority transformed the legal system into a matter of consensus and tradition, despite its colonial character. In practice, unjust ordinances were disobeyed.

"Marginal" also describes the social status of the promoters of this type of citizenship; the poorest people in the countryside enacted and practiced a marginal citizenship. This statement might seem a radical departure from studies of civil culture and citizenship because of its focus on the countryside. The prevalent emphasis on urban living and cities had led many to ignore what was happening in the rural areas. As David Montgomery, in *Citizen Worker*, concludes for the case of the United States, civic consciousness materialized first among working people in urban America as they fought for the ten-hour day, male suffrage, abolition of imprisonment for debt, and equal and universal education. Like Montgomery's, studies of civic culture tend to emphasize the city as the cradle of civility.[38] However, I argue that it was among the poorest sectors of rural society that a series of claims to social and legal equality developed in Puerto Rico mainly to defend the inviolable right of a person to live decently. After all, the great majority of Puerto Ricans lived in the countryside.

Marginal citizenship seems more progressive than the version of citizenship offered by liberals in Puerto Rico and classic liberals around the world. Elizabeth Dore affirms that classic liberals in Latin America, as elsewhere, "promoted freedom of property, not freedom of persons." They sought, adds Dore, land privatization and often organized forced labor systems relying on "first, the ideology that Indians, mulattos, blacks, and peasants in general were primitives who had to be forced out of their natural laziness into the world of work; [and] second, the material reality that, in the absence of a market in labor power, the landed elites had to use overt violence to recruit and discipline a labor force if they were going to enrich themselves from export agriculture." [39] In contrast, marginal citizenship often confronted the landed elite by promoting freedom of persons and the abolition of social hierarchies before the law. [40] Because marginal citizenship opposed the landed elite and did not form part of the written code, it materialized only in praxis.

The practical belief that everyone is entitled to eat, work, and move freely to make a living formed the core of marginal citizenship. This idea is clearly part of natural law—the claim that each person deserves to live appropriating from earth what she or he needs—and enjoyed communal understanding because it grants to everyone, without social distinctions, the right to live and use resources. It also serves as an ethical code to judge those who create social unbalance and hunger by taking too much from nature and the majority of people. This sense of community gave substance to the rural poor's claims to their own labor, time, and leisure. As Jelin states, "It is the sense of community that promotes that consciousness of being a subject with the right to have rights. The civic dimension of citizenship is anchored in the subjective feelings that unite or bind a community, in contrast to the seemingly more rational elements of civil and social rights." [41] The transformation of the belief in natural law into practice, using the courts to challenge powerful opponents, and evasion of authorities became the engine for the development of a civic culture that considered living a right for everyone despite socio-economic differences. The lowest social sectors of the countryside emphasized natural law to justify their access to property; theoretically this interpretation is closest to Locke's understanding of natural law. Locke believed that each person rightfully can only appropriate what he or she needs to survive and that every person has also a natural-law-binding interest in his or her own person and labor. In this sense, the civil law is "valid insofar as it conforms to the law of nature."[42] Hence, many people gave credence to land occupation and evasion and sought confirmation in the established law.

Natural law does not necessarily oppose privatization but rather certain elements such as excessive accumulation and disregard for the human community. Both natural law and privatization, however, strongly identify land with the individual. As J. G. A. Pocock states:

> *Since about 1700, when the juristic ideal of citizenship seemed to have attained theoretical completeness; the nature of property—of the person's interaction with the world of things—began to change and to be seen as changing. It had been known as "real property," the possession of an inheritable tenure in land, and this in turn was based on a process of appropriation very closely associated with arable cultivation. Humans appropriated the earth, and in so doing became persons and citizens, because they ploughed it and exchanged its fruits.*[43]

Within natural law, labor and property are inseparable because labor justifies appropriation and labor is intrinsic to a person. Poor people, after all, did not reject private property for subsistence but opposed the rich who clearly owned more than they could use. Also, many believers in natural law owned property and were interested in establishing an equal standing with those who owned even more in order to protect their few belongings. The issue here is what gave property its value—either the title of ownership, as large landowners suggested, or the labor poured into working the land, as the poor would argue. The concept of natural law was not alien to Spanish law; in fact, it remained part of the Spanish legal system from the Middle Ages to the late nineteenth century.[44] The poor made sure that Spanish authorities did not discard this principle by constantly invoking it in order to access resources and evaluate human behavior, rejecting what seemed unfair to the majority even when it was enacted as a law. Interpretations of land use and rights were also translated into the arena of human behavior. Natural law was used to measure fair and unfair treatment and self-worth in the social and legal spheres, and marginal citizenship developed as a consequence.

Marginal citizenship had its limits, however. Because it borrowed extensively from established policies and elitist ideals, in particular the patriarchal family and the subordination of women, it maintained a very conservative stand and could not effectively transform the social and political privileges of elite white men.[45] Marginal citizenship continued after 1898 with the change of sovereignty on the island, as many of its claims were incorporated into the legal system throughout the twentieth century. Mobility rights, for instance, were guaranteed for every Puerto Rican after 1898, and in the 1910s organized labor, in particular trade unionism, took the flag of marginal citizenship and demanded social equality for all rural laborers.

This study begins with a brief description of the social, economic, and political landscape of Caguas at the end of the nineteenth century and the early twentieth century (chapter 1). It continues with an in-depth view of the local political scene of Caguas by examining the municipal law of 1878, with an emphasis on low-ranking officials (chapter 2). Chapter 3 analyzes the social and cultural effects of land privatization for the majority of the population in Caguas, where people developed alternatives to the strictest notion of private rights by using natural law to gain access to land. Natural law was also the basis for the multiple challenges to forced labor and the struggles to obtain mobility rights, which is the focus of chapter 4. The discussion concludes in chapter 5 with an analysis of the meanings of a marginal citizenship for women in the countryside of Caguas.

Our Landless Patria

Mapping Caguas, Mapping the Country
The Political and Economic Bases of Citizenship

Caguas was a "typical" town in the sense that the majority of its population lived in the countryside and that its population was socially stratified according to land ownership. Caguas shows a pattern of land use characteristic of rural capitalism that illustrates social and political differences among people. Wealthy men owned the most fertile soil in the valley, while the landed peasantry usually occupied the most mountainous and least valued territory. These differences were expressed in the political life of nineteenth-century Puerto Rico as state officials differentiated between city and country, between citizens and laborers.

Origins of Caguas

In the early days of Spanish colonization in the Americas, Spaniards mispronounced the Arawak name of Caguax, a cacique who ruled the northeastern part of Puerto Rico. Spaniards called him Caguas, which later became the name of the region.[1] Beginning in 1508 Spaniards traveled from Caparra (today's San Juan area and the first Spanish settlement in Puerto Rico) to the south, reaching the valley of Caguas in order to acquire agrarian products. As in the rest of the Caribbean, indigenous people were soon wiped out in Caguas, and in 1625 the Spanish Crown gave a land grant, comprising Caguas and adjacent territory, to Don Sebastián Delgado de Rivera for his services in the colonization of the island.[2]

Delgado de Rivera and his family constructed their house and exploited the land in the valley. His children and grandchildren married and lived in the region. The original land grant was divided among Delgado de Rivera's descendants. For instance, he gave his daughter, Doña Domitila Delgado Manso, land to live on when she married Don Tomás de Castro, for whom Barrio Tomás de Castro was named. Delgado de Rivera's descendants continued subdividing the land among their offspring, but they were not the only settlers of the region. Many workers, slaves, and sharecroppers also moved into the region, as did white families from Spain and the Canary Islands, from the seventeenth century on. Although the land had been granted to Delgado de Rivera, people lived on and cultivated it without any legal or political obstacle.

Semi-nomadic agriculture allowed poor white families, runaway slaves, and poor colored families to make a living from the land without much intervention from the government. Peasant settlers obtained the majority of their food from the land and were the subjects of many government officials' complaints. This way of living continued unchanged for generations.[3] Black, mulatto, and white peasant settlers interacted with each other, sharing every aspect of life, including sex. The mulatto population became a numerical majority. Juan David Hernández, Caguas historian, estimates that by 1873, 8,196 Cagüeños were mulatto (and *pardo*, or people of color of the lightest skin color), 4,747 were white, and 961 were black (523 slaves and 438 free).[4]

In the early nineteenth century, another wave of European migration arrived on the island. The wars of independence in Spanish America forced wealthy Spaniards and Creoles to resettle in areas loyal to Spain, particularly the Caribbean. Between 1815 and 1820 thirty-one of these loyal families established their residency in Caguas.[5] Don Antonio Grillo, for instance, moved from Venezuela to Caguas in the 1820s. He established his family there and soon became part of the political life of the region. Don Grillo benefited from Spanish policies to improve the economic life of the island by offering land grants.[6] Most beneficiaries of the 1815 immigration policies were Europeans who brought slaves with them to work the land. The population of Caguas increased considerably in the early nineteenth century. Fray Iñigo Abbad in 1782 visited Caguas and calculated that there were 722 inhabitants. Caguas had 6,422 inhabitants by 1819 and 7,585 by 1842.[7]

In 1855 the road from Caguas to San Juan was finished, augmenting the volume of travelers and commercial interchange. Previously the trip took days, but with the new road it was a matter of hours, facilitating commercial production of sugar, tobacco, and coffee on a larger scale than before.[8] The population of Caguas had increased to 11,835 inhabitants by 1882 and to 19,857 by the end of the century.[9]

Caguas's Views: Valley and Mountains

The valley Caguas occupies, averaging 3 to 4 miles in width and with a total area of 42.5 square miles, is one of the largest on the island and borders the municipalities of Gurabo, Juncos, and San Lorenzo (see map

1). Until approximately the 1950s the valley offered the richest soil in Caguas, with an annual average rainfall of 60 inches.[10] Barrios Bairoa and Cañabón had the largest share of the valley (see map 2).[11]

The valley is bordered on the north by a narrow fringe of humid foothills with elevations of 600 to 1,000 feet. Barrios Río Cañas and San Antonio occupy most of these northern hills (see map 2). The humid mountains to the south of the valley represent the largest part of Caguas and continue to the Sierra de Cayey. These mountains average approximately 900 feet in height, but in the Sierra de Cayey elevations of 1,800 to 2,100 feet are common. The mountains contained Barrios San Salvador, Borinquen, and Beatriz. Barrios Cañaboncito, Turabo, and Tomás de Castro were mostly mountainous with some flat areas (see map 2). The soil of these hilly and mountainous areas was inferior to that of the valley, but both hills and mountains received more annual rain. In the hills the annual precipitation averaged seventy inches, and the mountains received from seventy to ninety inches or more, depending on elevation and exposure.[12]

In the late nineteenth century farmers who owned land in the valley exploited commercial agriculture to a larger extent than farmers of other areas mostly because of better roads, easier access to the downtown area of Caguas, and superior quality soil. In general, the valley was divided into big farms that were owned by the wealthiest men in the region. Large landowners produced tobacco, sugar, and meat to export to the capital. In 1860 the *ayuntamiento* (municipal government) of Caguas informed the governor that Barrio Cañabón was the richest barrio in the municipality, as measured by the level of production of commercial agriculture.[13] Because large landowners dominated commercial agriculture, their presence in a barrio served to measure wealth in any particular barrio. There were farms in Barrio Cañabón of over 1,000 *cuerdas* between 1880 and 1900 (see appendix A).[14] In 1880, for example, Don Pascual Borrás had a farm of 1,400 cuerdas in Barrio Cañabón.[15] Large landowners also maintained a constant presence in other barrios, such as Turabo, Beatriz, and Borinquen.

Commercial agriculture constituted a modest sector of the economy in the hills and mountains of Caguas in the late nineteenth century, while subsistence agriculture represented its main economic activity. The hills had "infernal roads," as described by Luciano Santos, which made transportation to the downtown almost impossible.[16] In this inhospitable environment, intermediary rural sectors and the landed peasantry made a home. In the ayuntamiento report of 1860, Barrio Quebrada Puercos

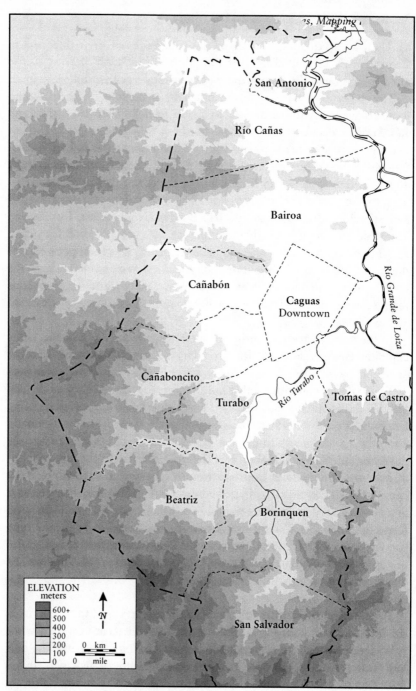

San Antonio

Río Cañas

Bairoa

Cañabón

Caguas
Downtown

Río Grande de Loíza

Cañaboncito

Turabo

Río Turabo

Tomas de Castro

Beatriz

Borinquen

ELEVATION
meters

600+
500
400
300
200
100
0

N

0   km   1

0   mile   1

San Salvador

Topographical and Political Divisions of Caguas

(later San Antonio) was the poorest and least inhabited barrio of Caguas and had no farm larger than two hundred cuerdas (see appendix A).[17]

In the twentieth century, many landowners in the valley became independent sugar producers (*colonos de caña*). Others dedicated their farms to the production of tobacco for commercial use, installing cigar factories in the downtown.[18] The landscape of Caguas became characterized by commercial agriculture, where some made large profits and others sweated in the heat for miserable wages.[19] Sugar and tobacco fields alternated with pasture, the basis of the small dairy industry. By the end of the 1930s there were thirty-seven small dairies, making Caguas the dairy center of the island.[20] In the second half of the twentieth century, urbanization projects (middle-class housing) covered the valley with cement. Today, the valley is a conglomeration of houses, one after another, interrupted by malls and stores of all kinds.

Concomitantly, mountain farmers in the twentieth century started growing tobacco as a cash crop along with their fruits and vegetables, eventually replacing subsistence crops with tobacco. The introduction of tobacco was minimal for farmers in the hills, who continued subsistence farming as their major economic activity.[21] The incorporation of tobacco as a cash crop in the countryside of Caguas corresponded to a crisis in Puerto Rican rural society that started around 1911 and has been attributed to the economic and social pressures of U.S. capitalism in the island.[22] The low tobacco prices depressed the income of many peasant families by the early 1930s.[23] Increasingly pauperized, many farmers in these areas were forced to try other economic activities to make a living. In the 1950s and 1960s a large number sold or lost their land and migrated to the cities: Caguas, San Juan, New York, or the Connecticut Valley.[24] Those who stayed combined agriculture with working in the new industries created by Operation Bootstrap (or state-led industrialization).[25]

However, there were pockets in the hills and mountains where the landed peasantry continued a lifestyle based on traditional farming.[26] Today, these pockets of peasant farming are practically extinct. The mountains have undergone a process of urbanization similar to most areas of the Caribbean, characterized by minimal food production and a decline of commercial agriculture.[27] This urbanization of the countryside has also been described as "reverse migration," referring to the development of suburbialike housing in the mountains.

In contemporary Puerto Rico, reverse migration often symbolizes personal achievement and monetary success. The house that the popular merengue singer Olga Tañón bought in Barrio Turabo in the late 1990s stands in contrast to the houses of her neighbors for whom, even after years of struggle, poverty is a day-to-day reality. When Tañón throws a big party other Puerto Rican celebrities and important public figures bring their glamour, their makeup, and their expensive cars to the mountain. Some Turabo residents are hired to help run the festivities, and Tañón generously invites a few other neighbors. The event becomes part of local talk for months to come, and the news spreads to the United States by phone.

Return migration has contributed to the accelerated urbanization of recent years, which has blurred the spatial distinctions between country and city. An extensive net of paved roads links all corners of the island. The island resembles a tropical forest covered by a thick cobweb of metal, concrete, and pollution. Motor vehicles, cable TV, radios, computers, and antennas are as popular in the mountains as they are in the valley. Thus living in the country does not represent an obstacle for most people who commute daily to their non-agricultural jobs. In spite of this obvious urbanization, the area that once was "country" (mostly the mountains) continues to be thought of as rural by everyone. Likewise, the expansion of the city today does not preclude the essentialism of past concepts of city versus rural, for people still consider the downtown the center of city life, or at least the center of the municipal government. Present notions of country and city evoke past cultural notions of space that go back to the beginnings of Spanish colonization in Puerto Rico and in the Americas.[28] According to Angel Rama, Spanish cities in America became "focal points of ongoing civilization." The plazas surrounded by the city hall, the Catholic church, various commercial stores, and the residences of important political figures became the architectural emblems of political, religious, commercial, and social power.[29]

Rama's description of the plaza or downtown was still valid for late-nineteenth-century Caguas and for Puerto Rico in general. The downtown area of Caguas was the center for market and government transactions for country people of all social classes. Like cities in England before the nineteenth century, the town of Caguas grew as an "aspect of the agricultural order itself," as part of the changes within the rural society.[30] From the late nineteenth century to the early twentieth century, numerous workshops in downtown Caguas manufactured tobacco and cigars in particular.[31] As late as the early 1950s, rural and industrial activity in Caguas was still largely confined to processing and distributing agricultural products.[32]

Despite this interdependency, state officials contrasted the order of the plaza with the nature and culture of the rural populations. The plaza

1. A busy street in Caguas (author's collection)

and its surroundings were located in the middle of the valley of Caguas (see map 2). For state officials, hills and mountains were obstacles to the progress that was being fostered in the valley, specifically the downtown city life, and this way of thinking had repercussions on the political life.

The Economic Pull: Life and Resources in Caguas

In the late nineteenth century, the Puerto Rican economy was rooted in an agrarian capitalism oriented to the production of export crops and

Table 1.1.   Cuerdas of land planted by crop in Caguas and Puerto Rico, 1897

Crop	Caguas	Puerto Rico
Sugar	607	61,498.23
Coffee	303	122,399.76
Tobacco	132	4,264.07
Grass	20,957	127,537.55
Subsistence crops	788	93,511.08
Other crops	92	16,277.23
Wood and forest	12,334	—
Total	35,213	—

Source: Coll y Toste, *Reseña del estado social, económico, e industrial*, 8 and 91.

was characterized by an increasing privatization of the land and of the labor force.[33] The production of sugar and coffee took a relatively large area of the island's territory. In 1897, for example, Puerto Ricans planted 122,399.76 cuerdas of land with coffee and 61,498.23 cuerdas with sugar (see table 1.1). The commercial production of sugar and coffee might serve as an indicator of capitalist social relations in the late nineteenth century. However, there were regional differences in spite of the relatively small area of the island. The economy of the western part of Puerto Rico presented earlier and more pronounced signs of capitalist development than the eastern part. Coffee production and the world of *haciendas* dictated social relations in the west, while sugar production and factorylike sugar mills (*centrales*) dominated the landscape on the coasts (see map 1). In these regions, concentration of land ownership in the hands of a few was more common than in the eastern interior of Puerto Rico. Jorge Seda Prado argues that municipalities of the eastern interior formed part of a particular economic structure, characterized by a large peasant sector. In this area, export-oriented agriculture represented a marginal sector of the economy. The eastern interior lacked large farms. Peasants had secured and maintained access to the land. With their own and their families' labor, peasants cultivated the land, raised cattle, or both. Yet this produc-

Table 1.2.   Rural and urban population in Caguas and Puerto Rico, 1899

	Caguas		Puerto Rico	
	Population	Percent	Population	Percent
Total	19,857		953,243	
Rural	14,407	72.55	814,540	85.45
Urban	5,450	27.45	138,703	14.55

Sources: Departamento de la Guerra, *Informe sobre el censo de Puerto Rico, 1899*, 162; and U.S. Bureau of the Census, *Thirteenth Census of the United States*, 3:1183.

Table 1.3. Rural and urban population in Caguas and Puerto Rico, 1910

	Caguas		Puerto Rico	
	Population	Percent	Population	Percent
Total	27,160		1,118,012	
Rural	16,806	61.88	893,392	79.91
Urban	10,354	38.12	224,620	20.09

Source: U.S. Bureau of the Census, *Thirteenth Census of the United States*, 3:1183 and 1185.

tion was linked to the local markets, where peasants exchanged part of their produce for goods not produced on their farms.[34]

Seda Prado includes Caguas within the economic structure of the eastern interior. However, the economy of Caguas showed characteristics in the late nineteenth century common to both the west and east of Puerto Rico, setting the patterns of land tenure of Caguas outside the categories of east and west.[35]

During the period under study (1880–1910), most Cagüeños, like most Puerto Ricans, lived in the countryside. By 1878 less than 20 percent of the total population of Caguas lived in urban areas, and by the end of the century the percentage was still almost identical (27.45 percent) (see table 1.2).[36] In 1910 the rural population of both Caguas and Puerto Rico still represented a large majority, 61.88 percent of Cagüeños and 79.91 percent of Puerto Ricans (see table 1.3). Rural Cagüeños and Puerto Ricans depended on the land to make a living. In 1882 occupations directly related to agriculture, day laborers, sharecroppers, and farmers constituted 93.72 percent of the working population in the rural barrios of Caguas (see table 1.4). According to the U.S. Census of 1899, 71.43 percent of the working population of Caguas worked in agriculture, fishing, or mining. Occupational patterns for most Puerto Ricans mirrored those of Caguas; 62.83 percent of the Puerto Rican working population that year engaged in agriculture, fishing, and mining (see table 1.5).

Although the majority of people made a living from the land, patterns of land tenure in Caguas and other areas of Puerto Rico were highly diversified. While there was an important presence of large landowners in Caguas, most owners held smaller farms (see appendix B).[37] In fact, the farms of more than half of the landowners were 30 cuerdas or smaller; about one-fourth of the farms were 31 to 70 cuerdas; and about one-sixth were 71 to 199 cuerdas. Despite differences in the number of tax bills for country land (*planillas de riqueza agrícola*), the pattern seems consistent between 1880 and 1900. Based on the number of small farms, the landed peasantry in Caguas constituted a permanent sector of the population,

Table 1.4.   Number of workers by occupation in the rural barrios of Caguas, 1882

Occupation	Workers	Percentage
Jornalero (day laborer)	1,436	58.85
Labrador (sharecropper)	542	22.21
Farmer/property owner	309	12.66
Launderer	37	1.52
Merchant	24	0.98
Seamstress	20	0.82
Cashier	19	0.78
Cook	10	0.41
Artisan	9	0.37
Teacher	5	0.20
Industrial worker	5	0.20
Carpenter	5	0.20
Mason	3	0.12
Maid	3	0.12
Overseer	2	0.08
Butcher	1	0.04
Writer	1	0.04
Not working	9	0.37
Total	2,440	

Source: AHMC, SEC Secretaría, SSEC Archivo, SER Censos, SSER Habitantes, 1882–83, C26.

maintaining access and title to the land despite large landowners' greed and interest in obtaining more land and despite even the law of land privatization that clearly favored the rich. After 1880 more people acquired titles of land, and the number of small farms increased steadily. In 1881 there were 210 small farms in Caguas, representing 53.03 percent, 331 (58.27 percent) by 1896, and the number rose to 341 small farms (58.19 percent) in 1900. While the number of small farms increased, the territory remains practically the same. In 1881 small farms occupied 3,343.25 cuerdas, or 12.32 percent of the registered rural property, increasing slightly to 4,583 cuerdas (13.76 percent) by 1896 and to 4,708.5 (12.49 percent) by 1900 (see tables 1.6–8). On average, small farms were becoming smaller. While in 1881 the average small farm was 15.92 cuerdas, a small farm averaged 13.85 cuerdas in 1896 and 13.80 cuerdas in 1900. This period thus witnessed a progressive parcelization of the land, a process that intensified under U.S. rule.

Many more Cagüeños secured title to a piece of land after 1898, taking advantage of a new U.S. colonial measure that facilitated the formalization of property titles. In 1899, as an effort to promote individual property at every level, the U.S. colonial government issued an ordinance that reduced

Table 1.5. Occupational categories in Caguas and Puerto Rico, 1899

	Caguas		Puerto Rico	
	Number of workers	Percent	Number of workers	Percent
Working population	6,140	100	316,365	100
Agriculture, fishing, mining	4,386	71.43	198,761	62.83
Commerce, transportation	476	7.75	24,076	7.61
Manufacture, industries	460	7.49	26,515	8.38
Professional services	44	0.72	2,194	0.69
Domestic and personal services	774	12.61	64,819	20.49

Sources: Departmento de la Guerra, *Informe sobre el censo de Puerto Rico, 1899*, 286 and 298.

the number of years of proven use required to formalize titles of land from thirty to ten. In addition the new colonial government exempted from taxes any farm valued at less than $100 as well as these farms' tools and production.[38] In 1900 there were 341 Cagüeños who owned farms of 30 cuerdas or less, and yet their territory was not too much larger than in 1881. The landed peasantry controlled 4,708.5 cuerdas of land or 12.49 percent (see table 1.8). The trend of smaller farms continued, and by 1910 farms of 49 acres (47.6 cuerdas) or less constituted 78.25 percent of the land farm in Caguas (see appendix B). The price of land after the U.S. occupation of the island increased considerably, from about thirty dollars to three hundred dollars per acre, inducing "many a small holder to sell his land and join the ranks of the laborers."[39]

The persistence and survival of the landed peasantry, albeit impressive in harsh circumstances is not indicative of what happened to the majority of the lower classes in the rural barrios of Caguas. In fact, small farmers in 1882 (about 235) represented 2.72 percent of the rural population in Caguas, and by 1899 their numbers remained practically the same (about

Table 1.6. Number of farms by size and area, 1881

	Number of farms		Area of Farms	
Size (cuerdas)	Farms	Percent	Cuerdas	Percent
0.25–30	210	53.03	3,343.25	12.32
31–70	97	24.49	4,482.75	16.52
71–199	66	16.66	7,634.75	28.14
200–400	13	3.28	2,818	10.39
401 and over	10	2.52	8,854.5	32.63
Total	396	100	27,133.25	100

Sources: AHMC, SEC Finanzas, SSEC Contribuciones, SER Planillas de Riqueza, SSER Agrícola, 1880–81, C80, C81.

Table 1.7. Number of farms by size and area, 1896

Size (cuerdas)	Number of farms		Area in Farms	
	Farms	Percent	Cuerdas	Percent
.25–30	331	58.27	4,583	13.76
31–70	118	20.77	5,816	17.46
71–199	88	15.49	10,365	31.12
200–400	22	3.87	5,086.5	15.27
401 and over	9	1.58	7,453	22.38
Total	568	100	33,303.5	100

Sources: AHMC, SEC Finanzas, SSEC Contribuciones, SER Planillas de Riqueza, SSER Agrícola, 1896, C95.

337, or 2.33 percent; see appendix B).[40] While a title of ownership measured formal access to land, it neither indicated its informal counterpart, which was prevalent in the rural barrios of Caguas, nor accounted for the hundreds of landless laborers. Changes in the number of day laborers across time might suggest a reorganization of land resources at the local level, which is exactly what happened in Caguas. In 1882 day laborers represented 16.62 percent (1,436) of the rural population, while in 1899 they constituted 30.44 percent (4,386).[41] Thus, the percentage of rural laborers almost doubled, indicating clearly the effects of land privatization. More and more people lost access to land and were forced into wage labor. The law of land privatization precisely attempted to eliminate informal access to land in order to improve the numbers and "quality" of workers, and judging by the increased number of rural laborers, the law was successful in this aspect.

The ways in which the land was used also reflect the fact that Caguas does not conform to the east-west divide. In 1897, for example, subsistence agriculture, mostly corn, rice, tubers, and plantains, occupied 788

Table 1.8. Number of farms by size and area, 1900

Size (cuerdas)	Number of farms		Area of Farms	
	Farms	Percent	Cuerdas	Percent
.25–30	341	58.19	4,708.5	12.49
31–70	114	19.45	5,700.5	15.12
71–199	97	16.55	11,125	29.52
200–400	23	3.92	6,640.5	17.62
401 and over	11	1.87	9,517	25.25
Total	586	100	37,691.5	100

Sources: AHMC, SEC Finanzas, SSEC Contribuciones, SER Planillas de Riqueza, SSER Agrícola, 1880–1900, C99–100.

cuerdas of land, while 607 cuerdas were used for sugar, 303 for coffee, 132 for tobacco, and 20,957 for grass. Commercial crops—sugar, coffee, and tobacco—accounted for a little more than subsistence crops (1,042 cuerdas). However, cattle raising represented a major avenue of commercial agriculture as represented by the land dedicated to grass (see table 1.1). Many large landowners sold meat to the capital. Meat suppliers needed a license from the municipal government, which created opportunities in Caguas for the development of a quasi-monopoly. First, authorities regularly punished any person who killed any farm animal without a license.[42] Second, licenses were obtained at public auction, but often the council granted special permits that depended on the solicitor's ability to influence the council. For example, Pedro Zoilo Solá, in 1882, solicited permission to supply meat in Barrio Borinquen. He had obtained a temporary permit for a month and in October reapplied for a permanent position. When the motion was discussed in the council, the first person to advocate in his favor was his brother, Celestino Solá, who was supported by his friends.[43] Eventually, Zoilo Solá became a regular meat supplier and a zealous observer of the law, reporting those who killed animals without the license.[44]

As the large percentage of land dedicated to commercial agriculture reveals, Caguas large landowners held a significant share of the wealth and political influence in Caguas. Between 1880 and 1900, there were a few landowners in Caguas with estates of over 401 cuerdas (see appendix B). Though they were few in numbers, large landowners controlled a significant amount of the territory. In 1881, for example, ten individuals had farms of over 401 cuerdas; together they owned 8,854.5 cuerdas of land, or 32.63 percent of the territory registered as rural property (see table 1.6). In 1896 nine Cagüeños had title of ownership to 7,453 cuerdas, or 22.38 percent of the registered land. After the U.S. occupation of the island, large landowners continued to dominate a large part of the territory (see table 1.7).[45] In 1900 eleven large landowners controlled 9,517 cuerdas, or 25.25 percent of rural property. From 1881 to 1900 large farms with over 401 acres acquired a very small portion of the territory (662.5 cuerdas). In comparison, more modest farms of 200 to 400 cuerdas gained a significant percentage of the territory. In 1881 these farms occupied 2,818 cuerdas (10.39 percent), increasing to 5,086.5 cuerdas (15.27 percent) in 1896 and to 6,640.5 cuerdas (17.62 percent) in 1900 (see tables 1.6–8).

Large landowners relied heavily on rural laborers and sharecroppers to develop their land. The significance of rural laborers and sharecroppers is not immediately obvious in the archives because they were often hired

Table 1.9.   Number and percentage of farm owners and tenants by race, 1910

	White	Percentage	Black and non-white	Percentage
Farm Owner	531	60.41	151	17.18
Tenant	158	17.97	39	4.44
Total	689	78.38	190	21.62

Source: U.S. Bureau of the Census, *Thirteenth Census of the United States*, 7:1001.

through informal, verbal contracts. However, it is possible to reach an estimate of how many sharecroppers and day laborers lived and worked in Caguas. According to the census of 1882, there were 1,436 *jornaleros*, or day laborers, in the rural barrios of Caguas, who constituted 58.85 percent of the working population. As the term suggests, jornaleros worked for a daily wage. The second largest group were *labradores*, or sharecroppers (see table 1.4). Literally, *labrador* means a person who plows for his or her own benefit. Historically, in Spain, labradores did not own land but rather a plow team. Their level of success cultivating the land varied enormously.[46] Moreover, jornaleros and labradores often shared social positions as many labradores hired themselves for part of the year and some jornaleros owned land. For example, the census of 1882 identifies 309 farmers or property owners, but this figure is slightly different from the tax records, which note 383 property owners (see appendix B). Some 74 property owners must have identified themselves as either jornaleros or labradores or lived in the downtown (which was common among a very small number of families of the landed elite). Nonetheless, the term *labrador* gives an idea of how many people farmed for their own benefit, without necessarily owning the land.[47]

The persistence of sharecroppers throughout the nineteenth and twentieth centuries suggests that they were an important part of the population, whose rights and ideals were often caught between landowners and rural laborers, the subject of chapter 3. Sharecropping was preferred to salaried labor by many Cagüeños because of the physical and cultural constraints imposed by the latter, to be detailed in chapter 4. In 1910, 197 Cagüeños rented land for cultivation, either by paying with cash (85) or with a share (112). Tenants, who represented 22.1 percent of all farmers, cultivated about 8,091 acres.[48] The census of 1910 also gives an idea of the racial profile of farmers and sharecroppers, who were mostly identified as white (78.38 percent). Blacks and mulattoes were drastically underrepresented in landownership (17.18 percent) and tenancy (4.44 percent), while they represented the majority of the population as mentioned before (see table 1.9). The limitations imposed by slavery, forced labor, and the laws of land privatization account for their unequal access, as discussed in detail in chapter 4.

The Political Space of Marginal Citizenship

While the process of land privatization imposed economic constraints for many Puerto Ricans, colonialism and its project of modernity limited the possibility of political representation and full citizenship for the majority of the racially mixed population. Puerto Rican elites attempted to work with the system in order to get some political benefits and were often successful, but for the majority of the population this possibility was remote. Puerto Rican elites joined metropolitan power in establishing social, economic, racial, and political hierarchies as long as they found themselves at the top of the pyramid. They also aided metropolitan power to force the racially mixed population to work in order to enrich themselves and increase the government revenues. Nonetheless, their situation was also precarious because for the most part Spanish authorities distrusted and excluded them from the highest sphere of government by naming only Spaniards to the most important positions. For this reason, many elite Puerto Ricans found in the municipal government the most important forum available to them, an effective way to influence their surroundings, as will be detailed in the next chapter.

In the late nineteenth century, political changes in Spain created new hopes for political participation for Caguas's and Puerto Rico's elites. The creation of the Spanish Republic of 1868 opened avenues for political expression in Cuba and Puerto Rico, when the Spanish courts accepted colonial representatives. In 1871 the state declared Puerto Rico a Spanish province, giving, at least in theory, citizen status to all Spanish subjects on the island. However, this measure never took effect, and Puerto Ricans lacked the civil and political liberties enjoyed by those born in Spain, known as *peninsulares*, who gathered in Puerto Rico under the Spanish Unconditional Party, founded in 1869.[49]

Puerto Ricans, in particular large landowners frustrated with the civil and political inequalities of their time, organized the island's first liberal party.[50] In 1871 the Puerto Rican Autonomous Party envisioned a larger degree of political autonomy for Puerto Rico under the tutelage of Spain.[51] Creoles initiated what Astrid Cubano-Iguina calls a "mass-party formation," reuniting professionals, landowners, merchants, and powerful administrators under the same party and taking upon themselves the representation of the popular classes in both urban and rural areas.[52] Liberal claims of representing the masses were mostly rhetoric because the Municipal Law of 1878 restricted the suffrage to literate men who were twenty-five years and older and who paid taxes of a minimum of 125 pesetas. The stipulations of the 1878 were more rigorous than earlier laws that set the age of voting at twenty-one and taxes at 25 pesetas.[53] In this way the suffrage restrictions of 1878 made a clear connection between landownership and citizenship because in the countryside only those with land were able to pay that amount of taxes.

Throughout the late nineteenth century, Spanish governors in Puerto Rico disregarded Creole concerns and petitions, making an inhospitable administration for liberals. Luis Muñoz Rivera, one of the liberal leaders on the island, finally proposed a solution to cope with conservative governors in Puerto Rico and the Spanish system: to unite the island's liberal party to the most powerful party in Spain, led by Segismundo Sagasta. The fusion materialized in the last years of the century, which coincided with colonial political reforms. In 1897 Spain declared Puerto Rico and Cuba autonomous states in a late attempt to quell the war for independence in the latter. The autonomy of 1897 provided court representation for Puerto Rico and Cuba, established parliamentary government in the islands, bestowed full citizenship upon Creoles (equal rights for both peninsulares and Creoles), and conferred universal male suffrage. As a result, Muñoz Rivera became the secretary of government in 1898.[54] He headed an impressive campaign throughout the island, registering party sympathizers in every barrio and won municipal elections in most towns on the island.[55]

The electorate increased from 4 to 16 percent of the total population in 1897. But "mass-party formation" had an interesting twist with the intervention of the United States in the island. The U.S. colonial government abolished universal male suffrage until 1904, when the administration realized that in order to defeat Muñoz Rivera's disfavored party, many illiterate men would have to vote.[56] From 1898 to 1904 the U.S. colonial administration limited suffrage to literate men mostly because U.S. authorities considered Puerto Ricans racially inferior and lacking any type of civil culture. The military governor, Brigadier General W. Davis, was concerned about possible "bad results" if universal male suffrage were allowed in Puerto Rico. For Davis most Puerto Ricans were "no more fit to take part in self-government than our reservation Indians," and "far inferior in the social, intellectual, and industrial scale to the Chinese." Davis was convinced that the masses were easily manipulated and did not deserve to vote.[57]

Most large landowners in Caguas were Muñocistas, followers of Muñoz Rivera. They brought to power their clients from business, family, politics, and religion.[58] They remained in power after the U.S. occupation of the island, as Muñoz Rivera's followers dominated municipal elections throughout Puerto Rico.[59] Subsequently, however, the United States took over the financial and legal prerogatives of the municipal government without removing the local land barons from office until at least the mid-1910s. The colonial government reformed the municipalities by stripping them of any significant power and leaving Muñocistas with token control.[60] Nonetheless, the Muñocistas maintained control of the increasingly feeble local government from the late nineteenth century to the mid-1910s in Caguas.

Muñocistas in Caguas and Puerto Rico embraced classic liberalism and the modernizing policies of the Spanish government in the island. Modernization in Puerto Rico was part and parcel of the nineteenth-century liberalism of Europe and Latin America that sought economic growth of the country and justified racial and ethnic inequities in favor of a white minority.[61] I maintain that liberals on the council of Caguas for the most part supported Spanish modernizing policies, albeit often only rhetorically. This notion of modernization is partially opposed to Alvarez Curbelo's proposal that argues that the discourse of modernity in Puerto Rico developed independently of the national state and its institutions. Only through its entrance into the world market did the national state partially help the emergence of the discourse of modernity in Puerto Rico.[62] While this conclusion holds for most of the nineteenth century in Puerto Rico, it does not account for the last two decades of the century. The Spanish state in Puerto Rico advanced an ideology of modernity, progress, and civilization in its administrative practices and procedures. Municipal centralization, on the one hand, was a clear attempt at political modernization. On the other hand, by reorganizing economic resources the state mobilized people and financial resources in order to increase its tax collection.

Officials propagated the idea of progress and applied liberal policies in conjunction with increased state intervention. Teresita Martínez-Vergne explains that for nineteenth-century liberals, the most important element in strengthening the social order was increasing the productive capacity of the individual. However, not all individuals professed a commitment to hard work, affecting the public welfare. Therefore, Martínez-Vergne argues, "only an interventionist state that sought control over every aspect of the nation's welfare could ensure that all individuals enjoyed the benefits of 'the good society' equally."[63] In Puerto Rico propertied classes used the narrative of modernization to present themselves as "natural guides" of the popular masses, excluding their poor countrymen from access to power.[64] In this sense nineteenth-century modernization, sponsored by both state officials and propertied classes, promoted a highly exclusive citizenship whose members were only white men with property.

Under Spanish authority modernity in Puerto Rico served to justify political control and an exclusive citizenship, but the United States sought the transformation of Puerto Rico and its people in order to serve capitalist interests, strengthening corporate liberalism. From the 1880s onward, state and federal courts increasingly gave corporations in the United States "stronger standing as 'natural entities' with contractual and due process rights of persons."[65] Martin Sklar concludes that imperialist countries reproduced capitalist relations with non-industrial societies by establishing "state-to-state relationships" with either a colonial or independent country, "in which the investing country's government adopted the goal of 'modernizing' (or 'civilizing') noncapitalist societies as a matter of state policy," transforming the host country's laws and social relations to achieve this end.[66] The U.S. colonial government in Puerto Rico took it upon itself to transform the living conditions and infrastructure of the island and controlled the political apparatus by appointing U.S. officials to the most important positions within the insular government.

After 1898 business grew hand in hand with the "enterprise of knowledge" in Puerto Rico and Latin America.[67] Modernization under the auspices of the United States in Puerto Rico took the form of a cultural project, in which the ideals of U.S. middle-class educators, hygienists, doctors, and reformers often informed the practices of the government. Politicians and reformers alike used a language that has been described as "the idiom of Improvement," in which the colonial metropolis is presented as a model for the colony.[68] Improvement in practice meant that Puerto Ricans required a period of tutelage and learning before they could govern themselves, before they could become full citizens. The Supreme Court of the United States in 1898 established an important precedent that justified colonialism in the island: Puerto Rico and its inhabitants were property of the U.S. government. As Efrén Rivera Ramos argues: "treating people as property was part of the American political and legal heritage. It was part of the ideological justification of slavery and of the subjugation of women."[69] As property, Puerto Ricans were excluded from full citizen rights, just as they had been under Spanish rule. Both Spanish and U.S. notions of modernity had colonialism as a cornerstone and precluded civic rights for the great majority of the population. Policies of modernization therefore helped define the community of citizens and those excluded from it.[70]

In the late nineteenth and early twentieth centuries, citizenship also had a spatial element; modern citizenship was to be found in the city. As mentioned earlier, the Spanish government measured civilization by the degree of urban living, recreating a bipolar order that counterpoised city versus country, valley versus mountains. This bipolarism reflected in large measure the process of commercial exploitation in the most fertile areas of the island, pushing peasants to the least valued lands, such as hills and mountains.[71] Thus, rural and country were understood as a state-political demarcation of a space (physical and social), a culture, and a people that were different from urban and city forms. As Federica Morelli argues, "[in Latin America] until the nineteenth century, an economic and social space independent of an institutional system was unimaginable."[72] The state in Puerto Rico represented and recreated a bipolar order, city versus country, in its policies, political debates, and public speeches. State policies and governmental organization described a spatial conceptualization of country and city that favored and characterized the city as modern and saw the country as wild, backward, and pre-modern. State officials assumed that the countryside, and for that matter country people, lacked every worthwhile quality of the city, its urban order, civilization, cultural and economic growth, and progress.

In contrast, the municipal government's main office, city hall (*alcaldía*), was centered in the downtown of Caguas. State officials, councilmen, and the mayor worked and often lived in the downtown area. It was not uncommon for wealthy Cagüeños to have a house in the downtown area and another in the countryside. The councilors Modesto Solá, Celestino Solá, and Odón Somonte owned farms in the countryside but lived with their families in the center of town, close to the plaza.[73] Like these councilors, modern citizenship was rooted in urban areas and was to be brought to the countryside by government policies, sometimes only by forcing the majority of the population to labor in commercial agriculture, the subject of chapter 4. Because land ownership was the most common guarantee of citizenship, the great majority of Puerto Ricans were excluded from this small community. Citizenship, as the privilege of a white male minority, needed for its fulfillment the labor of politically excluded individuals of the countryside.

The city of Caguas in the late nineteenth and early twentieth century thus constituted a political representation of power rather than an actual structured place, and it was full of contradictions.[74] First, the boundaries

2. Main street in Caguas (Mawson and Buel, *Leslie's Official History of the Spanish-American War*, 475)

between country and the city were not clearly demarcated. The valley might hold the city, but the city was small and many large and small farms as well as landless peasants were also there. Second, the mountains in Puerto Rico were not excluded from the project of modernization and colonization. In fact, nineteenth-century mountain towns of the Puerto Rican west were the leading producers of cash crops and a major source of government revenues. Third, in Puerto Rico Spanish cities were never an important instrument of colonization.[75] Instead, the plantation colonized the Caribbean.[76] However, city versus country was a spatial reality because state officials ordered social relations and distributed resources accordingly, recreating bipolar political spaces. The countryside was the space for economic production where people with property had to force their subordinates to work. Politically, the countryside was a place that was excluded from political power precisely because it was the opposite of the city, which was the center of power. Therefore, country people who did not participate in the administrative tasks of the municipal government or who did not belong to political parties lacked representation in city life and the center of power. In short, the country was the space of political exclusion.

Even the most progressive thinkers of the period supported this exclusionist civic understanding. Classic liberals in Latin America supported free trade rather than personal freedom and fiercely supported racial and ethnic hierarchies with exploitative and inhumane systems of labor.[77] In Puerto Rico also, liberals, despite their attempt to reach popular sectors, supported a hierarchical order in which elite white males were naturally called to guide the masses to work for society's benefit and progress.[78] Likewise in Caguas, rural laborers, sharecroppers, and part of the landed peasantry were excluded from formal citizenship, in particular, from political representation. However, these sectors of rural society had civic obligations recognized by the state and wealthy Cagüeños mostly in the form of labor. The main objective, then, of modern citizenship was to impose political and civil obligations upon the majority of the population in order to validate the citizenship of wealthy Cagüeños and Puerto Ricans in general. White men with property participated in and dominated formal politics to ensure a political system that supported a citizenship of privilege for the few. For this reason, people belonging to the lowest social classes sought alternatives to formal politics, either by challenging authorities or by relying on the courts to protect their own interests, as discussed in the following chapters.

From Crown to Citizen
Local Politics and Centralization

After the Paz de Zanjón (February 1878) put an end to the Ten Years' War in Cuba, the Spanish Crown attempted to reorganize local governments in its American colonies, Cuba and Puerto Rico. In an effort to restore order, the Spanish Crown issued the Municipal Law of 1878 (May 24), in part because the "peace" treaty did not achieve pacification of the whole island.[1] The new law's primary goals were to centralize administration and tighten control of the rural population. With centralization, the Spanish government sought to undermine the power of local elites and, more important, expand its power to the countryside. During the war in Cuba, the rural population constituted the majority of rebel recruits, offered food and weapon supplies to the revolutionary army, and linked the revolutionary army with civilians. Rural people represented the backbone of the revolution and became the focus of Spanish authorities in their attempt to crush any rebellion. As Ada Ferrer states, after 1878 new municipalities were created in Cuba "so that the power of the colonial state could reach deeper into the countryside and extend its presence to the kinds of small and remote communities that had helped sustain guerrilla war for ten years in eastern Cuba."[2]

The goals of the Spanish Crown were the same for Puerto Rico, even though the possibility of an armed rebellion in Puerto Rico was very remote. In general local elites were loyal to the Spanish Crown. For years they used the council and the municipal government to promote their vested interests in the land, enforcing social and political hierarchies and defining citizenship for a few. The new law, however, threatened their control of the council. The local elites resented this intervention but quickly learned to manipulate the law in their favor. This chapter discusses the municipal government and the 1878 law in order to understand why the majority of Cagüeños did not consider formal politics an option and developed marginal citizenship outside its realms.

The ultimate goal of the municipal law was the control of rural populations through government centralization. In this context, low-rank officials, specifically *comisarios* (sheriffs) and *alcaldes de barrio* (constables), acquired great administrative significance because they brought state power to rural people and the countryside. The effectiveness of the municipal law, as well as any other edict, depended on making comisarios and alcaldes de barrio good state representatives. However, alcaldes and comisarios de barrio were mostly recruited from the lowest social segments of rural society; they were members of the landed peasantry, sharecroppers, and sometimes rural laborers who were often coerced into their administrative positions by the municipal government. This chapter establishes the relationship between land and office holding by investigating the social background of local officials and discusses at length the role these officials played in the operation of the municipal state after the Municipal Law of 1878, focusing primarily on the lowest rank of officials—comisarios and alcaldes de barrio—because ultimately they were the enforcers of Spanish law in the rural areas.

The Roots of the Reform: Municipal Government before 1878

Historically, municipalities in Spanish America were established following the formation of towns, villages, or parishes.[3] Since the eighteenth century, the ayuntamiento had functioned as a legislative and administrative body to regulate local life and local interests on a daily basis. In Puerto Rico, although the *audiencia*, or high court, in San Juan reviewed and evaluated each ayuntamiento's ordinances, the municipalities enjoyed a fairly large degree of administrative and judicial autonomy.[4] Within the municipal government, the judicial and administrative organs were not separate, and the mayor was thereby the head of the municipality directing both the administration and the local courts.[5] Other officials, like councilmen and even comisarios and alcaldes de barrio, also carried administrative and judicial responsibilities.

The most important administrative body of the municipal government was the council (*cabildo* or *concejo*), which was made up of the most important landholders of the area.[6] The council imposed local taxes, supervised the construction of roads and public buildings, administered local hospitals and jails, provided local police, regulated parties and public events, and established and evaluated market prices.[7] The town council also recruited officials to represent the ayuntamiento in the countryside. Comisarios and alcaldes de barrio linked the ayuntamiento with the rural population by publicizing and enforcing state laws, requirements, and demands in remote areas in the countryside. The ayuntamiento depended on the work of comisarios and alcaldes de barrio for daily operation.

From the late eighteenth century to the nineteenth century, the centralizing Bourbons revived town councils as the link between the Spanish Crown and its subjects. The Municipal Law of 1878 followed this tradition, revamping the link between the Crown and the majority of the population in Puerto Rico, who lived in the countryside. The ayuntamiento increasingly responded directly to the office of the governor of Puerto Rico, who had quasi-dictatorial powers over colonial administration.[8] Holding authority over each state official, the governor was the highest colonial official in the island.[9] It was in his interest to name mayors who would facilitate the implementation of Spanish laws.[10]

The Spanish Revolution of 1868 gave new life to Puerto Rican municipal governments by making the position of mayor an elected one without changing the terms of suffrage. The monarchy was restored in 1875, but despite the short life of the liberal republic, enough changes were made in Puerto Rico that it was impossible to return to the status quo ante. For instance, until 1870 there were only three municipalities in the island— San Juan, Ponce, and Mayagüez. The Municipal Law of 1870 permitted Puerto Ricans to create new municipalities, requiring a minimum of two thousand *vecinos*, or male household heads, to establish a municipality. As a result most towns in Puerto Rico became municipalities after 1870.[11] The broadening of municipal organization was not synonymous with increasing municipal autonomy; on the contrary, the laws of 1870 and 1878 strengthened the governor's control over municipal affairs. In 1878 the goal was clearly to tie country people to the Crown, eliminating any possible obstacle posed by local politicians' influence.

The law of 1878 gave the Crown-appointed governor of the island the authority to name the mayor, who was charged with ensuring compliance with Spanish laws at the municipal level. The governor also had the power to intervene in municipal finances.[12] Inevitably, this meant that the mayor was more likely to represent the governor than local interests. Frequently, mayors were even outsiders to the municipality.

The Municipal Law of 1878 also restricted suffrage. Before 1878 all men over twenty-one years old who were literate and who paid any type of taxes to the Spanish government, at the local or provincial level, could vote. In 1878 the age for voting was increased to twenty-five and a minimum of 125 pesetas of taxes was established.[13] Undoubtedly, the Municipal Law of 1878 sought to disenfranchise the rural poor by increasing the amount of taxes and thus restricting suffrage. This law practically excluded men without a title of land ownership as well as some of the landed peasantry in the rural barrios from voting. Literacy remained a requirement until 1904. Public employees of the municipalities were included in the category of voters.[14]

The effect of the law on the electorate of Caguas is hard to assess because many of the electoral records in Caguas for the late nineteenth century have been lost. The only conclusive observation deriving from the electoral lists is that the number of voters before and after the law of 1878 was very small. In 1873, 727 men, or 5.62 percent of the whole population, turned out for Caguas's election; and in 1899, 953 men, 4.8 percent of the inhabitants, went to the polls.[15] The percentage of voters thus decreased in the last decades of the nineteenth century, and it is clear that formal politics was the prerogative of a very few in Caguas.

The law of 1878 intended to transform the ayuntamiento into an administrative tool for the governor, which would inform him about local conditions and needs. For most wealthy Cagüeños who belonged to the liberal party and advocated for municipal autonomy, the centralizing character of the law was intrusive at best and retrograde at worst. Even though the mayor responded first to the governor, liberals still managed to control the council and, in the last year of the nineteenth century, the office of the mayor as well, and their influence continued until the mid-1910s. Their strengths and weaknesses within the municipal government responded in part to class alliances formed inside and outside of government.

Councilmen of Caguas: Transforming Centralization

From the early days of Spanish colonization in the Americas, town councils, or *cabildos*, were the legitimate interpreters of local interests. They were responsible for administration and municipal finances, regulating local life through ordinances subject to the approval of the governor.[16] The council formed committees and commissions of research and action, which investigated the conditions and needs of the population as well as conflicts among the people. The council also appointed municipal employees and imposed local taxes. With such important tasks and responsibilities, participating in the council carried not only public prestige but also a real possibility to influence the economic and political events of the region. The council gathered individuals whose economic means and personal interests were embedded in the economic growth of the municipality and who could serve the government without pay. In fact, the most important landholders in the region formed these councils.[17]

In the late eighteenth century, the Bourbon reforms followed a state-interventionist policy that translated into governmental centralization. As part of that policy, the Bourbons revitalized town councils in order to strengthen the link between the Crown and its subjects; this effort led to the establishment of new councils in Puerto Rico. The liberal Constitution of 1812 had provided the original legal basis for the formation of the council in Caguas.[18] In 1814 the liberal regime in Spain was suppressed and so was the council of Caguas. Throughout the nineteenth century, liberal constitutions in Spain periodically reestablished the council of Caguas.[19]

The Municipal Law of 1878 was also intended to mitigate the historical tension between the Crown and the council. Traditionally, powerful town figures had made the council into a base of personal power that was largely independent of the Crown, and the law of 1878 attempted to curb that tradition. By limiting the suffrage and increasing the number of councilmen, the Crown hoped to diminish the influence of large landowners in town councils while weakening the potential threat of the majority of the rural population, those "possible rebels." In 1878 the number of councilmen was doubled (see table 2.1), and the council opened its doors to men whose estates were more modest than those of previous councilors. Large landowners on the council had to contend with men whose interests and social background were sometimes at odds with their own. After 1878 some men with farms of less than two hundred cuerdas became councilmen and thus had a vote in the council, and conflicts with prominent large landowners were part of the discussions and debates in the municipal records. Large landowners were forced to redirect their approach in the council in order to maintain their influence in town.

Large landowners found new ways to continue controlling the council as before. Because large landowners who could hire agricultural laborers were able to dedicate more time than poorer men could spare to serve on the council, they maintained group membership within the council for an extended period of time, often holding office for more than a decade. They also allied with men of all social sectors, including mid-size and small farmers, sharecroppers, and rural laborers, in order to control the council's projects and programs. Large landowners recruited allies using two intertwined mechanisms—party politics and patron-client politics. By granting political and economic favors to councilors of the middling sectors, large landowners tied new councilors to their political interests.

Party politics became the main strategy for large landowners to influence the council after the law of 1878 and the main reason for liberals to try to reach the masses. Recruiting allies along party lines bridged the nu-

Table 2.1. Number of councilmen according to number of inhabitants, 1870 and 1878

	Number of Councilmen	
Inhabitants	1870	1878
8,001–9,000	7	15
9,001–10,000	7	16
10,001–12,000	8	17
12,001–14,000	9	18
14,001–16,000		19
16,001–18,000		20
18,001–20,000		21

Sources: Barceló Miller, *Política ultramarina*, 23; and *Leyes provincial y municipal de 24 de mayo de 1878*, 43.

merical gap created by an increased number of councilmen. Most Caguas councilmen held liberal ideas and followed Luis Muñoz Rivera and the liberal party. Pedro Grillo and Marcelino López Aponte, both councilors in 1880, were active members of the Puerto Rican Autonomous Party.[20] Other followers of Muñoz Rivera on the council of Caguas between 1880 and the early 1900s were Celestino Solá, Modesto Solá, Marcelino Solá, Diego Lizardi y Echevarría, Vicente R. Muñoz Barros, Santiago Franqui, Landelino Aponte, Nicolás Quiñonez Cabezudo, Manuel García, Juan Ramón Quiñonez, José A. Grillo, Rufo J. González, Federico Diez y López, Juan Díaz Hernández, Antonio de Jesús, José Rosario Santiago, Nicolás Aguayo, Pablo Héreter, Ramón Álvarez, Benito Polo y Giménez, and Gervasio García. In 1904 North American Harrison Johnson joined the council of Caguas as a member of the Union Party (see appendix C).[21]

While allying with middle sectors in party politics, large landowners maintained an exclusive, elitist circle that only society men were able to enter. At balls, wealthy men's clubs, and family celebrations, large landowners and the top party leadership excluded most mid-size- and small-farmer councilmen. Large landowners established close friendships with Muñoz Rivera and were active members of the liberal party. For instance, Don Landelino Aponte, one of the founders of the liberal party in 1868, was part of the municipal government from the late nineteenth century to the twentieth, serving as assistant to the mayor in 1880 (see appendix C).[22] Don Lilá, as relatives and friends called him, was president of the liberal party in Caguas. He became a councilor in 1900 and held that position until he died in 1904 at eighty years of age.[23]

Vicente Muñoz Barros, uncle of Muñoz Rivera, was also a well-known liberal in Puerto Rico and owned one of the largest and fastest-growing land estates in Caguas.[24] Muñoz Barros, who came from a prominent family in Barranquitas, moved to Caguas in 1874 after marrying a Cagüeña and promptly became involved in the municipal government. He served on the council between 1880 and 1904 (see appendix C).[25] He was influential in Muñoz Rivera's early education and shared his books and ideas with his nephew.[26] Indeed, Muñoz Rivera considered his uncle his teacher in "his love of freedom."[27]

During his years in Caguas, Muñoz Barros, along with Muñoz Rivera became friendly with the Solá family, who actively participated in the municipal government. Their alliance strengthened and facilitated their lengthy political careers in the council. Muñoz Barros and the Solá brothers—Celestino, Marcelino, and Modesto—held political offices from the late nineteenth to the twentieth century (see appendix C).[28] Their alliance also reflected large landowners' political power and maneuvering. With solid friendships, large landowners dictated the development of the liberal party in Caguas and thus controlled the council.

Large landowners' success in influencing the municipal government relied in part on the impact of party politics and particularly on the ideals of classic liberalism, which embraced patriarchal values appealing to all social sectors.[29] In particular, Puerto Rican liberals combined elements of what Carole Pateman describes as traditional and modern patriarchy. The former uses the trope of the family, and the authority of the father as its head, as a model for power relations of all kinds; the latter is defined as fraternal, contractual, and able to structure capitalist civil society.[30] Pateman's discussion clarifies the apparent contradiction between large landowners' promotion of the liberal image of the "Great Puerto Rican Family" and their interest in controlling the council to the detriment of poor Puerto Ricans. Liberals gave prerogatives of political representation to male household heads but also established hierarchies within the party. As in most Latin American countries, "liberals asserted that the right to rule derived from the social superiority of elite males. They believed it was the natural right of men with wealth or professional status to exercise political authority."[31] Party and business favors influenced people's actions within and outside government.

Party politics became the medium to resolve differences within the council. Large landowners maintained a prominent position by emphasizing party agreement and consensus in order to incorporate middling sectors into their agenda. Councilors of modest background entered willingly into this type of relationship, which proved beneficial to them. It gave them a better chance to stay on the council for a longer period of time by using the machinery of a political party and the opportunity to raise their social position through business relations and friendship with the wealthiest families of the region.

Between Party Alliance and Barrio Praxis

On December 31, 1883, José Eduvijes Rivera, a tax collector, solicited money from the ayuntamiento in order to pay transportation costs, alleging that most of his "clients" lived in the countryside, "scattered in the barrios." Rivera added that often debtors worked and resided on different farms, making it very difficult, if not impossible, to collect taxes.[32] Rivera described a situation that concerned the ayuntamiento and Spanish authorities in general: most of the Puerto Rican population lived in the countryside, far away from the centers of civilization and state authority (the downtown areas). In order to mitigate the distance and extend its authority, the council appointed alcaldes and comisarios de barrio to facilitate state representation in the countryside.[33] The ayuntamiento conferred state authority on alcaldes and comisarios de barrio to represent the law and the municipal administration in the rural barrios. They had the authority to investigate, survey, and control in the name of the ayuntamiento both space (rural roads, rural schools, farms, and houses) and people (social interactions and people's bodies). Theoretically, there was a distinction between alcaldes and comisarios de barrio. The alcalde de barrio was supposed to focus on administrative tasks, while the comisario de barrio helped the police. In practice, however, both comisarios and alcaldes de barrio simultaneously policed the countryside and represented the municipality in administration. Alcaldes and comisarios maintained order and pursued fugitives.[34] State officials and country people often understood and addressed these two positions as one, and the same people often occupied both offices.

One of the most important functions of the alcalde or comisario de barrio was to maintain lists of the vecinos by family in each barrio as the basis for assessing and collecting municipal taxes. With these lists, the ayuntamiento prepared an annual census, which was used in locating individuals and granting residence permits.[35] These officials usually commanded a detailed knowledge of the geography and population of their barrio. When a state representative or commission, including the civil guard and the army, visited a barrio, they were called to guide, escort, and help.[36] They also provided transportation, usually horses, to state representatives who visited their communities.

The alcalde or comisario de barrio informed rural populations, as a group and individually, of their responsibilities to the state and advertised the state's projects, issues, and policies. They visited people house by house and posted ads in popular places, such as the barrio store.[37] They also called meetings of the residents to announce municipal laws or activities.[38] Alcaldes and comisarios not only informed individuals in the countryside of their civil duties but also made sure that their neighbors responded. They had the responsibility to investigate vecinos who excused themselves from municipal duties for illness or any other reason, and under these circumstances, they had the authority to enter people's homes. For example, when the alcalde of Barrio Turabo, Luis Acosta, informed Sandalio Ortiz of a citation, Ortiz excused himself due to illness. The mayor ordered Acosta to investigate Ortiz's condition, and Acosta found that "Sandalio Ortiz is ill because a bull kicked him in the right testicle; his wound is two inches long and I think it is very serious."[39] The reach of the municipal authorities apparently included the most intimate parts of people's bodies.

Alcaldes and comisarios also reported to state authorities the opinions, circumstances, and attitudes of rural residents. They gave voice to the beliefs and feelings of many people, including those who could not read or write. José María Rodríguez, alcalde of Barrio San Antonio, claimed to repeat the exact words of a defiant farmer ordered to appear before the mayor of Caguas: "I inform you that the individual Catalino Donis is aware of your notification and says that he will not show up and has nothing to do with your notification so you will know that I did my part."[40]

Alcaldes and comisarios were full members of their communities with the additional function of speaking for the people among whom they lived and reporting conflicts among neighbors in the countryside. They also reported the participation and collaboration of rural residents with the municipal state and wrote about the social and physical needs of rural residents. They channeled petitions, demands, and concerns from country people, rich and poor, to state authorities.

Each barrio in Caguas had one or two alcaldes or comisarios de barrio. Alcaldes de barrio in Caguas were first recruited in 1814; by 1822 there were six of them. The first comisarios de barrio in Caguas date to 1847, and after that year there was at least one for each barrio in Caguas. The ayuntamiento was supposed to select only literate male residents with property, twenty-five years or older to fill these positions. However, the data shows that between 1880 and 1900, a minority of alcaldes and comisarios de barrio were illiterate and had no property. Luterio Núñez, from Barrio Tomás de Castro, refused his nomination as alcalde de barrio because "not knowing how to read or write and with no one in my home who could, I might incur a responsibility through ignorance and obstruct the administrative work."[41] In 1882 Cesareo Mangual, a small farmer in Barrio Turabo, rejected his nomination as comisario on the grounds that he could not legally occupy the position since he was neither a taxpayer nor a voter.[42] He added, "I live in my father's house and lack even a horse to bring me to obey the City Hall's orders."[43] Despite his argument, the ayuntamiento did not accept Mangual's refusal, and he served the state as an alcalde and comisario of Barrio Turabo from 1889 to 1903.

When a comisario or alcalde de barrio attempted to leave his position temporarily or permanently, the ayuntamiento demanded that he suggest someone from the community as his replacement.[44] For example, Francisco Grillo, alcalde of Barrio Cañaboncito, assigned Don José Millán as his substitute until "my condition improves or I return from the baths that I have to take."[45] Illness, change of residence, and loss of property were three reasons for resigning frequently cited among comisarios and alcaldes de barrio.[46] Often, the ayuntamiento accepted resignations due to illness when certified by doctors but ordered the official to return to his post when he recovered. José Santos Rodríguez, for example, resigned his post as comisario of Barrio Turabo in 1883 and returned to it in 1898.[47] Similarly, Francisco Rivera resigned in 1893 due to illness but returned as alcalde and comisario of Barrio Bairoa in 1895.

In sum, comisarios and alcaldes de barrio were direct intermediaries between the ayuntamiento and rural populations.[48] But because this was a tough job with little monetary remuneration, the majority of countrymen did not accept the commitment willingly.[49] Why did some men resent the demands of the office while others turned the office into a means to gain power and influence? For a man able to take the time, the office offered an opportunity to meet and socialize with the mayor of Caguas and the councilmen and often represented the first step in a political career. Mayor Gervasio García began as an alcalde de barrio. Also, a number of councilmen, among them Benito Díaz, Gervasio García, Marcelino Solá, Joaquín Aponte, Juan Jiménez Saurí, Benito Polo y Jiménez, Manuel Muñoz, and Raimundo Faura, initiated their public careers as alcaldes de barrio.

The mayor, according to the Municipal Law of 1878, named alcaldes and comisarios de barrio, who surveyed private property and enforced the law. However, mayors were often outsiders who did not know the territory, its people, or their needs, and they delegated to the council the task of filling those positions. Councilors successfully arranged and controlled the assignments of alcaldes and comisarios de barrio. For example, Don Ramón Álvarez, a municipal councilor in 1900 who owned a big store in Barrio Beatriz, supported the nomination of Don Demetrio López, who before 1889 was the cashier in Álvarez's store, as alcalde and comisario of Barrio Beatriz. Likewise, the Solá brothers owned land in Barrio Borinquen, and in 1880 Marcelino himself worked as an alcalde of that barrio. Another close relative, Narciso Solá, occupied the position of alcalde of Barrio Borinquen for the years 1890–91 and 1895–96.[50] Thus, large landowners often positioned friends and relatives as alcaldes or comisarios de barrio to protect their own interests.

In addition, the authority conferred by the office situated comisarios and alcaldes de barrio above most of their neighbors. Rural residents were legally bound to obey and respect them, and some alcaldes and comisarios used their public position to advance their own private interests. In 1893, for example, Vicente Díaz, alcalde and comisario of Barrio Cañabón (1889–92), tried to buy some coffee from Ambrosio Román. When Román refused to sell, Comisario Díaz accused Román and Benedito Rodríguez of stealing the coffee. Román was able to prove his ownership of the coffee, but although the mayor of Caguas was informed of Díaz's behavior, he levied no punishment for the false accusation.[51] Even though Comisario Díaz did not acquire the coffee, his case illustrates the ways in which the office could be used for personal advantage.

Also, a small percentage of comisarios and alcaldes de barrio increased the size of their farms during or after their terms of office.[52] However, most men in the Caguas countryside sought to avoid serving in the offices because of their financial and social burdens. Their positions as comisario or alcalde de barrio did not generate any income, despite the fact that the duties and responsibilities of the office were multiple, varied, and time consuming. In general comisarios and alcaldes de barrio owned small and mid-size farms. Financial information is available for 98 of the 104 comisarios and alcaldes de barrio who served between 1880 and 1900 (see table 2.2). Of those officials, 45 percent owned less than 70 cuerdas of land. Additionally, 10 alcaldes or comisarios de barrio had no property; 8 were day laborers who knew how to read and write, 1 was a school teacher, and another was an artisan. Not a single official owned more than 401 cuerdas of land while serving as comisario or alcalde de barrios. In fact, the farms of 4 officials decreased in size during their terms.[53]

Alcaldes and comisarios brought their concerns to the council with loud and lively protests.[54] In June 1880 the ayuntamiento assigned Alberto Torres y López as alcalde of Barrio Cañabón. Alberto believed that

Table 2.2. Financial estate of the alcaldes and comisarios de barrio, 1880–1900

	Number of comisarios/alcaldes	Percent of Total[a]
No Property	10	9.62
Businessman	6	5.77
.25–30 cuerdas	34	32.69
31–70 cuerdas	13	12.5
71–199 cuerdas	18	17.31
200–400 cuerdas	6	5.77
401 cuerdas and over	0	0
Sold Property[b]	4	3.85
Bought Property[b]	7	6.73

[a] I found information for a total of 104 alcaldes and comisarios from 1880 to 1900. I did not find financial information for 6 of them (5.77 percent).

[b] This transaction changed their categories within this table.

Sources: AHMC, SEC Finanzas, SSEC Contribuciones, SER Planillas de Riqueza, SSER Agrícola, 1880–1900, C81–100; AHMC, SEC Secretaría, SSEC Archivo, SER Censos, SSER Habitantes, 1882–83, C26.

this nomination would force him and his family into starvation: "My appointment as alcalde de barrio is clearly unfair and to the detriment of the administration. First, it would ruin me and would leave my family, my woman and four children, without bread. My oldest daughter is not even seven yet. Second, as a poor man who does not know how to read or write, I could not serve well despite my desire to do so."[55] Despite this plea, Don Gerardo Darder, secretary of the ayuntamiento, rejected Alberto's petition.[56]

Antonio Ramírez de Arellano, comisario of Barrios Río Cañas and La Mesa in 1883, protested the ayuntamiento's order that he must add the barrios of Barra and Jagua to his responsibilities. In 1883 he owned sixteen cuerdas of land in Río Cañas and a small store. In order to supervise the additional barrios, Antonio would have had to leave his property unattended. In a letter to the mayor of Caguas, he alleged, "The writer has no way to earn his living beyond a small store and as he has no help, he must always be present, and if he left, he would have to close up. . . . You would not of course want to cause irreparable harm to the father of a family, who must live from a business that demands his constant personal attention."[57] The mayor ignored his petition and Ramírez de Arellano eventually neglected his duties by failing to pursue an outlaw.[58]

Regino García found himself in similar circumstances. After a month of serving as the comisario of Barrio Cañabón, García was desperate. He headed a large household of ten, and his farm demanded his continuous presence. In his resignation letter, García alleged that he was illiterate and poor and claimed:

> *My fortune, or rather the capital I have, is so insignificant that it consists of only twelve cuerdas of poor quality land, a pair of oxen and two beasts, and I have to attend to their needs, as well as my wife with our five small children, my in-laws, and my mother, all of the latter in their 70s, making up, including myself, a family of ten. . . . If I am forced to assume the office of comisario, I and my family will be ruined and left in misery. To avoid that, I would have to sell my bit of land and move—A situation that I don't believe will be forced upon me, since you are the head of a family yourself, wise and with the humanitarian feelings that are the product of a sensitive heart, you will not force ruin upon one of your subjects and his large family.* [59]

Because of the precarious conditions of many alcaldes and comisarios, they left office as soon as possible. Some comisarios de barrio resigned immediately after serving the obligatory period of two years. For instance, Juan Solano, comisario of Barrio Río Cañas, submitted his resignation in 1885, stressing that "I have performed the duty of comisario for two years and I want someone else to be named in my place." [60]

Because the ayuntamiento often ignored their concerns and needs, many comisarios and alcaldes de barrio opted to neglect their duties. There are multiple examples in which they failed to inform rural people of municipal projects, summons, and policies, leading the mayor to notify alcaldes and comisarios de barrio a second time and sometimes to fine them. [61] Fines for disobedience fluctuated between two and ten pesos. [62] In March 1881 the mayor of Caguas fined Ruperto Caballero, alcalde of Barrio Borinquen, five pesos for disobedience. [63] Caballero was fined again for similar actions some months later. [64] In 1895 the tax collector complained that people in the countryside did not even know when to file residential addresses (*cédulas de vecindad*). The official stressed "the necessity to inform such vecinos, since frequently many vecinos are fined for failing to file a document, due to the fact that the comisarios do not bother to inform them." [65]

Negligence often bordered on disobedience. [66] In 1897 the mayor of Caguas, José María Solís, warned the alcaldes about failing to fulfill their duties: "Very frequently some alcaldes de barrio of this town do not return the orders addressed to them, which results in harm to good public service."[67] Likewise, on numerous occasions, alcaldes and comisarios de barrio did not attend government meetings, such as those called by the commission on property taxation, delaying the collection of taxes in the whole municipality.[68] Also, many citations to appear in court were never delivered.[69]

The non-cooperation of state officials with the law appears to have reached a peak in August 1885, when the municipal court (*juzgado municipal*) advised the mayor of Caguas to insist upon the cooperation of the alcaldes de barrio. Because the officials had refused to serve civil or judicial citations, the court assigned one of its own constables (*alguaciles*) to take the place of the alcaldes de barrio in rural areas. But the costs of transportation as well as the constable's failure to reach all the rural barrios forced the municipal court to once again demand the cooperation of the alcaldes de barrio.[70] Two months later, José Garriga, a representative of the municipal court, frustrated by the attitudes of some alcaldes de barrio, wrote again to the mayor of Caguas, accusing the alcaldes of disobedience. He began his letter by referring to the recommendation that a constable be appointed in place of the alcaldes, stressing that some alcaldes de barrio still failed to cooperate with the municipal court. Garriga cited the example of Juan Portela, alcalde of Barrio Bairoa, whom he had ordered to "give judicial notice to his neighbor Don Ramón López, whose order was returned yesterday the 18th by the above-named alcalde de barrio, Don Juan Portela, without executing it and with the following note = 'The comisario of Barrio Bairoa is not Portero.'"[71] Mocking Garriga and the court, Portela ignored Garriga's order on the grounds that his name had been misspelled.[72]

Comisarios and alcaldes de barrio also faced pressure from neighbors. Rural residents found various ways to punish their local officials when they believed those officials had failed to represent or protect the community. For example, Gregorio Arroyo was a small farmer who had served as alcalde of Barrio Tomás de Castro since 1895. He owned thirty-two cuerdas of land on which he cultivated rice and starchy roots, using the one horse he owned to patrol the barrio. On the night of May 8, 1899, Arroyo's horse was stolen from his farm. The thief left the horse on the property of a nearby farmer, who brought it to the *depósito municipal*, an office that surveyed and controlled cattle and domestic animals. The municipality charged the owner for each day the animal spent in the depósito, and Arroyo did not have the money to pay the fines. The thief was never located, and without the horse that remained in the depósito, Arroyo could not patrol the barrio.[73] Unfortunately for Arroyo, protests turned violent. The teacher of the barrio, Francisco Díaz Rezino, in a long letter to the mayor, accused Arroyo of corruption. Allegedly, Comisario Arroyo falsely accused Díaz Rezino of drinking alcohol in the classroom in order to avenge the fact that the teacher had listed Arroyo's children among the absent.[74] In his defense, Díaz Rezino stressed how unpopular Arroyo was among barrio residents: "You cannot ignore that the neighborhood does not approve of some of [Arroyo's] doings, because once acting as the comisario, he was beaten and wounded to the point that he was forced to go to the hospital."[75]

Arroyo was not the only alcalde de barrio who suffered injuries after delivering a municipal order. In fact, people's challenges to government authority were directed first toward low-rank officials who were physically closer to country people and who generally shared a similar class background. In the line of duty, alcaldes and comisarios suffered verbal and physical aggression from people who refused their authority as municipal officials.[76]

The Municipal Government after 1898

After the U.S. invasion of the island, municipal governments at first maintained the same functional and organizational structure as before, keeping the same personnel and offices. In 1898 only three alcaldes de barrio in Caguas—Benito Polo, Serafín Acosta, and José Santos—refused to swear loyalty to the United States. They were removed from office in December of 1898.[77] All the others continued their duties as usual, informing rural populations of state projects, ordinances, and dispositions and assisting U.S. representatives when they visited their barrios.[78]

However, in the early twentieth century the U.S. colonial state on the island attempted to further centralize administrative functions and, as a consequence, considerably reduced the tasks, responsibilities, and powers of the municipal government. In 1901, for instance, the legislature transferred the judicial functions of the mayor to a justice of the peace named by the governor, with the objective of achieving judicial neutrality and making the functions of the judiciary in Puerto Rico more like those in the United States.[79]

The Municipal Law of 1902, the first large-scale U.S. government revision to municipal administration, further reduced the capacities of the mayor of Caguas. This law reorganized the town council, making it independent of the mayor, who was no longer its president or member. However, any council resolution or ordinance required the mayor's approval.

The council appointed the comptroller, and the mayor named all other officers.[80] The law gave the governor the authority to suspend mayors and to fill any vacancy in the offices of either the mayor or the council.[81]

The Municipal Law of 1902 maintained the comisarios' effectiveness, providing for the council to regulate their prerogatives and responsibilities.[82] Basically, the council stipulated in 1902 the same duties and responsibilities of comisarios as before but emphasized sanitary and hygiene surveillance (see appendix D). However, the new colonial state relied less and less upon alcaldes and comisarios de barrio as intermediaries between its officials and the rural population. As the pressures from the municipality decreased, the alcaldes and comisarios de barrio gradually became community leaders who voluntarily organized neighbors to ask favors and services from the municipal state, in particular, the construction and repair of rural roads. Some were very active and found in this activism the key to entering the power structure of the municipal government.

As community leaders, some alcaldes and comisarios de barrio embraced and voiced political ideas among their neighbors. Affiliated with the liberal party led by Muñoz Rivera, some of them became important links between the party leadership and country people. They prepared various visits of the Muñocista leaders to the rural barrios and helped the party recruit members. Hilario Coto, comisario of Barrio San Salvador (1900 and 1908) and an active member of the Union Party, was instrumental in the party's victory in Barrio San Salvador in the campaign of 1908.[83] In the first decade of the twentieth century, the leadership of men like Hilario Coto facilitated the political triumph of the Muñocistas in Caguas.

The Landed Elite after 1898

Cagüeños and Puerto Ricans in general perceived the United States as a nation of freedom and civil liberties and welcomed the occupation of the island as an opportunity.[84] However, the United States established a military government in 1898 that eliminated the political advantages achieved with the Spanish autonomy of 1897.[85] The military government took control of the higher levels of the colonial administration, appointing North Americans to those positions. At the local level, the military government allowed Puerto Ricans to manage municipal governments.

In the early twentieth century, followers of Muñoz Rivera occupied most positions in the municipality of Caguas, from the mayor to the councilors. As in the rest of Puerto Rico, liberals sought control of municipal governments in an attempt to curb the increasingly oppositional colonial policies of the United States in the island. Liberals achieved their goal, winning over most municipalities in Puerto Rico, until the mid-1910s.[86] Their party changed names—Autonomous, Federalist, and Unionist—in the twentieth century, but its membership remained basically the same. In the municipal elections of 1899, the Federal Party triumphed in Caguas with 880 votes over 73 Republicans.[87] In part the change of sovereignty in 1898 abetted the dominance of Muñoz's liberal wing in Caguas. Most Spaniards who occupied positions within the municipal council left office in 1898, eliminating this competition.[88]

The landed elite as part of the liberal party remained in control of the council, but the number of businessmen and professionals increased throughout the twentieth century.[89] Some businessmen and professionals joined the party and became close friends with the landed elite, among them were Nicolás Aguayo, Harrison Johnson, and Enrique Moreno.[90]

After 1898 liberals also controlled the office of the mayor without challenge and some members of the landed elite became mayors. In 1898 U.S. general John R. Brook named Celestino Solá mayor of Caguas, the first mayor born in Caguas.[91] Don Gervasio García, a good friend of Muñoz Rivera, entered the town hall of Caguas as mayor from 1900 until 1906 and returned in 1908 and in 1911.[92]

García's successor, Doctor Gabriel Jiménez Sanjurjo, was a well-known ophthalmologist who owned a large estate in Caguas.[93] Jiménez Sanjurjo began his political career within the conservative party, but in 1887 he joined the liberal party and followed Muñoz Rivera.[94] In 1909 the Unionist councilor Harrison Johnson occupied the position of mayor of Caguas for a couple of months.[95] He was the first American to participate directly in the municipal council in Caguas and to hold the office of the mayor. In 1909 voters in Caguas elected José Domingo Solá y López as the new Unionist mayor of Caguas. Solá y López was the son of Celestino Solá, former mayor of Caguas, then serving as a municipal councilor.[96] He was active in the public life of Caguas before his election, constructing a building that later became a theater, loaning a warehouse for political meetings, and donating land to build a hospital.[97]

While the landed elite took control of the municipal government in Caguas, their administrative prerogatives under largely shrank. Nonetheless, the landed elite's demise points to a rich past of struggles and changes. It is clear that the twentieth-century transformations of the municipal government are rooted in the struggles for power that took place in the nineteenth century. The political power of the landed elite was solidified by their advantageous position in the economy of the island. Their position, however, was not a comfortable one because of the many challenges posed not only by the colonial government but also by popular sectors. The struggle for economic resources and for the legitimacy of interpreting this fight is the topic of the next chapter.

In the Face of Inequality
Land Privatization and Racial Hierarchies

Land privatization set off struggles in the rural barrios of Caguas that eventually favored large landowners, mainly because they had the economic means to deal with the bureaucracy and had the police at their service. However, people from lower social ranks sought alternatives to the notion of private property. This chapter discusses the nature, meanings, and implementation of private property in Caguas in the day-to-day life of common, non-privileged people and their coping mechanisms, illustrating the ways in which people used and interpreted natural law, a pillar of marginal citizenship, to claim access to the land and its products. Specifically, people's notion of natural law in Caguas focused on need and ability to work to justify access to land.

Land Privatization in Puerto Rico

The antecedents of land privatization in Puerto Rico began in the late eighteenth century with the Royal Order of 1778, when the Spanish Crown legalized private ownership of land, woods, and pasture. Created exclusively for Puerto Rico, this order treated squatters and land-grant recipients equally by requiring that the owner cultivate or raise cattle on at least half the territory in question. Otherwise, the Spanish Crown reassigned the land to someone else who could cultivate it.[1] The criterion for property ownership was personal use, although the Crown maintained the ultimate power over Puerto Rican land.

The order of 1778 served throughout the nineteenth century as a principle and method to foster economic development by populating and taxing the land. In 1815 the Cédula de Gracias established free and permanent land grants to immigrants in the hope of promoting European immigration to Puerto Rico in an effort to revitalize the economy through agriculture, commerce, and industry. These granted areas were not empty but inhabited by numerous peasant squatters. The Cédula de Gracias of

1815 thus precipitated a displacement of peasants from the land in favor of European immigrants who brought capital (money and technology), labor (families and slaves), and the knowledge to exploit the land commercially. European immigrants successfully maintained their land titles over a long period of time by paying taxes to the government. In comparison, squatters found multiple obstacles to registering land: the costs were prohibitive for most of them, and they depended almost exclusively on family labor. Even with land titles, taxes pushed many farmers into debt and eventually caused them to lose their titles of ownership. Seized land was often annexed to the European immigrants' estates.[2] In order to accelerate economic growth, the Royal Order of December 28, 1818, created the Superior Board for the Allocation of Common Land (Junta Superior de Repartimiento de Terrenos Baldíos y Realengos), which offered squatters mechanisms to legalize their informal arrangements. For most of the century the board pressured subjects to formalize their land possession with the state. All legal titles were subject to occupation and agrarian production, the requirements of the Royal Order of 1778. Thus, the conditioned privatization of the land, as expressed in 1778, was generalized in Puerto Rico until 1880.[3]

In the 1880s and the 1890s property rights increasingly became individual and absolute. The Law of Mortgage and Property Registry of 1880 mobilized credit and created new pressures for the segregation and registration initiated in the early nineteenth century. Land-title holders used agrarian credit to engage in and profit from commercial agriculture and acquire more land under their titles. Michael J. Godreau and Juan A. Giusti emphasize the importance of this law in Puerto Rico and claim that the Mortgage Law of 1880 initiated the regime of private property because it left the formalization and legalization of land titles to individuals. In the interest of obtaining agrarian credit, individuals themselves paid the fees for land registration, influenced government agencies, and defined boundaries in the area. The law thus concretized land privatization, whereby wealthy people had a better chance of obtaining land titles than those without money. At the same time, this law gave an unprecedented significance to land titles by effectively protecting registered property. It also fostered land registration because mortgage loans required titles of ownership, which served as guarantees for obtaining credit, and gave moneylenders legal power in case of unpaid debts, making them legally entitled to confiscate property.[4] The law also punished individuals who did not register land by subjecting their land to the possibility of new occupations. Because people who failed to register their land could lose their property under the new law, its urgency was immediately communicated to the majority of the population. On April 1, 1880, the mayor of Caguas urgently recommended that Cagüeños legally register their land because there was a month left before the new law would take effect and its consequences were serious.[5]

In 1884 the Regulations for the Composition and Sale of Unused Land legalized long-term occupation of the land, revising old land grants in the island. In the 1880s and the 1890s the Superior Board for Allocation of Common Land took away land titles from owners who did not comply with the regulations. The regulations of 1884 entitled owners only to the portion of the territory that was cultivated or used for cattle. Thus, the regulations represented both an incentive and a pressure to formalize people's access to the land.[6] Many of these old grants were not occupied by the title-holder but by numerous peasant squatters who lacked the means to formalize their access to land. Many lost their informal access to land in addition to the opportunity to formalize it, as people with money took the opportunity to acquire titles of ownership. Once the title was revised, the squatters were often forced by the new owner to leave or pay with their labor. The service of the police was constantly needed, for the older users felt it their right to question the new ownership. Even though the main impetus behind the laws was to formalize titles, it also recognized and legitimated use as the basis of land possession. This legal principle is an ancient corollary of the natural law—natural resources are available to those who exploit them—which formed part of the Spanish legal system until the late nineteenth century.[7] However, the recognition of land use as a legal principle is limited because the 1884 law ultimately sought the formalization of titles and the total privatization of land. The law also disfavored peasant squatters who practiced semi-nomadic agriculture and would have a difficult time proving the use of the same territory for more than a couple of years.

The Civil Code of 1890 theoretically left intact the two laws of 1880 and 1884; for this reason, Godreau and Giusti consider that the Code of 1890 "consecrated" private property over the land and other goods in Puerto Rico.[8] People with economic means embraced this legislation and used it to their advantage, acquiring land that peasant settlers used to occupy.

The 1880s legislation maintained its effective vitality throughout the nineteenth and twentieth centuries. In fact, the U.S. government found that the laws "scientifically" protected private property and its interest in the island.[9] The U.S. government even recognized use as a legal basis of possession, albeit with revisions providing for the elimination of this type of property in the long run. The 1884 law formalized titles of ownership after a person proved consecutive use of the same territory for thirty years, a provision that intentionally excluded the majority of peasant squatters who practiced semi-nomadic agriculture. The U.S. government significantly reduced the period (to ten years) with General Order Number 82 of April 4, 1899. This legislation made many title owners uncomfortable because it entitled many sharecroppers (*agregados*, commonly known as *agregao's*) to a legal title of land, promoting individual property at all levels. However, sharecropping was a common practice throughout the twentieth century.[10] The Civil Code of 1902 reestablished the term to thirty years from ten. Finally, in 1912 the U.S. government in the island prohibited any informal occupation of state territory, but sharecropping continued to be an important part of the Puerto Rican economy.[11]

Municipal Taxes on the Land

Land taxation was the main source of revenue for the municipal government in Caguas, which in appearance taxed its constituency in a democratic way. The municipal government met annually to approve a budget for the following year, which provided tax commissions the basis for levying taxes on the population. The amount of money projected for the budget was distributed among taxpayers according to what they produced that year. In this regard, people from different social classes had a similar standing before commissions: productivity, not the value of estate property, was the basis of taxation. Even day laborers were called upon to contribute with a third of their annual salaries.[12] After tax commissions finished their task, the mayor organized a meeting with taxpayers in his barrios to assess their productivity, giving them an eight-day period to review their taxes.[13] Taxpayers also had an opportunity to write to the mayor and councilors questioning and protesting taxes, and the municipal government was obliged to rectify errors.[14] People from all social sectors could participate in the process of tax revision, writing affidavits to the municipal government and demanding tax reductions. Most arguments stressed the system's inequality by comparing their assessment to that of other neighbors, and a few asked for a revision of land titles.[15]

This system was subject to manipulation, abuses, and discriminatory practices against people of the lower classes. Obtaining an affidavit was difficult and costly, and poorer people were left vulnerable to the eventual confiscation of their property. In April 1882 Doña Leonor Donis wrote to the municipal government outraged by the fact that authorities confiscated seven head of cattle from her farm in Barrio Cañaboncito. She emphasized her old age and invited the administration to think of a better, fairer tax system. She suggested that the municipal government "adopt another system that respects property, instead of relying on the tax commissioners' whimsical will, disregarding reasons and documents. They [tax commissioners] continue committing those very hateful acts that *totally ruin poor neighbors who do not have the means to speak out*; poor neighbors have no other choice but to publicly give up their property public lest they become debtors to the State or the Municipality" (my emphasis).[16]

Illiteracy also weighed on the landed peasantry. In a largely illiterate society, authorities asked for written documents proving people's claims, a requirement that excluded or alienated a lot of people. For instance, Mercedes Rodríguez de Negrón, a widow in Barrio Culebras, protested the confiscation of some cattle despite the fact that she paid her taxes. She found that the municipal government had duplicated her record, once under her name and again under her deceased husband. When authorities asked for the receipt, Mercedes explained that because she was illiterate she never asked for or even thought of a receipt. However, authorities kept asking for a receipt, accusing Mercedes of fraud and disobedience.[17]

The tax rate was also biased against the poor, as it was the same for people who had a small farm of any value and those few who had farms over two hundred cuerdas of land, whether for family consumption or commercial purposes. The landed peasantry had to pay taxes on their own subsistence while large landowners, who had the best soil in the territory, paid the same percentage for cash crops that yielded considerable wealth. This system favored the accumulation of land to the detriment of small farms, prompting one local newspaper to predict the disappearance of small farms.[18] The tax rate was also the same for sharecroppers, who paid taxes on what they produced and on their rent. Taxation was even worse for day laborers, who paid a third of their already miniscule annual income.

In addition, powerful figures in the local government and their friends influenced tax commissions in order to obtain lower taxes. In 1889 the newspaper *El Buscapié* denounced how tax commissioners followed orders issued by the mayor or by any other powerful politician ("algún cacique poderoso") rather than the law.[19] Members of the council, who according to Pedro Garay of Barrio San Salvador knew nothing about their barrio, formed tax commissions with the assistance of alcaldes and comisarios de barrio.[20] Moreover, the council and the mayor made corrections to tax files and thereby had the opportunity to lower their own taxes. This situation was exposed not only by ordinary taxpayers but even by honest councilors. In 1887 Miguel Puig, a tax commissioner who had joined the council in 1885, denounced the corrupt character of tax revisions in Caguas. He protested against the unfair tax reductions of powerful landowners, among them Don Jaime Vilá and Don Nicolás Quiñonez Cabezudo, who both had large farms and connections within the council (Quiñonez was a councilor himself). Puig objected: "Don Nicolás Quiñonez's property in Cagüitas, undoubtedly one of the most valuable properties with a large number of cuerdas cultivated in the best sugar cane, also produces a large amount of coffee. He has another extensive property in Jagua in very good conditions. For these two properties, he obtained a reduction to seven hundred *pesos less than half what the tax commissioners indicate*. Sirs, is this equity? As commissioner, I cannot accept this, and as a taxpayer, I protest"[21] (my emphasis)

The worst part of these reductions, according to Puig, was the direct consequences for property owners who had small farms; the municipal government increased their taxes in order to compensate for Quiñonez Cabezudo's reduction. Puig claimed, "As a consequence of the reductions, or rather the granted concessions, [the municipal government] has increased the taxes of many other properties that could not remotely produce that amount."[22] Puig described the system well: powerful landowners usually benefited from tax reductions, increasing the amount of taxes to be paid by less powerful landowners. In 1884 the municipal government lowered the taxes of four individuals by a total amount of 1,272 pesos, which was redistributed among thirteen other property owners.[23]

Puig's words seemed to be truthful, considering that he did not show any preference for family members, although his brother Gerardo tried to obtain a reduction because he was taxed with an "exorbitant amount."[24] Puig also forced the municipal government to investigate the finances of Jaime Vilá, who in exchange wrote to the mayor demanding an investigation of Puig's financial status.[25] The commission validated Puig's complaint and found that Vilá was in fact exaggerating his claims in order to obtain lower taxes. Vilá owned a farm of 481 cuerdas of land and rented from a neighbor 264 cuerdas of the best quality, where he produced sugar, tobacco, and other crops and raised cattle. The investigator recommended against reducing Vilá's taxes.[26]

Likewise, Felicita Santos denounced another case of corruption. She sold half of her farm to the brothers Pascual and Bartolomé Borrás, who were councilors, but was taxed for the whole farm. Felicita understood the high taxes to be a clear matter of abuse and corruption. She argued that because Pascual Borrás was part of the tax commission, he and his brother obtained tax reductions while her taxes increased.[27]

Councilors were not the only beneficiaries of this type of corruption. One alcalde de barrio who formed part of a tax commission also lowered his own taxes. In 1884 Pedro Pablo Grillo was alarmed by the high taxes assigned to his small store in Barrio Cañaboncito, particularly when the tax commissioner and alcalde de barrio, Manuel García, had lower taxes for a larger store. They both sold rum but García had a large-scale business, which paid less tax than Grillo.[28]

The requirements to produce the affidavits, the flat tax rate for large and small farms, and the influence of the powerful within tax commissions clearly indicate that the municipal government depended on the lower classes for its financial support. For the landed peasantry and the working population, this was a severe consequence, and often taxes were simply too high to pay. The government gave extensions in special circumstances, such as illness, and debtors received various notifications.[29] But most debtors were treated without mercy, and the municipal government confiscated anything of value on their farms—the harvest, domestic animals, furniture, tools, and so on—in order to cover the taxes.[30] Undoubtedly, losing chattel exacerbated the living conditions of many farmers, who were forced into destitution and had to sell their land.

In other cases in which chattel was not available, the municipal government confiscated part of or the whole farm.[31] In Barrio Beatriz, Rufino Díaz described his sad circumstances of debt and poverty. In 1883 he had a small farm of twenty-five cuerdas of land that was highly taxed, forcing him to sell twenty cuerdas of the best soil in order to pay taxes. He was forced to make a living on five cuerdas of land of poor quality.[32] The great limitations of his small farm likely forced him to hire out his labor for part of the year in order to make a living. Likewise, Ramón Villafañe was convinced that no matter how much he produced, he could never pay his taxes. He owned forty cuerdas of land in Barrio Tomás de Castro, but most of it was composed of woods, and the rest was poor quality grass where he could barely maintain three to four skinny cows. His production was not even enough to pay an annual tax.[33]

Many farmers who could not pay taxes just left their farms and moved away. Their farms stayed "without owners" for years, until the municipal government took possession and often resold the land, usually to large landowners in the vicinity.[34] During the time that the farm was left "alone," peasant squatters and neighbors took advantage of its resources, cultivating and harvesting the land, extracting wood, water, and so on. The former owners became part of the landless peasantry that traveled around looking for a place to sharecrop or work. Spanish taxation made the living conditions of the landed peasantry similar to those of day laborers and sharecroppers because it impoverished them. Many landed peasants had to hire out their work temporarily or permanently in order to pay taxes and make a living.

This system of taxes was in effect until the U.S. government took control of the island. In 1898 taxes were collected as usual, but on January 19, 1899, the U.S. military government on the island ordered a comprehensive revision of finances, which began to transform the Spanish taxation system.[35] U.S. authorities provided for the formation of a tax board in each municipality to assess the quality of property and levy taxes. The new order implemented a tax system based on the productive potential of the property; the territory was classified according to the quality of the soil, assessing "valleys at one dollar per acre, midlands at fifty cents, and highlands at twenty-five cents."[36] The new system borrowed some features from the former one: land classification remained basically the same, and the boards were similar to the former tax commissions. The new system also penalized absentee owners with a 50 percent surcharge.[37] The tax board needed the assistance of alcaldes de barrio, as the old tax commissions had.[38] More important, the assessed taxes were similar to those of the Spanish system because the real productivity of the land remained more a theoretical principle than an effective practice, and farmers who did not engage in intensive commercial agriculture paid the heavy bulk of taxes.[39]

The tax order of 1899 was debated among Puerto Ricans who favored and condemned it, but they agreed that the ordinance was going to change the status quo. A newspaper article described the changes as "patriotic" and "fair" because what had happened before was common knowledge: "Everyone knows what has happened in this island with land taxes; small-property owners have always carried the burden of taxes, while the politicians [*caciques*], those who influence the government and politics, the large landowners, with rare exceptions, have always appear to have less wealth than they actually possess."[40] However, the journalist foretold some problems with the new ordinance. The land classification would force small producers, who cultivated mostly subsistence crops, to pay the same tax percentage than those who produced cash crops and had larger farms, just as before.[41]

Two years later the U.S. government in the island made substantial revisions to the fiscal system. With the Hollander Bill of 1901, U.S. authorities openly announced the end of the Spanish system of taxation.[42] The bill began by eliminating the municipal boards and creating a central bureaucracy to assess the value of property and its taxation. It eliminated the fines against absentee owners and taxed property according to its real value and actual production. Property owners across the island protested the bill, favoring the Spanish system as highly civilized and condemning the new one as hateful and abusive.[43] Once again alcaldes and comisarios de barrio were called to assist, notifying tax delinquents.[44] The Hollander Bill favored small producers, at least in theory, by exempting from taxes land valued at less than one hundred dollars as well as these farms' tools and production. In practice, however, the law effectively released farmland from the control of local elites and made it available for U.S. corporations.[45]

Liberal Cagüeños criticized the bill and felt threatened when the first tax agents arrived in Caguas. The agents came from San Juan, representing for liberal Cagüeños the unwelcome intervention of the U.S. colonial government in town.[46] Liberal Cagüeños had lost forever their capacity to influence and often dictate taxes at the local level. Under the new law a central bureaucracy would direct and supervise taxes. However, they applauded the agent's decision to name Landelino Aponte and Nicolás Quiñonez Cabezudo, two well-known liberals, to the tax board.[47] Most historians would agree with Angel Quintero Rivera, who claims the Hollander Bill accelerated the development of agrarian capitalism, transferring land to U.S. corporations.[48] However, in Caguas, at least in the initial years of the twentieth century, large landowners began to lose territory not to U.S. corporations but to the middling sectors of the countryside, mostly because U.S. corporations targeted coastal lands first. From 1881 to 1900, large farms gained about 4,485 cuerdas, but proportionally their territory remained the same (see tables 1.6, 1.7, and 1.8). Large landowners successfully maintained control of the land after 1898 too. Eventually, Caguas joined coastal Puerto Rico in the intensive production of sugar, but U.S. corporations had limited control of the land. The local elite in Caguas continued controlling much of the land. Many large landowners became colonos de caña, farmers who sold cane to sugar factories, and Caguas's large landowners continued influencing politics at the local level. They arranged the beginnings of foreign investment in Caguas and the formation of large-scale sugar factories.[49]

Large Landowners and the Law in Caguas and Puerto Rico

It is always a challenge to interpret individual actions within societal processes and vice versa. There are always individuals, as in today's world, who contradict not only what their own social group proclaims but also their own individual actions. Historians try to explain such contradictions within a framework of possibilities that embraces most people's reality. In Caguas ideas and practices of private rights generally reflect class groups and alliances. However, individuals of all social classes used principles of both private property rights and natural law; their choices and preferences were bound by the limitations and possibilities of their own realities. The landed elite favored private property rights, while the poor and part of the landless peasantry supported the natural law of land possession, specifically the principles of use and need.

In the late nineteenth century, Spaniards and many wealthy Puerto Ricans believed property rights in Puerto Rico had a positivist, modern character. Lawyers at the time maintained a vision of law as science in which the application of formal reasoning could resolve the problems of social organization.[50] According to Spanish statesmen, guaranteeing private property constituted legitimate promotion of progress and modernity in any society. For instance, Fernando López Tuero, engineer and director of the Agronomic Station in Rio Piedras, saw privatization of the land as the only way to achieve social progress. In pursuit of this goal, the state called all social sectors to work and commit to the improvement of private property. Everyone, according to López Tuero, must contribute their efforts and resources; large landowners must commit their knowledge, land, and capital to the production of agrarian goods. But social progress also demanded the commitment of people without economic resources. In particular, progress demanded that rural laborers and peasants contribute their labor to the advancement of the general welfare. In a society where wealth measured progress, social order, and the general welfare, workers were judged by their contribution to economic growth.[51] The government took on the responsibility of guaranteeing that every person contributed to the general welfare.

López Tuero, voicing the view of Spanish authorities at the time, firmly believed that the state functioned mainly to protect property rights.[52] His ideas about the police and private property were incorporated into the organization of the police force at the end of the nineteenth century: the Municipal Law of 1878 gave municipalities the power to organize and administer their own police forces.[53] All the municipal governments in Puerto Rico formulated ordinances to establish the rural and urban po-

lice, though according to *El Buscapié* the ordinances for the establishment
of a municipal police were ignored throughout the island.[54] In the countryside of Caguas, for the most part, policing activities were carried out
by comisarios and alcaldes de barrio.[55]

In 1890 the municipality of Caguas placed guards on private farms.
For example, the municipal government assigned rural guards (*guardia
particular del campo*) to protect the private property of councilors Don
Bartolomé Borrás, Don Landelino Aponte, Don Víctor Fernández, Don
Rafael Rodríguez, and Don Nicolás Quiñonez Cabezudo. Guards were
usually white men who had retired from the Spanish Civil Guard or the
Spanish Army.[56] Large landowners also employed workers who collaborated with the police to protect their farms. In 1891 Don Joaquín Jiménez,
after a series of tobacco thefts from his farm, named two of his laborers
as vigilantes, or guards. The guards caught Ysidoro de la Cruz with a
sack of tobacco; he was tried and sentenced to two months and a day in
prison.[57]

In sum, policing was the mechanism that guaranteed landowners a
social order based on respect for private property; this association between
policed private property and social order continued after U.S. rule. A
Federalist (liberal) writer living in the Caguas countryside with the pen
name of Vecinet defined social order in this manner: An effective and
non-partisan insular police force "will end the turmoil and unrest, the
thefts and robberies in the town and the countryside, games and all kind
of vagrancies, and the people of Puerto Rico will be happy, dedicated to
work in the arms of a perfect order."[58] The press announced that policing
was the "true and unique guarantee for honorable men who live in the
countryside."[59]

Policing, however, became more centralized. In 1898 the U.S. government established a rural guard that reported directly to the governor and
not to the mayor of Caguas.[60] The municipal police force was still in effect,
but it was finally disbanded in 1901, centralizing completely the police
force in the island.[61] By 1902 comisarios and alcaldes de barrio had lost
all their police privileges, circumscribing their duties to administrative
tasks.[62] The municipal government thereby was stripped of any police
power. After losing control of the police, large landowners and liberals of
Caguas were no longer sure of the social order established by the police.
Some political leaders even opposed the creation of a centralized police
force. *La Democracia* published multiple examples of police abuse and
political partisanship, forcing the governor to order an investigation.[63]
In 1904 Raimundo Faura, the Republican judge named by the governor,

was replaced, but the issue of justice and police abuse for Federalists in Caguas was never resolved.[64] In fact, police abuse against civilians in Caguas continued being an important issue for liberals; a reporter in 1907 stressed, "Not even during the most turbulent times has Caguas experienced the type of abuses perpetrated today by the Police force, and the chief is to be blame for all this. . . . We just want to prove one more time that today's Insular Police force is the same as in 1902, and it is not more abusive because it does not count upon those judges who not only approved their abuses but also promoted them."[65] In 1907 a new surveillance organization was established in Puerto Rico, the National Guard, aimed at assisting the Insular Police and promoting social order.[66]

Large landowners' position in relation to the social role of the police changed dramatically after the U.S. occupation. During Spanish rule, they strongly supported the power of the police, when their political standing within the municipal government allowed them to control the police. From a position of power, they proclaimed a world where everyone, including people without property, followed the rules of private ownership. However, when the police were outside their control and when the U.S. colonial government disfavored liberals, they began to protest police brutality—an interesting contradiction, since the Insular Police had a strong commitment to protecting private property. In fact, the social role of the police that protected private property continued without much alteration from the nineteenth to the twentieth century. What changed was large landowners' capacity to control it.

Alternative Access to Resources

After the Mortgage Law of 1880 the principle of natural rights, specifically use as a legitimate claim to land possession, did not disappear; rather, it was more prominent than before, despite greater police surveillance, which failed to eliminate it but tried hard at least to contain it. Natural law acquired greater value after 1880 precisely because it was in jeopardy. As mentioned earlier, the landed elite had at its disposal the police and the municipal government to enforce boundaries and protect private property. Policing and protecting private property became a priority of the municipal government. After 1880 there was an expressed zeal in favor of private property that condemned any other form of property or appropriation. People with property titles grew less tolerant of popular forms of redistribution and had the police at their service to express this intolerance. Intolerance was exacerbated by economic circumstances, such as the drought of 1880, wood scarcity, and increased competition for land, which forced the lowest social sectors of the countryside to look for supplements to semi-nomadic agriculture and sharecropping.

Aggravating circumstances, as Astrid Cubano Iguina observes, subsistence agriculture and fruit cultivation were practically destroyed during the 1880s in order to reorient resources toward export agrarian production. Commercial agriculture in this decade depended on currency devaluation to compete in the international market. This strategy helped Puerto Rican merchants improve and advance competition in the international arena, but it also had devastating consequences for the rest of the country, impoverishing the whole economy. In fact, currency devaluation and salary reductions went hand in hand. In 1884 the currency was devalued 14 percent. By 1898 it had been devalued by 70 percent (see table 3.1). The wages of urban workers suffered a gradual, parallel deterioration, as did their living conditions.[67] In the countryside landless laborers, sharecroppers, and even farmers with land titles suffered the consequences of the financial crisis of the mid-1880s. In particular, the living conditions of the rural poor significantly deteriorated because increasingly they were forced to buy food imports to survive. Life in the countryside became very expensive because most resources were used for commercial agriculture, decreasing the overall food production for the island. Food imports were expensive, and with pauperizing wages the rural poor had to face unbelievable obstacles just to stay alive.[68]

On top of this, the municipal government of Caguas decided to impose an extra tax on food, drinks, and fuel in order to alleviate its own shortages.[69] Taxes on food had a direct and negative effect on the lives of most Puerto Ricans because the island depended heavily on food imports (47.6 percent of total imports in 1895).[70] Impoverished conditions went hand-in-hand with land privatization so that more and more avenues to make a living considered legal by government authorities were closed to the laboring classes. The legal system supported title-holders, who obstructed laborers' access to the land. Therefore, people sought alternative forms of economic subsistence, based on previous experiences and traditions but with new consequences.

The lowest social classes responded to harsh conditions by squatting, which in the last two decades of the nineteenth century became harder than before because of land privatization and the increased policing of fences and titled property. The poor in the rural barrios turned their attention to the products of the land, which were easier to appropriate than land itself. Specifically, the poor redistributed resources from the rich to themselves through small pillage, giving new interpretations to and justi-

Table 3.1.   Currency devaluation in Puerto Rico in the late nineteenth century

Year	Percent devaluation
1884	14
1889	25
1893	40
1898	70

Source: Cubano Iguina, "El autonomismo en Puerto Rico, 1887–1898," 408.

fying their actions with old principles of natural law. As E. P. Thompson states in his study of the English countryside, "customary consciousness and customary usages were especially robust in the eighteenth century: indeed, some 'customs' were of recent invention, and were in truth claims to new 'rights.'"[71] Those "new" customs in the Puerto Rican countryside caused concern among government authorities and intellectuals of the period. Some intellectuals wrote about the communal understanding of property with alarm. Doctor Francisco del Valle Atiles, for example, considered problematic rural laborers' notion of ownership:

> *A jíbaro [peasant] does not believe that he breaks any law when he takes a bird from the pen, a bunch of bananas or other small something, which is still private property in spite of its small value and should therefore not be appropriated without the permission of its owner. Or if he does believe it, it is not because he is convinced that such an act is wrong, but because he knows that he will be punished if he is caught. Of course, not all jíbaros profess this kind of communism, but there are many who show no scruples in practicing it.*[72]

This re-allocation, however, does not imply equality or the primitive communism suggested by del Valle Atiles. On the contrary, natural law made natural resources available to everyone but differentiated the individual capacity to work and obtain natural resources. Greater capacity to work resulted in greater results from nature. However, in the context of the 1880s natural resources had social and political constraints because the land was being privatized. In this sense, enacting natural rights was often against the law, showing some characteristics of social banditry. As Eric J. Hobsbawn argues in his discussion of social banditry, a man (and I add "or a woman") becomes a bandit because he or she does something not regarded as criminal by local conventions but which is so regarded by the state or the local rulers. Social banditry is also a modest and non-revolutionary protest and seeks certain limits to traditional oppression.[73]

Redistribution of goods in the countryside of Caguas may have saved some rural residents from starvation; however, it did not change their socio-economic situation.[74] Small pillage might have provided a meal or two but did not improve living conditions as a whole.

However, people who held the principles of natural law were not always outside the realms of the law. Natural law did not exclude private property rights because the goal of many people was to guarantee access to the land, and privatization was the ultimate, best-known way to do so. The main objective was to legitimize use as a form of privatization.

Fair distribution of resources was an important principle for laborers, sharecroppers, and even the landed peasantry because practicing it became a matter of survival for the lowest social sectors of the countryside. Poverty and harsh living conditions partially unified sharecroppers, rural laborers, and the landed peasantry.[75] In some ways, the social position of the landed peasantry was deteriorating; they were in-between the dispossessed and the landed elite. Land ownership ranged widely, from .25 to 30 cuerdas or more, and so did production, quality of the soil, and value of land. Hilly areas, usually characterized by poor quality soil and poor roads, had a much lower value than farms in the valley, where good roads and rich soil made them accessible and profitable. Ownership of land parcels of different sizes and values was the common characteristic among the landed peasantry. But while their titles of ownership separated them from the sharecroppers and rural workers, their vulnerability to scarce resources often pushed them toward the poorest end of the economic spectrum.

Throughout the nineteenth century, Caguas experienced a process of land privatization that fragmented the holdings of the landed peasantry. As shown in chapter 1, the number of landed peasants steadily increased from 1881 to 1900, even though the territory under their control remained essentially the same. Their vulnerability was also assured by the Spanish system of taxation; they supported the finances of the municipal government through high taxes, which forced many landed peasants to hire out their labor. Indeed, throughout the late nineteenth century, the daily life of the landed peasantry became closer and closer to that of the sharecropper and often to the day laborer. In many instances, their positions were indistinguishable, as even the landed peasantry recognized. Francisco Osuna, for example, abandoned farming, stating, "Since three or four years ago, I have not farmed that land because it does not yield anything of value."[76] His soil was of such poor quality that Osuna was forced to look for waged labor to satisfy his and his family's needs. Osuna experienced extreme poverty even though he was healthy enough to work the land for himself or others.

Illness or any other inconvenience, albeit temporary, crushed the economic resources of other landed peasants. Mercedes Negrón, for example, explained, "I had been sick for over ten years, someone else has to feed me because I cannot even use my hands. I have a small piece of land that does not yield anything."[77] She was trying to sell her farm of ten cuerdas in Barrio Borinquen, but it was difficult to sell because its soil was of poor quality ("peña pobre") in a hilly area.[78] The landed peasantry certainly shared with sharecroppers and rural laborers poor living conditions.

People like Mercedes Negrón and Francisco Osuna, along with many sharecroppers and rural workers, pushed authorities to reconsider the implications of the law. The Regulations for the Composition and Sale of Unused Land of 1884 reaffirmed that work or use justified land possession, based on the idea that natural resources are universal and available to those who exploit them, a concept that had been part of the Spanish legal system since the Middle Ages and that maintained its legal vitality after 1898.[79] The law of 1884 gave powerful ammunition to sharecroppers, rural laborers, and some landed peasants who refused to pay rent for land. Their work gave them permanent right to the land to the dismay of private property owners. For example, José Esterás complained about the "frequency" with which workers refused to pay him rent, describing the situation as "fatal."[80] Those "workers," however, asserted their natural right to land with their actions, refusing to pay rent and tilling the land to satisfy their own needs.

The law of 1884 referred exclusively to the land, but many people from the lowest social classes applied it to objects, crops, and animals, finding themselves at odds with legal authorities and the landed elite. In order to cope with the devastating effects of an impoverished economy and land privatization, marginal sectors in the countryside resorted to small pillage, which followed a particular pattern that helps clarify cultural concepts of ownership among the poorest sectors in Caguas. To a large extent, theft occurred among people who knew each other. There were 153 robbery cases in the countryside of Caguas from 1880 to 1900, of which 75 reveal information about the perpetrator or the suspect. Out of these 75 files, the plaintiffs knew the transgressor as a neighbor in 30.72 percent of the cases (as shown in table 3.2). "Neighbor" meant someone who lived close by or in the same barrio, a person the plaintiff could easily recognize and locate. This level of intimacy might suggest that people incorporated small

Table 3.2.   Relation of the perpetrator/suspect to the plaintiff in judicial cases

Years	Number of Cases	Neighbor	Unknown	No Suspect
1880–1885	40	10	2	7
1886–1890	5	*	*	*
1891–1895	28	5	0	7
1896–1900	80	32	2	10
Total	153	47	4	24
Percentage	100	30.72	2.61	15.69

Sources: Archivo Histórico Municipal de Caguas AHMC, Archivo General de Puerto Rico AGPR, *La Democracia*, and *La Correspondencia*.

pillage into their daily activities and that small pillage had a quasi-casual nature as dictated by circumstances.

People who took fruit or any other small object frequently did not even bother to cover up their acts. For instance, early in the morning on January 9, 1880, Victorio Álamo, a rural laborer of Barrio Turabo, took a bunch of bananas from the farm of his neighbor Gumersindo Santos, a sharecropper of the same barrio. After appropriating the fruits in question, Álamo crossed a small stream from Santos's banana trees directly to his house, leaving a clear set of footprints, which he did not bother to erase. Santos followed the set of prints to Álamo's house and found the bananas hanging on a stick. Afterward, Santos reported the incident to the alcalde de barrio, Luis Acosta.[81] In another case, the sisters Gabriela and Pola Ortiz, residents of Barrio Cañabón, entered the house of the small landowner Lope Muñiz on the night of November 2, 1900, and stole some women's and children's clothes. The next day, Lope Muñiz went to downtown Caguas and, on his way, saw the Ortiz sisters wearing his daughter's clothes in public and in the company of three other neighbors.[82] The fact that they did not try to hide the evidence and, more importantly, that they went out in public with the clothes suggests that they felt at ease about stealing needed clothes.

One might accuse these perpetrators simply of being bad thieves, but when comparing their actions to those of other perpetrators, often outsiders, the evidence points toward something different. The acts of these neighbors seemed casual, even spontaneous, and not planned. In contrast, perpetrators who targeted valuables such as cattle or large amounts of coffee or tobacco rather than small objects seemed more systematic in their acts and tried to hide their tracks. Various techniques were used in stealing cattle. For instance, a perpetrator spent some days observing a cow or horse, until he or she could isolate the animal in a distant corner

Table 3.3. Distribution of robberies in kind, 1880–1910

	1880–85	1886–90	1891–95	1896–1900	1901–05	1906–10	Total
Num. Cases	40	5	28	80	9	23	185
Agrarian Products	8	1	6	23	0	0	38
Domestic Birds	5	0	2	17	0	0	24
Tools	1	1	0	3	0	0	5
Cattle	14	2	13	11	8	17	65
Money	3	0	0	2	1	0	6
Other	6	0	1	5	0	0	12
Non Specific	4	1	6	21	0	6	33

Sources: Archivo Histórico Municipal de Caguas AHMC, Archivo General de Puerto Rico AGPR, *La Democracia*, and *La Correspondencia*.

in the farm. Sometimes, the thief tied the animal, waiting for darkness to steal it.[83] Others stole cattle in surrounding towns and hid them on their relatives' farms.[84] Exchanging an old mare for a better one proved successful for one thief.[85] Thus, stealing cattle or large objects required more caution and planning than small pillage. However, between 1880 and 1910 police reported a similar number of cases of large and petty theft. There were sixty-seven robberies of produce, agrarian tools, and domestic birds; sixty-five robberies of cattle; and fifty-six robberies of money and other objects (see table 3.3).

It seems that Cagüeños made a distinction between small theft and planned pillage, giving some degree of tolerance to the former. Large landowners might tolerate certain redistribution because it was also convenient for them. It was in land-title holders' best interests to maintain laborers and sharecroppers close to their farms in order to guarantee easy access to labor. Rural laborers and sharecroppers could move from the area if landowners did not meet their needs. Thus, property owners tolerated small pillage, which allowed social leverage and guaranteed workers in the area.[86]

In contrast, people lost patience with thefts of big, valuable objects or even systematic small thefts. Cagüeños showed this intolerance by reporting to the police any robbery case that involved some sort of planning or that involved high-value objects and animals. The use of traps, for example, strongly suggested forethought. Simeón Ríos was caught with three chickens that belonged to Luciano Lindor. In the investigations, the police found a chicken trap in his house.[87] In Barrio San Antonio, Mariana Estrada commanded her three sons Nicolás, Agustín, and Ramón Estrada, to take some bananas from the medium-sized farm of Don Marcos Estrada.[88] In their efforts, Mariana's sons destroyed part of the banana fields. Mariana and Don Marcos were neighbors and knew each other. When Don Marcos realized that his banana fields had been robbed and partially damaged, he relayed the incident to the alcalde de barrio. Don Marcos, who had neither "malice" (*malicia*) nor "suspicion" (*sospecha*), went to Mariana's home accompanied by a couple of men and the alcalde de barrio in order to collect information that might lead to the thief. But to Don Marcos's surprise, when the men arrived at Mariana's home they found about nine hundred banana peels badly hidden in a small pit near the house. The men counted only the recently peeled bananas but the report stressed that there were other peels as many as four to six days old.[89] How the Estrada brothers used the bananas is never mentioned, but it was clear that they stole too much and had to face the police as a result.

In Barrio Tomás de Castro, Felix Rodríguez and Julián Morales were known among neighbors as chicken thieves. Reporting some stolen chickens in 1900, Jesús Cortés, a proprietor in the same barrio, suspected Rodríguez and Morales since they were "accustomed to that kind of robbery."[90] Indeed, Rodríguez and Morales had been accused before of the same crime.[91] The alcalde de barrio forced Morales to pay for the chicken.[92] Meanwhile, Rodríguez took three chickens from the small farm of the alcalde de barrio, Gregorio Arroyo. After investigations, Arroyo found a feather from one of his chickens next to the house of Juan Colón, left from the Colón family's dinner. The Colón family enjoyed the chicken that night thanks to the generosity of Rodríguez, who had brought the chicken the day before.[93] Colón never questioned Rodríguez about the origins of the chicken but enjoyed it with his family. The report also made clear that there was no sales transaction but that Rodríguez gave the chicken to Colón. Intentionally or not, Rodríguez's actions effectively redistributed resources in Barrio Tomás de Castro. Obviously, Arroyo owned more than one chicken and Colón owned none, and yet, Colón's family enjoyed dinner without paying for the chicken. Colón was never accused of stealing, but Rodríguez was accused because he had been caught before with a large number of stolen birds.[94] The calculating nature of Rodríguez's actions was not tolerated by large landowners and the police.

A similar number of small and planned thefts might also testify to the success of small pillage. Perpetrators could erase the evidence by simply eating it or hiding it. They could be accused only if caught in the act, and this proved much more difficult for property owners and the police. Even though evidence is scarce, the context and words of some complaints suggest that petty robberies were common. For example, on September 7, 1900, Jesús Cortés, a proprietor in Barrio Tomás de Castro, went to the police to report some robberies in his farm. He complained that "in this barrio one cannot work, since every night there are robberies of female pigs, chickens, turkeys, ropes, and fruits; I already have lost ropes and other things."[95]

Small pillage was not the sole terrain of the destitute. The landed peasantry had a problematic relation with small pillage. Some landed peasants practiced small pillage, while others accused neighbors of stealing their fruit, as shown in previous examples. However, this contradiction illustrates an ideal of justice in the countryside, where the powerful were called to give more than the poor. It was acceptable to steal from those who had a lot but punishable to steal from sharecroppers or the landed peasantry. As Brendan McConville documents for eighteenth-century New Jersey: "An assault on the rights or property of a community member was a crime, but the pillaging of wealthy enemies for profit was an entirely different matter."[96] It was acceptable to steal from a rich man because he was not using most of his land anyway, but the poor man was using all his resources to make a living. For instance, Gumersindo Santos, a sharecropper in Barrio Turabo accused his neighbor of stealing a bunch of bananas in 1880, but in 1885 the tables turned, and Santos was brought to justice for trespassing on state property. Santos had two horses grazing along the roads for which he was fined two pesos. Santos stole from the state but did not tolerate a neighbor stealing from his sharecropped farm.[97]

Even rural laborers expressed the notion of justice that stealing from the poor was considered a crime. On the night of January 7, 1900, Juan de Mata Torres y Rodríguez, a rural laborer of Barrio Cañaboncito, and his wife, Juana León, went to a party in the house of a neighbor. When the couple returned from the party, they caught Agustín Osorio, a rural laborer from the same barrio, inside their house trying to steal four pounds of meat that the couple left inside a box. Osorio ran away leaving a machete and a straw hat that served as evidence for Juan's accusation. Juan stressed that his house was unguarded because they went to the party.[98] This sense of justice was also expressed on a large scale throughout the island in the 1898 popular revolts against *hacendados* (hacienda owners) in Puerto Rico. Rebels looted and destroyed haciendas and property of powerful owners, in particular Spaniards.[99]

Property was not only re-appropriated and pillaged but also voluntary redistributed, which is often undocumented because it did not violate any law. Most sharing in fact went unrecorded. However, there is evidence that voluntary redistribution formed an important part of daily living in the rural barrios of Caguas, and it involved the rich as well as the poor. Modesto Solá, the large landowner and councilor, gave his workers in Barrio Turabo some sugar cane of poor quality, unfit for sale. Solá cultivated two cuerdas of sugar cane for experimentation but because the result was so poor, he gave it away.[100] Even though people like Solá sought wealth, they understood that some concessions to the community were necessary for the well-being of the whole society.[101] Their support for redistribution was minimal but instrumental in maintaining the social order. Oral history also reveals that redistributive practices lasted into the twentieth century and often took the form of sharing information and crop surpluses.[102]

Critics might suggest that the image of redistribution in oral histories might account more for romantic memories than for reality, but people's insistence on an image in which sharing was one of the most valuable characteristics of their communities served as an inspirational concept that measured the past and the present and that opposed the claims and rights of private property. Indeed, redistribution constituted an ideal of justice among the rural poor in Puerto Rico. After an analysis of a collection of popular songs and stories in the twentieth century, Lillian Guerra states that stories of Juan Bobo, the main character of these popular narratives, "implied a mutuality of struggle transected by an awareness of community needs; principal among these was a perception of Self that would be geared toward the refutation of elite critiques while remaining aligned with community values."[103] In the case of Caguas, community values emphasized access to land and its products with work.

The Essence of the Unequal Race

The constant clashes between the police and people who asserted rights not only to the land but also to its produce reveal a larger social conflict that affected the whole island and the Caribbean and that had a racial dimension. Racial tensions during the aftermath of slavery exacerbated debates over access to natural resources. The Mortgage Law of 1880 intended to keep former slaves and their descendants readily available for work and away from subsistence agriculture by making it difficult for them to own or have informal access to land. The law attempted to reverse decades of history in which people of color gained access to economic resources. Free people of color in Cuba and Puerto Rico gained numerical and social significance before the abolition of slavery and represented a constant reminder to Spanish authorities of the "dangers" if all slaves were free. Spanish authorities feared mainly that ex-slaves would not work for a salary because many free people of color were self-employed and refused to engage in wage labor.[104]

In the last decades of the nineteenth century, Spanish authorities were also forced to deal with the reality that slavery was a dying institution. The Mortgage Law of 1880 (issued in May) in part anticipated the abolition of slavery in Cuba and attempted to curb the effects the *patronato* (apprenticeship) law established on January 30, 1880. This apprenticeship provided for an eight-year period of tutelage during which masters were compensated by their former slaves' work. At the end of this period, former slaves were set free, but because of political instability, slavery in Cuba was officially abolished in 1886, two years before the patronato had dictated.[105] Clearly, the law attempted to curtail the economic power and mobility of ex-slaves in Cuba. However, the law also applied in Puerto Rico, where slavery had been abolished seven years before, in 1873, and where slaves had ceased to be the largest share of the labor force by the late 1860s because the sugar industry practically collapsed and landowners had used waged labor for decades.[106] In Puerto Rico, the apprenticeship period that started in 1870 ended in 1876, four years before the Mortgage Law was issued in 1880. During these four years, former slaves were free to move around, buy land, and produce for themselves. But as in the rest of the Caribbean, authorities and the landed elite saw with terror how former slaves succeeded as small agrarian producers and how the lack of workers let their own fields go fallow.[107] The Mortgage Law of 1880, along with forced labor, discussed in the next chapter, dealt directly with this issue by attempting to eliminate informal access to the land. Former slaves and peasants were the main target of the law in Puerto Rico because historically they were the main practitioners of squatting and sharecropping. However, state authorities designed and distinguished between the categories of peasants and former slaves in order to create divisions among the working classes, further demoralizing and alienating them. In fact, former slaves were peasants before and after the abolition of slavery, and the peasantry was mostly a mulatto population, whose livelihood was almost undistinguishable from that of former slaves. Both former slaves and peasants were part of the lowest sectors of rural society and included rural laborers, sharecroppers, and landed peasants. They were equally affected by the Mortgage Law of 1880 and held tight to the principle of use to legitimize their access to land.

Even when slavery was still in effect, free blacks and people of color in Caguas had been successful in guaranteeing formal access to the land. The census of 1873, albeit incomplete, clearly suggests that blacks and people of color had access to the land in numbers comparable to white folks. In Barrio Beatriz, for example, there were six white farmers and seven non-white farmers (four blacks and three colored). Non-whites outnumbered white sharecroppers by two to one; there were ten of the former and five of the latter.[108]

Of the four black farmers, only one was able to retain title to land. Bibiano Ramos Ortiz and Hermenegildo Losado Salgado lost their land and became day laborers by 1882.[109] Domingo Ortiz Delgado apparently moved from the area after losing his land. Only Francisco Díaz was able to maintain his formal title to sixty cuerdas until 1896, increasing the size of his estate afterward.[110] However, Díaz faced many obstacles. In 1887 he assured municipal authorities that his neighbor's generosity saved him from hiring out his labor to sustain his family. He had been forced to sell most of his cattle the year before to pay taxes. His neighbor, seeing his precarious conditions, offered him gratis the use of some land to make a living.[111] Even though Díaz had a farm of sixty cuerdas in Barrio Beatriz, he experienced poverty and quasi-destitution because his farm was of poor quality soil, and the taxes were too high.[112] Among the black farmer's descendants, only Díaz's son was able to buy or keep some land. Francisco Díaz Figueroa bought twenty-eight cuerdas in Barrio Cañaboncito in 1891, but after 1897 he held no land in his own name.[113]

Colored farmers did a little bit better than black farmers in retaining land, as was the case in Brazil.[114] Two of the three colored farmers in Barrio Beatriz were able to secure titles to land for a prolonged period of time. Ramón Ramos Robles apparently moved from the area after losing his land, but both Aniseto Navarro Castro and Marcelino Medina Ramos owned small farms for more than a decade. Navarro Castro had fifty cuerdas of land until 1887, when he transferred the property to his son Joaquín. The farm was kept relatively intact, losing only about ten cuerdas, until 1900. Joaquín's brother, Pedro, bought land in the same barrio, after having worked as a day laborer until he was able to buy land. From 1897 to 1900, his estate had seventy-five cuerdas. In comparison, none of Medina Ramos's children secured a piece of land under their names. Medina Ramos kept eighteen cuerdas of land until 1897, when he sold the whole farm to Don Landelino Aponte, the councilor and owner of a very large estate.[115]

For former slaves, the circumstances seemed hardest. Although the Spanish government in the island stopped using color categories in the censuses after 1873, there are some clues that indicate that for former slaves and their descendants obtaining title to a piece of land was extremely difficult. The censuses continued designating the birthplace of the population, which makes it possible to trace the occupation of both those born in Africa and their children living in the same household. In 1882 there were nine people in the rural barrios of Caguas who were born in Africa, and four of their descendants are clearly identified. None of them owns land, and only one seems to have rented land. Bautista Polo, a freeman born in Caguas, lived with his parents in Barrio Río Cañas and possibly sharecropped.[116] Former slaves in Caguas seemed to follow the pattern of the Spanish Caribbean where, former slaves had a very slim chance of obtaining land.[117] After the Mortgage Law of 1880, people of color, who constituted the great majority of the population, began to lose access to land. As they lost access to land, people of color almost doubled their numbers in the waged labor force from 1882 to 1899. In 1899 rural laborers who were racially mixed constituted the majority of the working class in the rural barrios of Caguas (56.89 percent or 2,495).[118]

However, while the census sample of ex-slaves might be too small to draw a definite conclusion, the census speaks volumes for what it does not say. In 1882 Francisco Polo, Bautista's father, owned ten cuerdas of land in Barrio Río Cañas that, though they were of poor quality, allowed him to make a living for himself and his family.[119] Clearly, Polo might be considered by the conventions of the time either a farmer or a property owner. However, the census does not list any occupation for Polo, denying the former slave the possibility to identify himself with landownership. This rejection along with the stipulations of the Mortgage Law of 1880 effectively disqualified people of color from owning land. Three years later, when Polo was forced to sell some land, possibly to pay taxes, his farm was further reduced to eight cuerdas.[120] Eventually, Polo lost his piece of land. By 1889 the only Polo with title to land was Don Rafael Polo, the councilor and prominent landowner who very probably had owned Francisco Polo and his family before 1873.[121]

It is not possible to determine the exact number of people of color who had land titles in the late nineteenth century because after 1873 the census eliminated race from its categories and the tax records never registered it. However, the land patterns for Barrio Río Cañas shed light onto this

Table 3.4.   Number of farms by size and area in Barrio Río Cañas, 1881

	Number of farms		Area in Farms	
Size (cuerdas)	Farms	Percent	Cuerdas	Percent
.25–30	16	61.54	319	30.09
31–70	7	26.92	346	32.64
71–199	2	7.69	195	18.4
200–400	1	3.85	200	18.87
401 and over	0	0	0	0
Total	26	100	1,060	100

Sources: AHMC, SEC Finanzas, SSEC Contribuciones, SER Planillas de Riqueza, SSER Agrícola, 1880–81, C80 and 81.

issue because this barrio was hilly and of poor quality soil and historically known as the locus of the poorest sectors of Caguas society. Thus, Barrio Río Cañas represented a magnet for people of color, such as Francisco Polo. The land was divided mostly among small farms in the early 1880s. In 1881 sixteen farmers controlled 319 cuerdas of land, or 30.09 percent of the registered territory in this barrio. There was only one large farm of 200 cuerdas (see table 3.4). In sharp contrast, by 1896 thirty-six peasants held title to 500.5 cuerdas of land, or 12.43 percent of the registered land in Barrio Río Cañas, while three large farms occupied 2,105.5 cuerdas, or 46.91 percent (see table 3.5). Proportionally, landed peasants were losing territory to large farms. Moreover, there was a significant increase in the proportion of the territory that was registered throughout the late nineteenth century. In 1896 there were 2,967 more cuerdas of registered land than in 1881. It is safe to assume that this land was occupied by racially mixed peasants who had no official title to land and who were forced out by 1896. While the increase in land registration affected people of all social sectors, large landowners by 1896 monopolized the great majority

Table 3.5.   Number of farms by size and area in Barrio Río Cañas, 1896

	Number of farms		Area in Farms	
Size (cuerdas)	Farms	Percent	Cuerdas	Percent
.25–30	36	60	500.5	12.43
31–70	16	26.66	918	22.8
71–199	6	10	503	12.48
200–400	1	1.67	216.5	5.38
401 and over	1	1.67	1,889	46.91
Total	60	100	4,027	100

Sources: AHMC, SEC Finanzas, SSEC Contribuciones, SER Planillas de Riqueza, SSER Agrícola, 1896, C95.

Table 3.6. Racial profile of farmers in Caguas, 1910

	Farmers		Owners		Tenants	
White	700	78.48	531	59.53	158	17.71
Non-white	192	21.52	151	16.93	39	4.37
Total	892		682		197	

Source: U.S. Bureau of the Census, *Thirteenth Census of the United States*, 2:995 and 1000–1001.

of the territory at the cost of people who previously had informal access to land (see tables 3.4 and 3.5). Also, the large number of workers who were racially mixed by 1898 confirmed this trend in Barrio Río Cañas.

In the twentieth century, people of color represented a small minority in titled holdings. Only 16.93 percent of farmers in Caguas who were non-white owned their farms, while 4.37 percent were non-white tenants. In sharp contrast, 59.53 percent of farmers who were white owned their land (see table 3.6). Ownership among people of color was insignificant considering their numbers. In 1910 blacks and mulattos formed more than 40 percent of the total population of Caguas. These figures mark a process that had parallels in Cuba and in most of the Caribbean: the alienation of Afro-Caribbean people from the land and their conversion into day laborers.[122]

People of color in Caguas held tightly to the principles of natural law mainly because the Mortgage Law of 1880 excluded them from land privatization. Natural law became a stronghold among the underdogs because the Regulations of Unused Land of 1884 protected some their access to land, and the application of natural law to objects, crops, and animals in the form of small pillage was somewhat tolerated. The interpretation of natural law did not stop with natural resources but was also incorporated in the understanding of individual rights and claims of citizenship, as the next chapter discusses.

Stepping toward Liberation
Defense of Mobility Rights and Race

The concept of natural law was applied not only to land and natural resources but also to other aspects of human relations. Charles McCurdy finds that for anti-rent movement leaders in nineteenth-century New York, "natural law provided an acknowledged standard for evaluating the righteousness of human law."[1] In Caguas labor justified not only land possession but also social, economic, and political worth as reflected in the law and equal treatment before the law as expressed in popular claims to appropriate labor, time, and leisure. Elites agreed that labor was the most important asset of an individual, but their ideas about its use and worth drastically clashed with those of the working classes. Intellectuals and the municipal government believed that the value and purpose of labor was the development of private property. As a result, in 1881 they supported the enactment of the law of the *cédula de vecindad* (residential identification document) to force the poorest sectors of the rural barrios to comply with a labor ethic that directly benefited large landowners. The poorest sectors of the countryside constantly challenged the legality of this measure through civil disobedience, claiming equal standing with large landowners and political figures before the law. This chapter discusses a cornerstone of marginal citizenship: defiance of the system of forced labor and the poor's reclamation of mobility rights.

Science to Advance Forced Labor
In the rural barrios of Caguas, there were at least two competing notions of work that shared some similarities. One came from the working populations and the other from the government and the elites. Both elevated the importance of individual labor, but their ends and implementation differed sharply. Rural laborers, sharecroppers, and the landed peasantry assigned value to work as a matter of personal pride and honor, which justified possession of land and legal identity.[2] In contrast, the local elites in Caguas

and Puerto Rico perceived labor and the working classes through utilitar-
ian lenses, linking them to economic growth and scientific principles that
placed greatest importance on the productive capacity of the individual.
For authorities and liberals, labor was essentially another source of raw
material on the island that had to be exploited for the well-being of the
whole society; it was something to be extracted from the masses, using
force if necessary.

In particular, after the abolition of slavery, the landed elite in Caguas
and in the rest of Puerto Rico and the Caribbean attempted to impose a
labor discipline among former slaves and their descendants so that they
would accept salaried labor instead of relying on subsistence agriculture.
As discussed in the previous chapter, elites used Spanish laws of land
privatization to keep colored people from owning land. In fact, as in
the rest of the Caribbean, land privatization and the land question were
attempts to control labor.[3]

Limiting the mobility of former slaves and the racially mixed population was the principal goal of the official policies of labor discipline.
However, color and race were rarely mentioned in the official policies;
instead, economic scientific principles justified labor coercion. In Puerto
Rico, silence on the issue of race in official policies was not because Puerto
Rican leaders were above racial discourses of inequality and oppression
but because they thought it unnecessary, as they had no doubt that colored people's sole role in society was to work for a wage. Also, the leaders
perceived workers and laborers to have skin color that was darker than
their own. This association was so clear and obvious that, to elites, it did
not require further examination.

Rather than the color of their skin, what the leaders did carefully scru-
tinize were laborers' attitudes toward work and life in general. The peren-
nial obstacle to commercial agriculture, according to local elites in Puerto
Rico, was the lack of a reliable working population, for a large sector
of the landed peasantry, many rural laborers, and sharecroppers found
ways to avoid wage labor. The government issued a series of labor laws
to guarantee economic growth and progress by supplying workers for the
fields. Official reports condemned the habits of the working classes, who
were also indirectly referred to as racially mixed.[4] In 1893, for instance,
Fernando López Tuero, engineer and director of the Agronomic Station
of Río Piedras, stated,

> *The laborer, except for numerous exceptions that honor his class,
> has neither inclination to work nor a good labor education; does*

*not want to suffer any inconvenience against his way of being; a
minor correction suffices for him to leave work; has no motivation,
employs his intelligence, which is not little, to conspire against the*
master's interests; *frequently does his job badly on purpose, trust-
ing that it will pass for good, mocks the owner and when he has
attained enough money to satisfy, not his needs, but his caprices,
cares little about both work and commitments; leaves the task and
departs, even if he leaves a Virgin's altar [camarín] half finished.*[5]
(my emphasis)

López Tuero makes a clear, direct connection between workers and slavery
by referring to the "master's interests." López Tuero, like other intellectuals, superficially distinguished between peasants and former slaves and
their descendants but treated them equally.

Puerto Rican intellectuals also criticized the apparent liberties taken by
peasants in their labor contracts. For example, del Valle Atiles claimed,
"When the peasant decides to rent his services, he does it willingly [*con
buena voluntad*]; but in honor of the truth he neither follows contract
conventions strictly, nor does he make major efforts to take care of objects
that had been commended to him; he works, and works like few laborers,
if we consider his poor nutrition, but he maintains certain independence
that is often translated into work absenteeism, with no other reason than
his voluntary impulses."[6]

P. Morales Cabrera suggested that scientific, commercial agriculture
would eliminate inefficient producers such as small farmers and laborers.
He proposed:

*Let's then reform our laws, avoiding the dismemberment of rural
properties, the endless subdivision of farms, and, as the property
area expands, labor will take flight, substituting small production for
big ones, and small producers will find refuge within the towns. Let's
encourage the use of agrarian machines which, simplifying agrarian
work, will launch peasants out of their solitude, seeking employment. . . . The small-property owner will sell his farm to someone
who has better means to exploit it, putting his modest capital to
other productive business; the destitute will march behind the one
that can meet his needs.*[7]

Morales Cabrera links the scientific search for better agriculture to the social displacement of ineffective producers. He presents land displacement
as equally beneficial to peasants and large landowners because the latter

would care for the former with employment. Reformation and repression formed part of the rhetoric and practice of disciplining the labor force.[8] In particular, the availability of workers by the elimination of subsistence agriculture clearly addressed the ideal of separating former slaves and, more important, the racially mixed population from the land.

Authorities also sought the transformation of the working classes through the educational and the legal systems.[9] The *casas de beneficiencia* (charity houses), for example, openly sought to train individuals to work for wages in order to mitigate the labor crisis in Puerto Rico.[10] The police were also instrumental in addressing labor discipline. As Madeline Román argues, criminality in Puerto Rico was linked to the bourgeois project of imposing capitalist values and a capitalist ethic on the population's laboring sectors.[11] The capitalist labor ethic consisted of working enthusiastically for long hours, day after day, week after week, for employers with private property. Docility and contentment were also expected, but because workers did not readily adopt this ethic, the police were called upon to enforce it.

The municipal government used the police and the legal system in Caguas to constrain the so-called dangerous classes.[12] The chances that a rural laborer would be fined, accused of an offense, or imprisoned were higher than for a well-to-do person. In fact, the police system in Caguas processed more people from the working classes than from any other sector, and the "criminal" was very often a laborer. In cases of violent crime in which professional background is recorded, rural laborers constituted the majority of the assailants, while proprietors and farmers formed the majority of targets (see table 4.1).

Men represented the large majority of assailants, targets, and witnesses in violent acts that were reported to the legal authorities. Men constituted 92.91 percent of the assailants, while women represented only 7.09 percent (see table 4.2). In other areas of the island, criminal records showed a similar pattern in the 1880s.[13] In the 1890s and early twentieth century, Caguas police mainly processed the same suspects as in the 1880s, that is, men from the working class, but it is more difficult to determine the racial composition of this group.

Unfortunately, the data does not offer enough information to determine the racial background of all the people with whom the police dealt. In the 1880s and the 1890s in Caguas, authorities described carefully the physical appearance and racial profile of only those individuals who escaped prison or the courts. In general, they were non-white, but even those few files were not systematic. The descriptions usually referred to prisoners

Table 4.1.   Socio-professional background of targets and assailants, 1880–1910

Profession	Targets	Assailants
Jornalero/Labrador	12	40
Sharecropper	2	2
Sale person	1	4
Domestic	2	2
Housewife	2	0
Store owner	2	0
Teacher	0	1
Seamstress	1	0
Overseer	2	1
Road Patrol	0	1
Farmer/Proprietor	41	13

Sources: Archivo Histórico Municipal de Caguas AHMC, *La Democracia*, and *La Correspondencia*.

who had no contact with people in the community, whereas files for those who were known in their barrios did not offer any physical description. It was enough to name an individual of a barrio for the comisario or alcalde de barrio to search for him. Moreover, the Spanish censuses of the late nineteenth century had eliminated race from their categories. Nonetheless, policies and intellectual treatises about labor discipline made clear that their target was also racially specific. The working classes, including the landed peasantry, were perceived as non-white.

Nineteenth-century Puerto Rican intellectuals were in tune with Darwin's and Spencer's theories of the species and evolution, particularly with Spencer's "social" application of evolution. With scientific racism, these intellectuals affirmed their racial superiority over peasants in general.[14] They believed that the mestizo nature of peasants contributed to their degenerate condition and stressed that peasants who were white in appearance were not truly white since they were "polluted" with the conditions of living in the tropics and with their interaction with blacks.[15] Del Valle Atiles asserted that "the black's moral deficiencies have been able to

Table 4.2.   Gender of assailants, targets, and witnesses in cases of violence, 1880–1910

Sex	Assailants	Percentage	Targets	Percentage	Witnesses	Percentage
Female	18	7.09	67	33.17	21	9.95
Male	236	92.91	135	66.83	190	90.05
Total	254		202		211	

Sources: Archivo Histórico Municipal de Caguas AHMC, *La Democracia*, and *La Correspondencia*.

produce damaging results in the moral disposition of country men."[16] He also questioned the intellectual capacity of peasants.[17] Liberals in general adopted del Valle Atiles's vision of the peasantry.[18] The role left to the fathers of the nation was to guide the rural masses with culture and labor. Del Valle Atiles was convinced that the "weak races disappear before strong races: therefore, it is crucial in order not to be extinct, to achieve the proper organic strength through work and intellectual and moral culture."[19] Del Valle Atiles denies whiteness even to those peasants who looked white. In his opinion, whiteness was incompatible with working classes. However, perceptions of the peasantry's racial background dramatically changed after 1898.

The U.S. government in 1899 reincorporated race as a category of the census in Puerto Rico and Cuba.[20] In general, "whitening," passing as white, was feasible for more Puerto Ricans than for Cubans after 1898. Puerto Ricans supposedly had lighter skin color than Cubans. People of the mountains of Puerto Rico in particular were represented as white in the official studies and policies of the U.S. government on the island.[21] There was an interesting debate among U.S. officials regarding the racial composition of rural Puerto Ricans. While in general U.S. officials considered all Puerto Ricans their racial inferiors, army doctors popularized a discourse that stressed the white stock of the mountain people. On the one hand, U.S. officials emphasized the "indolence" and racial "difficulty" of Puerto Ricans.[22] On the other hand, descriptions of the rural folk after 1898 usually accented whiteness. George Cabot Ward, for example, was certain that the rural folk in Puerto Rico were "predominantly white" and thus had "remarkably quick intelligence and perceptions."[23] The U.S. Army's Dr. Bailey K. Ashford helped to solidify racial perceptions of the rural folk in the mountains with his anemia campaign. In his medical reports, Dr. Ashford reaffirmed that "the vast majority of the mountain people should be considered white."[24] Other medical experts in the United States challenged Dr. Ashford's scientific results. Dr. A. Huston, for example, questioned Dr. Ashford's theories:

> *You say that the* jíbaros *[peasants] are not lazy—that they are anemic. In your thesis you could almost prove that Anemia is a Spanish colonial disease. The "system" consisted in a moral degradation of the people, therefore, the physical degradation. The terrorized country people had to seek a refuge in primitivism, this being the only way of living tolerated by the government. Imposed primitivism, means degradation: as the organism must develop it wears out in the strug-*

3. Reinvigorating pills for white peasants. A newspaper advertisement that was popular after 1898. (*La Democracia*)

> gle. *Cod-fish, illiterate heads, Catholic friars, lyrism, militarism—such were the tools. You can not overlook these considerations in treating this subject!*[25]

Despite medical challenges, Dr. Ashford's observations that the rural folk were white prevailed in Puerto Rico.

Cagüeños also participated in and took advantage of this process of "whitening." While in 1899 whites comprised 45.65 percent of the population of Caguas, in 1910 that figure had risen to 58.83 percent. The increase was not only due to natural reproduction but also to a shift in general racial perception. People of mixed ancestry with a light complexion were counted as white. Only people with very dark skin were considered black. The black population of Caguas, according to the census, decreased by almost half from 1899 to 1910. The decrease of the mulatto population almost equaled the increase of the white population (see table 4.3).

People of unquestionable blackness, whose skin color was very dark, could not participate in the passing-as-white fashion of the twentieth century. They suffered the extra burden of being associated with brutishness because not being able to whiten was understood as not being able to improve culturally. Therefore, black Puerto Ricans were condemned to

Table 4.3. Number of inhabitants by race in Caguas, 1899 and 1910

	1899	Percentage	1910	Percentage
Total	19,857		27,160	
White	9,065	45.65	15,979	58.83
Black	1,116	5.62	789	2.91
Mulatto	9,676	48.73	10,392	38.26

Source: U.S. Bureau of the Census, *Thirteenth Census of the United States*, 3:1210.

manual labor, as they were unfavorably contrasted with highland peasants in twentieth-century official records.[26] Because of those representations, black Puerto Ricans were separated from the land and were cast as the epitome of salaried laborers, denying them any other possibility. As in Cuba, employers hired blacks as cane cutters, restricting their access to other sectors of the economy.[27] Not only in representations were black Puerto Ricans separated from the land; their alienation also mirrored their own reality. In 1899 people of color were underrepresented in professional services, commerce, and transportation, whereas in agriculture, fishing, and mining, they surpassed whites in number (see table 4.4). However, even though people of color were the largest group that participated in agriculture, most did not own the land, as was shown in the previous chapter.

In sum, in the nineteenth century authorities targeted the working population, former slaves and peasants, with a labor discipline that conceptualized them as racially inferior and mixed. As Frederick Cooper observes for Africa, "Neither slaves nor peasants faced the 'rational predicament' of choosing between wage labor and starvation . . . even if the former

Table 4.4. Racial distribution by occupation in Caguas, 1899

	Whites	Percentage	Non-whites	Percentage
Total	9,065	45.65	10,792	54.35
Agriculture, fishing and mining	1,891	9.52	2,495	12.56
Commerce and Transportation	342	1.72	134	0.67
Manufactures and Mechanical Industries	234	1.18	226	1.14
Professional Services	38	0.19	6	0.3
Domestic and personal services	238	1.2	536	2.7
Unemployed	6,322	31.84	7,395	37.24

Source: Departmento de la Guerra, *Informe sobre el censo de Puerto Rico, 1899*, 298–300.

were no longer under the 'brutal predicament' of slavery. In northern Nigeria, Kenya, and elsewhere, peasants and former slaves alike might have to be pushed by old authority patterns and new colonial constraints into producing for someone other than themselves."[28] After 1898 the U.S. government established various racial divisions among the working population, though they targeted them equally with policies of labor discipline—blacks along the coasts and highland peasants alike were part of the working classes that were considered dangerous and in need of containment.[29]

Forced Labor and Civil Disobedience

Even with the use of the police and the legal system, imposing a capitalist labor ethic was a daunting task. State officials, politicians, and intellectuals in Puerto Rico blamed the popular classes ad nauseum for lack of both job discipline and interest in their work and sought other practical ways to resolve "the labor problem." The "problem" consisted of the refusal to exchange labor for a salary. Many people preferred to sharecrop and move when the terms were not favorable. A series of vagrancy laws between the 1830s and 1874, popularly known as the notebook (*la libreta*), that tried to provide a labor force for large landowners and moralize the working classes failed to achieve their goals and earned great unpopularity among all social sectors. After the abolition of slavery in 1873, many former slave owners claimed that labor in Puerto Rico had become increasingly expensive and that agrarian production in the island competed with that of Cuba, where slavery prevailed and production was cheaper as a consequence. They added that peasant labor was erratic and unreliable because peasants focused on meeting their own basic needs and not on economic growth. As time progressed, the need for a reliable labor force increased because the abolition of slavery provided only for a three-year period of compulsory work with ex-owners. The law specified that by 1876 the government of Puerto Rico would grant civil and political rights, including those of mobility, to ex-slaves.[30] The Spanish governor of Puerto Rico, Gen. Segundo de la Portilla Gutiérrez (1875–82) followed the law and recognized, at least in theory, mobility rights for laborers.[31] Former slave owners worried that by granting mobility rights and eliminating la libreta, commercial agriculture would decay for lack of a labor force.

Authorities, however, found other ways to restrict laborers' mobility rights. In fact, la libreta was succeeded by the cédula de vecindad, an official document declaring the name, occupation, domicile, and so on of each person in Puerto Rico, to serve as identification papers.[32] The governor

Table 4.5.　Fee of the cédulas de vecindad in 1881

Type	Fee
First class	20 pesos
Second class	10 pesos
Third class	5 pesos
Fourth class	2 pesos
Fifth class	1 peso
Sixth class	40 centavos
Seventh class	20 centavos
Eighth class	10 centavos

Source: AHMC, SEC Secretaría, SSEC Archivo, SER Expedientes/Documentos, SSER Cartas de Vecindad, 1868–98, C124–25.

of Puerto Rico ordered all subjects in the island to be issued cédulas, and the order became a legal requirement on May 25, 1881.[33] The cédula de vecindad was issued in theory for any individual who was fourteen years or older, regardless of social sector or gender, but in practice, only male rural laborers, sharecroppers, and landed peasants were asked to show this official identification to municipal authorities. The law dictated that laborers give their cédulas to their employer, who held the document until the job terminated. Employers, backed up by municipal authorities, could punish laborers who came late to work by holding part of their pay—half a day's wage for being an hour late, a whole day's wage for being more than an hour late, and so on—and the ultimate punishment was fifteen days of forced work on the roads.[34]

The concept of the cédulas de vecindad was an old one within Spanish colonies, referring simply to a residential identification.[35] In 1881, however, Spanish authorities on the island gave a new interpretation to the cédulas by using them as a mechanism to enforce labor discipline. They established eight different types of cédulas that classified the individual's productive capacity and set a fee for each one from twenty pesos to ten centavos (see table 4.5). Women and handicapped men paid for second-class cédulas, while men with their full capacities to work paid for first-class cédulas. In Barrio Cañaboncito, for example, Ramón de Rivera solicited a second-class cédula because he injured his right arm and could not work.[36] Before 1880, free cédulas were common for poor families, but they were discontinued in 1881.

The cédulas also identified the color of the person as white, black, mulatto, *trigüeño* (wheat color), *pardo* (lightest skinned person of color), or *moreno* (between mulatto and pardo) and specified the individual's age, occupation, and some physical features, such as body scars and body

4. A *cédula de vecindad* of a black woman (AHMC, SEC Secretaría, SSEC Archivo, SER Expedientes/Documentos, SSER Cartas de Vencindad, 1886–98, C125)

build. These descriptions are reminiscent of ads for runaway slaves.[37] Another characteristic that might have reminded workers of a slave society was the direct correlation between a person's capacity to work and the value of the cédulas, as was clearly specified in the document. A cédula of a strong, young man was of higher value. The cédulas undoubtedly would have provided a wealth of information about rural laborers in Caguas, but unfortunately, most have disappeared. The few surviving examples give us an idea of their content and use. They are made of a poor quality paper cut in a square of about three inches on each side (see figure 4).

Municipal authorities attempted to contain rural laborers within the municipal territory, a response to the laborers' tactic of running away both to avoid unfair labor conditions and to gain better terms. Laborers were required to show their cédulas to the mayor before moving to another municipality, where they should already have had a contract with a known proprietor. Laborers were granted a three-day pass, no more than three times a year, to look for a job outside their municipalities. Those who failed to inform the mayor were fined and often charged with compulsory labor on the roads.[38]

At the time, it was clear that authorities intended to control laboring classes with the cédulas. For example, *El Buscapié* argued that the mayor of Caguas in 1880 used the cédulas de vecindad in an abusive way against rural laborers:

> *According to some reports from Caguas, it seems that there exists a zeal to abuse poor laborers for small faults for which other people are easily absolved. Not too many days ago, two honorable neighbors from Barrio Cañaboncito were brought to the city hall. They were accused of not having the cédula in their pockets. The mayor, who could have investigated in the office whether or not they had been issued a cédula, forced these individuals to return immediately to their houses, which were very distant from the downtown, and seek their documents. The two laborers did as demanded and presented their cédulas. One was condemned to six days in prison and the other to pay a fine of six duros.*[39]

Municipal authorities in Caguas, in particular the police, comisarios and alcaldes de barrio, and the road patrol, often stopped people on the roads, fields, streets, and so on and demanded their cédulas. Those who did not carry the identification with them were reported to the mayor of Caguas, who usually fined them.[40] For example, in 1881 the mayor of Caguas fined Wenceslao Cotto, who worked for Don Modesto Solá in Barrio Borinquen, because he did not have personal identification.[41] In 1897 when the Spanish conceded universal male suffrage to Puerto Ricans, a newspaper suggested that during municipal elections, politicians and municipal officials use the cédulas as a mechanism to bar individuals from voting.[42]

Invariably, the cédulas represented an economic burden that strangled the poorest sectors of society and directly benefited the ayuntamiento, as the money collected formed part of the municipal budget. If unable to pay the fines, laborers paid the municipal government with forced labor. Also, inability to pay taxes left rural laborers, sharecroppers, and landed peasants subject to forced labor. In 1882 the mayor of Caguas sentenced Pío Rodríguez and Aldino Flores of Barrio Borinquen to two days of public work because they could not pay the fine of one peso given for not paying their taxes.[43] The initial cost of the cédulas, the fines, and forced labor often pushed rural laborers and peasants into dependency and constant indebtedness to the government. Thus, the municipal government, through labor debts, created a mechanism that guaranteed the availability of workers for any town project.

Public work, in particular the maintenance and construction of roads, represented the most common form of forced labor throughout the nineteenth century. Puerto Ricans of all social classes paid the price for public work; proprietors paid road fees, and from 1838 laborers paid with their time and work.[44] The central government of the island demanded workers from the mayors, who turned to alcaldes and comisarios de barrio to find laborers for public work. Alcaldes de barrio issued annual lists of laborers and artisans in the countryside, which helped municipal administrators plan for public work.[45] In 1893, for example, the mayor of Caguas solicited laborers for the construction of the road from Cayey to Arroyo.[46] Various historians have documented the resentment this law created among Puerto Ricans and in particular among the working population.[47] In Caguas the situation was very similar. Rural residents expressed their feelings for the law by defying the authority of comisarios and alcaldes de barrio.[48] In December 1882 the alcalde of Barrio Cañabón accused José Otero, a thirty-two-year-old illiterate laborer, of disobeying authority and evading compulsory work on the roads.[49] Month after month, authorities attempted to correct his "rebellious attitude" because he ignored nine different court citations. In October 1883 the alcalde de barrio informed the mayor that Otero went into hiding every time he tried to deliver the citations.[50]

Like Otero, other laborers ignored or avoided municipal authorities as a tactic to escape forced labor on the roads. In 1883 Paulino Díaz Contreras, a resident of Barrio Borinquen, was accused of disobedience for not complying with forced labor. His ordeal of numerous notifications, citations, and denunciations had begun a year before. In 1881 Díaz Contreras was accused of being undocumented.[51] On December 6, 1882, a municipal official notified Díaz Contreras of his labor debt to the municipal government. Because Díaz Contreras acknowledged and yet ignored the notification, he was officially ordered to see the mayor of Caguas on January 2, 1883, and again on July 12. He again acknowledged both citations but did not comply. On August 8, municipal authorities issued another citation for Díaz Contreras, threatening to take him to court; he did not respond. Between August and November, he was repeatedly accused of disobedience in the municipal court.[52] Between 1881 and 1883 Díaz Contreras's debt to the municipal government increased, and he responded by ignoring state officials. After 1883 there is no record of Díaz Contreras. He might have paid his debt or just moved to another town. His example shows that by both open defiance and evasion of authorities, rural laborers claimed time and labor to be their own.

Evasion of the law was often achieved simply by running away. In 1888, for example, the municipal police of Cayey arrested Fidel Rivera, a resident of a rural barrio in Caguas because he did not have his cédula de vecindad. According to the police, Rivera presented a "sad sight," sleeping outside in the plaza.[53] In San Juan, the police arrested Nicolasa Rodríguez Álvarez, who lived in a rural barrio of Caguas, because she did not have legal documentation and worked as a prostitute (*vida licenciosa*).[54] Here, a homeless person and an alleged prostitute did not have legal identification with them, and consequently faced high fines.

Fleeing seems to have been a common response among rural laborers, as recognized by a newspaper of the period that warned the government of "detrimental" consequences. In order to avoid taxes and the payment of the cédula, the newspaper observed, "day laborers migrate from one district to another, to the detriment of their affections, their domestic responsibilities, and the sacred links of society and family; not considering that in this nomadic and errant style of life, there is no means to effectively take advantage of education and of other means employed to improve the social conditions of that unfortunate class."[55] The patronizing reporter does not seem to have considered that moving around was a preferred choice of the working population because it effectively protected them from forced labor. Moreover, the supposed benefits of education were non-existent for the working population anyway. Still, the article offers progressive suggestions inviting the government to eliminate the cédulas because their results were negative for the well-being of the whole society. However, the report did not find receptive ears within the municipal government, and the cédula de vecindad remained a requirement for any governmental transaction and a source of labor for public roads.

As the newspaper article mentioned, rural laborers fiercely hated compulsory work and did what was in their means to avoid it, including open defiance. In 1897 Tomás Benítez, a resident of Barrio San Antonio, refused to work on the roads without pay and told the alcalde de barrio that he would not return unless he earned fifty centavos a day.[56] By demanding to be paid, Benítez questioned authorities' claim that public work benefited everyone. In fact, laborers paid dearly for public work. Benítez's refusal to work without pay was also a demand for his own time and work, denouncing the repressive nature of forced labor. In November 1897 José María Rodríguez, alcalde of Barrio San Antonio, accused Benítez, along with Catalino Donis, Juan Flores, Isidro Díaz, Sotero Navarro, and Juan Jiménez, of deliberately missing days of work.[57] A month later they were again accused of open insubordination. Benítez and Donis did not comply with the labor ordinances and disobeyed Rodríguez's orders.[58] Rodríguez confronted major problems in imposing his authority among his neighbors of Barrio San Antonio. After two years of service, he strongly suggested to the mayor of Caguas that one of his constituents, Pedro Coto, be imprisoned for disobeying his authority, adding, "for him [Coto] there is no comisario since he does not obey me when I need him to give a message."[59] Coto might have been imprisoned for a day or two. If this were the case, he would eventually pay with forced labor in prison. Other alcaldes and comisarios de barrio expressed frustration in trying to discipline laborers, particularly when they became the target of violence. In 1888 Juan Rodríguez, alcalde of Barrio Quebrada Puercos, was badly injured while attempting to break up a fight.[60]

These examples testify to the repressive nature of the cédulas. Once in the system of forced labor, laborers found it almost impossible to get out of the cycle of debt. Inability to pay taxes or the cédulas brought many to prison where forced labor was a daily reality. In 1880, for example, José E. Delgado and José Vázquez of Barrio Turabo were arrested and sentenced to time in public works.[61] In effect, imprisonment was just another form to enforce compulsory work among the rural poor. Rural laborers, sharecroppers, and the landed peasantry worked side by side with prisoners, who were assigned to public work in the 1880s, 1890s, and early twentieth century.[62] Prisoners and others forced to work on roads were often indistinguishable because many laborers, unable to pay a debt, ended up in prison for a short period of time. Once they left the prison, some of them were forced to work with prisoners again. Moreover, prisoners were not entirely ostracized or locked away from society. Prisoners worked on the roads and spent time in front of the city hall, interacting with friends and passers-by.[63] Thus, forced labor created similar conditions of work and social interaction among prisoners and rural laborers, sharecroppers, and the landed peasantry. In her analysis of nineteenth- and twentieth-century folklore, Lillian Guerra finds a strong solidarity between peasants and outlaws, which can be explained by the fact that prisoners worked with rural laborers, sharecroppers, and the landed peasantry.[64]

Authorities also attempted to control labor with vagrancy laws and the prohibition of excessive drinking and games. In 1876 the governor of Puerto Rico reinstated the 1874 vagrancy law because he believed that vagrancy was the cause of most crimes in the island. The law considered anyone who lacked either a labor contract or a lucrative profession a vagrant and fined and forced vagrants to work.[65] The laws of the cédulas of 1881 attempted once and for all eliminate the "recurring problem" of vagrancy. Comisarios and alcaldes de barrio were supposed to provide bi-monthly lists of vagrants to the mayor. In 1880 Antonio Ramírez, alcalde of Barrio Río Cañas, wrote to the mayor of Caguas alleging that he had not seen Silverio Díaz and his two sons, Santiago and Juan, working.[66] In 1880 the mayor sent after "Críspulo Vázquez or Marquez" because he was an "obstinate vagrant" (*vago incorregible*) who would not even confirm his own last name to authorities.[67] However, the alcaldes often avoided denouncing people in order to minimize making personal enemies or confrontations, just as they had done in the past.[68] In 1880 the mayor of Caguas reminded the alcaldes de barrio that if they failed to provide the list of vagrants, they "would receive the proper punishment for concealing individuals without productive occupation."[69]

The governor also stated that vagrancy promoted vices among the popular classes, in particular drunkenness and participation in illegal games such as unofficial cockfights and card games, which incited people to violence and crime.[70] In Caguas, municipal authorities occasionally prosecuted individuals who engaged in what the governor defined as vices.[71] For example, in 1880 the mayor of Caguas ordered an investigation of "prohibited games" among rural laborers in the Hacienda San José in Barrio Cañabón.[72] However, cockfights were a popular entertainment among rural laborers, sharecroppers, and the landed peasantry, who engaged in this activity in spite of the law.[73] In 1890 two guards caught a group of twenty-two men and a woman participating in a cockfight that took place in a small building in Barrio Culebras. Participants tried to escape, but the guards blocked the entrances and arrested them, including the comisario of Barrio Culebras, Juan Jiménez Saurí, a landed peasant, who refused to cooperate with the guards.[74] Further investigations revealed that Jiménez Saurí had organized the event, providing the facilities for the fight.[75]

The municipality did not oppose cockfights in general, only those that provided no revenue to the state. Official cockfighting rings (*galleras*) were allowed in 1890 and 1891; Ignacio Lizardi Delgado and Regis Ramos of Barrio Turabo paid taxes for cockfighting rings.[76] Unofficial cockfights and other prohibited games continued to be entertainment for people in the countryside in the twentieth century.[77] The Hacienda San José in Barrio Cañabón continued to gather rural laborers who engaged in illegal games. In 1900 Bartolomé Borrás had ten laborers of the hacienda who played *chapas* arrested by the police.[78] In general, the police, not alcaldes and comisarios de barrio, reported prohibited games and cockfights. It seems that those alcaldes and comisarios de barrio who reported this type of entertainment to the mayor made enemies in the rural barrios, while other alcaldes and comisarios were actually participants in the games. Cockfights and games were forms of entertainment by which the rural poor, including some comisarios and alcaldes de barrio, claimed their own time. Hard working people deserved leisure time, a motive that was even accepted by some comisarios and alcaldes de barrio. The comisarios and alcaldes de barrio were the authorities closest to the laboring population of the rural barrios of Caguas, and through their complicity in illicit games they reinforced the right of the majority to enjoy themselves in games. In this sense, cockfights and games were considered harmless and legitimate despite legal prohibitions. Leisure and entertainment were the prerogatives of men who worked, and neither the mayor nor the governor could interfere with them.

The "tolerance" shown for leisure sharply contrasted with the attitude toward alcohol drinking. While alcaldes and comisarios de barrio seemed to ignore the law against vagrancy in relation to prohibited games, they willingly reported drunkards. For example, in 1880 Salvador López, comisario of Barrio Bairoa, brought Francisco Jiménez to jail for being drunk almost every day.[79] Municipal authorities defined drunkenness as another form of vagrancy because alcohol destroyed the individual's capacity to work.

Municipal authorities and people in general associated men's abuse of alcohol with adopting an unrealistic, violent bravery and with public scandal. For example, Joaquín Aponte, a storeowner in Barrio Borinquen, solicited the assistance of the comisario de barrio because Agustín Díaz insulted and challenged Aponte and people in the store to fight. Díaz felt he was strong enough to fight a group of men on his own. Aponte and the rest avoided confronting Díaz's insults and provocations because of his excessive drinking and instead reported him to the municipal authorities.[80]

Because They Are Still on the Move

By constantly evading authorities, the laboring classes of Caguas effectively disarmed the law of the cédulas de vecindad, and workers moved around without much difficulty. In a desperate attempt to contain laborers, authorities fell back on fines, which were equally evaded by the poorest sectors of society. One of the most common reasons for minor fines was the lack of legal documentation, but it was not the only one. Minor fines recognized public offense on an endless list of misconduct, such as disrespect for authorities, missing a day or arriving late to work, drinking, cursing, and so on. By the end of the nineteenth century, the mayor's strongest legal prerogative in Caguas and Puerto Rico was the ability to fine individuals for challenges to municipal laws.[81] As shown in multiple examples, the mayor of Caguas fined thousands of individuals for different reasons, but most of those who were fined had one thing in common: they were poor and could not pay the fine in cash and were therefore forced to work for the municipal government. In fact, many landed peasants, sharecroppers, and rural laborers did forced labor in lieu of paying fines, despite having land to till or a contract job. With the monetary crisis of the late nineteenth century in Puerto Rico, lack of cash was a common condition among people in the countryside. A fine of one or two pesos could create an economic crisis for many rural producers who were forced to work to pay. A day of work on the roads often caused the rural poor to neglect their small farms, which could lead to destitution and even starvation. For these reasons, the rural poor tried to overcome the negative effects of fines and forced labor with a strategy that was the least damaging to their condition: evasion of authorities.

Evasion did not necessarily imply open defiance and disruption of the legal system but was framed by the logic of the legal system itself, as Luis Roniger and Tamar Herzog argue.[82] Many people in the countryside expressed protest by evading legal authorities, in particular the courts. Many rural residents failed to attend court until the second, third, and sometimes fourth notification. With these delays, they denied the municipal state its claim to organize or demand citizens' time and cooperation. Legal authorities categorized those delays as "disobedience," a fault against the state, which was often fined one peso. However, they had very little success enforcing this punitive measure. The mayor of Caguas increased the fine for individuals who persisted in ignoring their citations but without success. In April 1880 the mayor of Caguas wrote to the alcalde of Barrio Cañaboncito: "Don Manuel Vélez, vecino of that barrio, has openly disobeyed my orders by not responding to a citation after being properly notified."[83] The mayor fined Vélez and ordered the alcalde de barrio to inform him "so that tomorrow, without hesitation, he will report to this city hall, *with a large fine* in case of disobedience"[84] (my emphasis).

The fact that the mayor fined many persons day after day and had to threaten some with a "large fine" testifies to the minor effect that fines had over the majority of the population. His threat was a cry for cooperation. The mayor increased the fine by one peso each time the person disobeyed the citation. In 1881 Fulgencio García, a resident of Barrio Cañaboncito, owed five pesos to the municipal state due to his constant disobedience.

He finally paid the fine to the alcalde de barrio but did not present himself at the town hall.[85]

The ways in which people avoided or defied authorities also reflected a general disregard for the consequences and sometimes even a cavalier attitude. For instance, rural residents alleged that they did not respond to state authorities because of their temporary or permanent incapacity to ride horses, when it was obvious to most that this was a false excuse. On December 15, 1880, Rosa Caraballo, from Barrio Tomás de Castro, refused to testify in a criminal case, claiming that she could not get downtown due to her inability to ride horses.[86] The mayor insisted on Rosa's cooperation without success, and three days later the alcalde de barrio found Rosa in downtown Caguas.[87] Either Rosa did not need a horse to travel to the downtown area or she intended to stay away from the court. Like Rosa, other people alleged that the large distances and the poor condition of the roads impeded the trip to the downtown of Caguas.[88] Other individuals avoided being counted in the census by moving from one place to another. As a result, alcaldes and comisarios de barrio were unable to locate them for summonses or any other civil duty, such as forced labor.[89] One individual did not receive a court citation from the alcalde de barrio for "three or four days" because he "was too busy."[90] Apparently, whatever else he was doing was more important to him than receiving a court citation.

By avoiding court citations and running away with such frequency, people of the rural barrios claimed their labor and time to be their own property, thereby asserting a civil freedom that for the most part defied authorities but avoided open confrontation. In this way, the rural poor pushed the limits of what was permissible, using the court when it was convenient but delaying and evading court citations as much as possible. Both strategies affirm their participation in the legal system because they entail recognition of court authority; their actions were framed by the possibilities of the legal system. Their challenge within what was permissible contradicts the assertion that peasants were afraid of the law. Muñoz Rivera observed, "The peasant thinks that laws are mysteriously made with the purpose not of protecting him but with the aim of oppressing him."[91] However, the rural poor's strategies proved to be more resourceful than critics have been willing to accept. Because those strategies did not seek to disrupt the established system, their challenge effectively transformed the very possibilities of the law. This constant challenge to the cédulas de vecindad made the law practically ineffective.

Mobility: The Essence of Freedom

Because by the late 1860s slavery had lost strength and vitality in Puerto Rico, the reduced number of slaves gave rise to some liberties that were unheard of in other areas of the Caribbean, including the right to marry at will.[92] But even before slavery was abolished, authorities confronted serious obstacles in containing the mobility of slaves. Benjamín Nistal Moret presents multiple examples of slaves who left the plantation and went to other municipalities to work as free agents. Among them, Tomás Tirado, a *moreno* slave of Caguas, left his owner's property for Naguabo, another municipality, and adopted a new name in April 1829. Tirado had gotten a five-day permit to leave Caguas, but he extended his stay in Naguabo for two months until authorities caught up with him.[93] He moved around so easily because even in the early nineteenth century, free people of color enjoyed some mobility rights.[94]

The Mortgage Law of 1880 and the 1881 reinterpretation of the cédulas de vecindad attempted to keep workers in the same areas where they had worked as slaves; at least this was the main objective for the island of Cuba. In Puerto Rico, these laws were redirected against the population of color, without distinguishing free blacks from former slaves, attempting to reverse the decades-old practice of free people of color moving freely throughout the island. In practical terms, it was impossible to distinguish slaves from free workers because even before 1880, former slaves had joined the majority of the free working population. Former slaves played an integral part in formulating and enacting the strategies to undo the consequences of the law of the cédulas. After slavery ended in 1873, freed slaves spent some years working for their ex-owners, but in 1876, when the apprenticeship period was over, many free people of color moved away from the plantation zones if they could, as was the preference elsewhere in the Caribbean.[95]

With the failure of the law of the cédulas, people of color moved around Caguas and other municipalities looking for better terms of employment and access to land. For example, Francisco Polo and his wife, Elena Polo, were former slaves who, in 1882, lived in Barrio Río Cañas. Judging by their last names, they had probably been owned by the prominent councilor Rafael Polo, who had a large estate in Barrio San Salvador. Francisco and Elena moved from Polo's large estate to Barrio Río Cañas, an area that was characterized by subsistence production and small farms.[96] As in Cuba, the hills had offered the possibility to form communities of free coloreds even before the abolition of slavery.[97] The municipal government of Caguas since the 1860s had described Barrio Río Cañas as the poorest barrio in the municipality. It did not have any large farms that produced cash crops; instead, small farms dedicated to subsistence agriculture sustained an impoverished population. This area represented a magnet for people like Francisco and Elena Polo.

In 1872 Marcelino López Aponte owned a young slave, Olaya López, who was eleven years old and did domestic work in her owner's house in Barrio Beatriz.[98] Unfortunately, there are no existing records of López's life, except that she made sure that she would not work for López Aponte after slavery was abolished. In the census of 1882 López Aponte lived with his family, and his house also sheltered various workers, a domestic worker, and a cook, but Olaya López was no longer in Barrio Beatriz.[99] The girl was not alone in leaving the barrio where she had been a slave. Petrona, Juan, and Andrés Naranjo also left Barrio Beatriz after the abolition of slavery.[100] López and the Naranjos joined the majority of the racially mixed working population in evading authorities to secure their mobility rights. However, for Olaya López, Petrona Naranjo, and most women, basic rights of mobility and access to resources were limited by gender roles of the time, as the next chapter discusses.

Mobility and Labor after 1898

When the U.S. government formally abolished the cédulas in 1898, there were no real consequences because the rural poor had already abolished them in practice. Ironically though, the Hurricane San Ciriaco and the effects of the change of sovereignty devastated the economy of the island and the crops of the majority of farmers, giving workers a reason to have work for the state. Many Puerto Ricans of the laboring classes found themselves without employment or any way to make a living. After the hurricane those who had refused under Spanish rule were desperately seeking to work on the roads. In 1900 public work on the roads offered a source of employment to many heads of household. By 1903 the U.S. colonial government in the island had officially terminated this source of employment, opting for a cheaper source of labor: unpaid convict labor.[101]

Cheap labor became a major consideration for U.S. colonial officials who tried to attract U.S. businesses to the island, even though laborers were often looked upon with disdain. U.S. officials emphasized the ignorance and lack of ambition and discipline among Puerto Rican rural laborers.[102] Environmental determinism and science were often used to explain the apparent "idleness" and "laziness" of Puerto Ricans. Governor Charles H. Allen believed that the tropical climate fostered idleness because "a man can lie in a hammock, pick a banana with one hand,

5. The public square in Caguas after the hurricane of 1899 (Allen, "Porto Rico," 1440)

and dig a sweet potato with one foot."[103] The allegations of idleness and laziness justified many employers' programs for low wages for Puerto Rican laborers, who were blamed for the poor economic production of the island.[104] Government officials also held laborers responsible for the economic stagnation of the island. Dr. Ashford explained, from a medical standpoint, why laborers appeared lazy and idle. He argued that most laborers in Puerto Rico suffered from anemia, which reduced their capacity to work by more than 50 percent.[105] Dr. Ashford promised a solution for the supposed laziness of the Puerto Rican laborer, convincing many large landowners in Caguas, who cooperated with the anemia campaign.[106] A U.S. reporter celebrated Dr. Ashford's scientific results and foresaw that Puerto Rico, "for centuries the heaven and haven of devotees of the idle existence, will in a short time become as energetic and hustling as Boston, Mass., or Butte, Mont." Puerto Ricans, he added, will not take pride in "their slouching shuffle, but are said to have already adopted the American pie-counter rush, while the man who lies abed half the day, once a favorite occupation, is now look[ed] upon with scorn." He could almost guarantee that "the siesta will be abandoned as a national custom and that the strenuous life will become popular in time."[107]

Environmental determinism and science did not overshadow the fact that numerous laborers in Puerto Rico were accustomed to work in the tropics, and their very low wages represented a "natural" attraction for the "new blood" of U.S. capitalists, who might find that "the return to capital is exceedingly profitable."[108] Thousands of rural laborers, in fact, were hired by U.S. companies throughout the island. Caguas became a center for tobacco production and manufacture, where many rural labor-

ers became factory workers. Caguas's factory workers took advantage
of the new rights of organization under the U.S. flag. The discussion of
the labor movement in twentieth-century Caguas is subject for another
book, but I would like to stress that the struggles of the labor movement
for better wages and a better standard of living were very similar to the
claims of marginal citizenship. Both marginal citizenship and the labor
movement emphasized social equality and relegated formal politics to
a secondary plane. In fact, the trade union movement did not consider
political partisanship until the Socialist Party was founded in 1915.[109]
Also, both marginal citizenship and the trade union movement found
their stronger support in the countryside. In general, the largest compo-
nent of the working class in the first half of the twentieth century was
rural. In the 1910s leaders of trade unionism found receptive ears among
rural laborers, who became the strength of the labor movement in Puerto
Rico.[110] Rural laborers began to demand the rights and liberties of the
U.S. constitution. As Joseph Marcus, a special agent of the U.S. Employment Service, observed, the Puerto Rican laborer "is no longer willing
to depend upon the employer's generosity"; rather, he "is beginning to
demand his rights to better living conditions." Marcus understood that
such demands resulted from a close contact between the rural laborer and
U.S. institutions.[111]

In Caguas the U.S. tobacco industry established some of the largest
manufacturers of Puerto Rico. The industry became the main source
of employment for the racially mixed majority. For the first time rural
workers, female and male, could be educated and organized en masse.
Tobacco factories became a school for many who for the first time heard
about socialism, anarchism, and workers' rights and struggles through the
most influential writings of the period from Europe and Latin America.
Some Caguas cigar makers developed a radical anarchist movement that
was typical of those found in Spain and Latin America. Free labor and
progress were the movement's most important goals. The U.S. government immediately suspected its radical nature and dismantled it through
violent repression. But even before the repression, the anarchist movement
attracted few rural workers in Puerto Rico.[112]

In contrast to anarchism, trade unionism was very successful among
rural workers in Caguas. The Free Federation of Labor, affiliated with the
American Federation of Labor, successfully recruited hundreds of workers
in Caguas. In fact, Caguas became the "cradle of the struggle" between
labor and capital in the first decades of the twentieth century, leading
organized labor to impressive activism.[113] For example, on October 14,

1913, about two thousand cigar workers in Caguas went on strike. The strike spread to other areas of Puerto Rico.[114] In the following years, Caguas tobacco workers initiated a series of strikes demanding better labor conditions and higher wages, and women also participated on the strikes.[115] Caguas' sugar cane workers also participated of trade unionism and organized various strikes in the 1910s. They also demanded better wages, an eight-hour work day, and better working conditions.[116] In 1915, two hundred sugar cane workers in Caguas went on strike, and in the 1930s they organized various strikes.[117]

Labor activism eventually led many rural laborers into formal politics, particularly after the foundation of the Socialist Party in 1915. As active members of the Socialist Party, laborers in Caguas attended meetings, rallies, and protests.[118] It is clear that this activism had its roots in nineteenth-century claims of marginal citizenship. The next chapter provides an analysis of women's role within both marginal citizenship and trade unionism.

Marginal but Not Equal
Gender and Citizenship

Marginal citizenship did not imply wide egalitarianism, for it distinguished between and privileged men over women, justifying women's subordination and circumscribing them to family roles just as elites and authorities did. The municipal government promoted bourgeois family values as the key to disciplining working classes, including the peasantry, and prescribed codes of behavior that stressed deference and obedience to adult men. People understood these codes well enough because they valued and incorporated many aspects of the bourgeois family; they also solicited government intervention in family matters only to demand or confirm their roles within the prescribed codes. While the long nineteenth century in Latin America has been portrayed as a progression toward gender equality, in fact nineteenth-century state policy had more negative than positive consequences for Latin American women.[1] In Caguas both governmental and popular perceptions of women's sexuality were re-created in the civil arena by subordinating women to men in every area of public life, including property rights, salaried labor, education, and political representation. This chapter discusses the process of subordination through an examination of mainstream sexuality and people's responses to it, followed by an analysis of women's civil status.

Promotion of Family Life and Righteous Sexuality in Puerto Rico

The nineteenth-century Catholic Church and Puerto Rican liberals agreed that the family was the key to improving the morals and values of the Puerto Rican popular masses. The Church envisioned the family as a sacred sphere, a spiritual unit or private church, while liberals thought of it as a social institution.[2] Despite their contrasting definitions, both the Church and liberals perceived that the family could be used as a mechanism to instill family values into the poorest sectors of the country.

The ideology of family life according to the Crown and wealthy Puerto Ricans recognized monogamous, heterosexual relations as the only legitimate reproductive unit of society. Basically a bourgeois ideal, this unit produced and raised children, cared for the development and well-being of its members, and represented a political entity headed by the father or the oldest man of the unit. Women had the important role and responsibility of creating a peaceful home for the family where all members looked for comfort and care.[3]

Women's education played a pivotal role in liberal policies because it represented an instrument for reaching future mothers and thus future generations.[4] Eileen Suárez Findlay argues that liberals in Puerto Rico called continually for the reform of the family itself, especially that of the rural popular classes; they aimed at reconstituting the family with "loving, faithful" wives and mothers and their moral energies.[5] The reconstituted family, liberals believed, would eventually reform the whole society.

As Christopher Ebert Schmidt-Nowara argues, the family within liberal ideology served elites in developing policies to integrate the working class peacefully into the market society created by the middle-class revolution.[6] Imposing family ideals on popular classes had the purpose not only of improving their moral condition but also of guaranteeing their disposition to work. Sexual misconduct, like violence, had the potential to waste the productive capacity of the individual; therefore, a major concern of family life was the imposition of righteous sexual behavior, which referred to marriage and fidelity, female virginity, and female chastity.[7]

Liberals and the Crown held together practices and ideas of proper sexual behavior with an elaborate system of honor and respectability based on a benevolent but hierarchical patriarchy. The liberal image of the "Great Puerto Rican family" intended to incorporate laboring classes into a respectable community under the leadership of wealthy Puerto Ricans, the most respectable fathers of the nation. Liberals eventually incorporated popular codes of respectability that linked male honor to hard work.[8] Liberals and state officials imagined a citizenship of fathers whose positions in politics responded to their social class and value. Dore emphasizes that classic liberals "asserted that the right to rule derived from the social superiority of elite males. They believed it was the natural right of men with wealth or professional status to exercise political authority."[9] Liberals believed, as Thomas C. Holt suggests, that the family home produced "reflective men capable of civilized discourse and norm-governed interactions."[10] Thus, imposing the ideals of bourgeois family on the working population also represented a mechanism to order the political arena, legitimating the power of state officials and wealthy Puerto Ricans within both public and private domains.

Family Relations and Patriarchal Intervention in Caguas

Many people of the countryside buttressed parental authority at home with that of the municipal government, soliciting governmental intervention to mediate family relationships. By allowing governmental authority within their homes, people ceded to them the last word on family matters, accepting the government as the ultimate source of patriarchal power. In this way, patriarchal relations permeated social expectations among men and women in the countryside of Caguas; men were supposed to fulfill the role of providers and protectors of their family, while women were expected to obey and care for their husbands and children. Men used governmental resources to stress parental authority with their own children and wives. In 1897, for example, the Civil Guard arrested Francisco Báez for injuring and threatening his own father.[11] In the same year, Rafael del Rosario solicited the assistance of the alcalde of Barrio Bairoa because his wife "had disappeared," taking their four children with her. She had left in the morning while Rosario was working, and he had no idea of her destination.[12] Rosario expected that authorities would bring his family back.

Women also used the authority of the mayor to demand a father's protection and support.[13] In particular, women mobilized government authority, forcing husbands to comply with their responsibilities as fathers and husbands. Women demanded economic support for their children. In 1880 Frutos Ramos, a resident of Barrio Cañabón, abandoned his family and went to Gurabo, a neighboring municipality. The alcalde de barrio, J. Y. Esterás, reported Ramos to the mayor of Caguas, stating that Ramos "has abandoned his family in this barrio, and for six months has not sent any food or provided means for them to obtain food . . . this family lives at the mercy of public charity, suffering nakedness and illnesses."[14] Ramos was forced to support his family. Likewise, in 1892 Celestina Torres, a resident of the neighboring municipality of Hato Grande (today San Lorenzo), wrote to the mayor demanding economic support from her husband, Bartolo González, who had moved to Caguas. Torres protested her husband's abandonment of their eight children and stressed that some of the children were sick. She claimed that her husband had moved to Barrio Tomás de Castro in Caguas, where municipal authorities found him. He answered that he was willing to take care of his children but not of his wife; he even offered to slap his wife's face.[15] Despite González's threats, Torres forced her husband to support their eight children.

Like Celestina Torres, other women learned to protect themselves by seeking the intervention of men, or what Steve J. Stern describes as the mobilization of powerful patriarchs.[16] In particular, women sought protection against husbands' abandonment and physical abuse. In 1880 Manuel Rodríguez of Barrio Tomás de Castro wrote to the mayor of Caguas accusing his son-in-law, Don José Domingo López, of abandoning his daughter for six months, stressing the recurrence of his action.[17] Rodríguez's letter does not provide the name of his daughter, and there is no other detail about the resolution of this case. However, in the census of 1882, Rodríguez had his married daughter, Berta Rodríguez Miranda, and Juana López Rodríguez, presumably his granddaughter, living with his nuclear family in Barrio Tomás de Castro.[18] The census might suggest that Manuel's daughter continued living with her father and that her husband abandoned her permanently. In 1884 Margarita Otero lived with José Díaz y López, her husband, in Barrio Cañabón, next to her parents' house. After a marital quarrel, Díaz y López began to beat Otero; her father intervened and stopped him and reported the incident to the police.[19] In these two cases, the fathers sought their daughters' protection by informing the police of misbehaving sons-in-law. In both cases, the women got rid of abusive husbands.

These examples testify to the flexible nature of patriarchy as both restricting and enabling. While paternalism limited the options for women in the countryside, it also offered them some economic and physical protection. Women sought the intervention of male relatives and state officials to stop husbands' physical abuse and abandonment. However, women's strategies to stop abuse also translated into justifying and affirming the patriarchal system that conditioned women to depend on men, solidifying their unequal social status.

Both women and men solicited the intervention of municipal authorities to reinforce their parental authority. In doing so, they also stressed the authority of the municipal government as the ultimate power to reestablish family order and patriarchal authority. By soliciting and choosing municipal authorities to help them, women and men in the countryside made the municipal government part of their family relations. In particular, by soliciting the intervention of authorities, women and men attempted to force relatives to behave and conform to patriarchal ideals. In these cases, the municipal government succeeded in stressing bourgeois family ideals among the rural population. This small triumph might suggest the transformation of the family into a "mechanism" of governmental control; as Jacques Donzelot has argued for eighteenth-century France, the growth of the police relied on the power of the family to extend its authority over the family's rebels.[20]

After 1898 authorities in Puerto Rico conceded some civil protection to women, but family relations still framed their social position. Married women had the prerogative to represent themselves and their property in court, but their husbands were still the sole representatives of the nuclear family and retained absolute rights to administer the couple's property. In 1902 women also gained the right to divorce. Suárez Findlay represents women's reactions to this new right as a revolution, for they "flocked" to the courts to get divorced.[21] This revolution confronted old ideologies that maintained women's subordination. They were still expected to fulfill their roles as submissive wives and loving mothers who would sacrifice their individuality for the well-being of the family.

"Sacrifices" often included tolerating adulterous husbands. In Barrio Bairoa, Ramona Neris was married to Pedro Cortés, a day laborer with whom she had five children. The couple was separated for over two years; while Cortés stayed with the children in his rented house, Neris was working as a seamstress. Apparently, they were separated because Cortés had a mistress who lived next door. After a violent confrontation, Cortés hit Neris and threw her out of the house. In July 1902 Neris returned to the house, claiming that she had returned to "govern her own house, as a woman she had a right to govern it." Cortés did not want to hear more from Neris and exited the room, but Neris, in a desperate attempt to stop him, began to hit him.[22] This was not the first time that Neris reacted violently, attempting to claim some respect. A month before, she had confronted Cortés's alleged mistress, Anselma Bernal, who was taking care of the children and doing Cortés's laundry. In the confrontation, Neris hit Bernal. Neris seemed at the end of her rope: for two years Cortés had kept their children and his mistress in the house. Her options to see her own children were limited to going to the house where the mistress constantly visited. Cortés took his wife to court, which sent her to prison for fifteen days, even though she blamed Bernal for her husband's abandonment.[23]

The law ruled against Neris because she left her house, husband, and children, even though she had left in the first place because Cortés hit her and threw her out. Because a woman was not supposed to leave her house under any circumstance, Cortés used the authorities successfully to punish his wife. Neris's position nonetheless signals a new era. Even though she lost the case, her few recorded words speak volumes about her assertiveness in a very precarious position. It appears that the first time she left the house, Neris was too afraid to talk about her situation; she did not even report it to authorities. But in 1902 Neris talked loudly of her "rights" as a married woman, demanding full control of her home and demanding to be the governess of family life.

Other women like Neris challenged gender inequality by using new rights and a newfound assertiveness to speak out against relatives and even authorities. The use of words in the past, mostly in the form of gossip, had proved to be a powerful weapon among women. Suárez Findlay exposes how women in Ponce used gossip to establish boundaries of acceptable sexual and social behavior.[24] Gossip was so effective that often the intervention of authorities was the only way to counter its effects, as shown in cases of slander. For example, in 1900 Encarnación Cruz informed Pedro Roque, her protector, that other women in Barrio Cañaboncito were insulting her. Roque solicited the assistance of the comisario de barrio.[25] The mayor of Caguas arranged a meeting with Cruz, Roque, the comisario, and the women who had offended Cruz to solve the problem legally.[26] Cruz felt she restored her reputation through the only means left to her: the intervention of municipal authorities.

Gossip was not the only option for women's verbal expressions. More women began to speak out openly about their needs and feelings, pushing the limits of what was permissible or feasible. In this way, women challenged men's roles as protectors. Miguel de Santiago, for instance, solicited the assistance of the alcalde of Barrio San Antonio because Anastasia Estrada had insulted his wife and family. The alcalde investigated the allegation and was insulted by Estrada as well. He stressed Estrada's dangerous character, reporting that she "is not afraid of the courts and reports say that Anastasia has declared that she cleans her rear with the comisario and that the comisario counts for nothing with her. Sir Mayor, we must determine what to do with this woman; otherwise, I will not continue as a comisario because she can compromise me. For instance, her brother Casimiro Estrada, armed with a sword, went to Miguel's house and defied Miguel."[27]

According to the comisario, Estrada represented a public danger because she compromised men and state officials in their roles as protectors. Casimiro and de Santiago almost had a bloody confrontation because of Estrada's provocations, and the comisario even considered leaving his position. There is no other record about Estrada, and the comisario continued in his post. Nonetheless, Estrada's words irreverently challenged authorities and male relatives who attempted to control her.

Love, Marriage, and Consensual Union in the Rural Barrios of Caguas
Despite the ideal of men protecting women and women's confinement inside their houses, women were an important element in the society outside as well as inside their homes. They worked in the fields, did laundry and bathed in the river, and hired out their labor for a wage.[28] Countrywomen, in particular those of the lower social classes, could not possibly practice the ideal of home confinement. Social and economic limitations, however, did not bar people from selecting and incorporating other elements of a bourgeois code of righteous sexuality.

Even though sources about sexual attitudes are scarce, those that do exist indicate some of the ways people thought of, dealt with, and transformed bourgeois family values. For the Church and the government in Puerto Rico, the ideal family was achieved only through an official marriage, sacred or civil. However, for the majority of the population marriage was not the only way to create a family. Even when marriage was the ultimate goal, people found different roads to reach their end. Authorities labeled this flexible attitude about marriage as the biggest obstacle to forming decent families among the poorest sectors of rural society. Their concerns led to a series of studies and governmental reports on peasants' attitudes toward marriage.

Spanish and U.S. authorities and Puerto Rican intellectuals believed that consensual union (*concubinato*) represented an anti-hygienic sexual vice among the poorest sectors of the population, including laborers, the landed peasantry, and sharecroppers.[29] They asserted that consensual union promoted sexual liberties, obscene behavior, and illegitimate offspring—in short, immoral and irresponsible behavior. Authorities believed that the proliferation of consensual unions among poor Puerto Ricans produced a status of immorality and vice that kept this sector away from the fruits of progress. A newspaper explained that the practice of consensual union among poor Puerto Ricans originated under the rough conditions of slavery; after all, the majority of day laborers in Puerto Rico were either black or colored (mestizo).[30] Thus, sexual degeneracy was linked to the black race. For instance, Dr. Francisco Del Valle Atiles attributed moral, cultural, and physical degeneracy of the Puerto Rican peasantry to the "black blood" infiltrated over time.[31]

Others blamed the requirements of the Catholic Church for the prevalence of illegal unions.[32] During the nineteenth century the Catholic Church monopolized marriages, although civil marriage had legally existed since 1889. U.S. authorities in the island condemned the practices of the Catholic Church and legalized civil marriages with an order on

March 24, 1899.[33] The secularization of marriage was intended to advance the social and moral status of laborers and peasants, as understood by authorities and intellectuals of the period. In 1913 Miguel Meléndez Muñoz asserted, "Consensual union, together with its by-products illegitimate offspring and bigamy, is being replaced by canon and civil marriage and, thus, the social status of the Puerto Rican peasantry, in relation to this vital and institutional organ of our society, is frankly evolving and progressively so."[34]

However, the legalization of civil marriage did not increase significantly the number of marriages, in part because consensual unions were well accepted by the majority.[35] There were only four civil marriages celebrated in Caguas between 1890 and 1898 and one in 1902.[36] Consensual union, in fact, represented a valid alternative for many country people in Puerto Rico before and after the U.S. government made civil marriage more accessible to the masses. In the early 1930s José Colombán Rosario, a sociologist, asked country Puerto Ricans their opinions about marriage and found that consensual union was socially acceptable; in fact, it was considered more stable than official marriage.[37]

Day laborers entered into official marriages, sacred or civil, as often as property owners did. There are 259 marriage documents that specify the profession of the groom, of which day laborers represented 60.23 percent (156) and property owners 21.24 percent (55) (see table 5.2). The number of marriages in each occupation is representative of each group's percentage in the whole society. In general, however, the number of official marriages for each occupation was relatively low, pointing to people's ideas about marriage and consensual union.[38]

Cagüeños valued consensual union as much as official marriages, obliterating their distinction in the census. In the census of 1882 most couples, independent of their class background, are listed as married (*casado/a*); more than 87 percent of all the day laborers, sharecroppers, property owners and merchants in the rural barrios of Caguas are described as married (see table 5.1). A critic might suggest that these figures measure census takers' values rather than people's, but other indicators point to the same results. Most children have their father's last name and are thereby considered legitimate, born of an official marriage, or at least born to a couple that could marry. There are few children with their mother's surname, who would be considered illegitimate by Spanish authorities, that is, born to an unmarried couple that could not marry because of the incestuous or adulterous nature of the relationship.[39] The high numbers of people who considered themselves married, whether officially or not,

Table 5.1.   Civil status by occupation, 1882

Occupation	Married	Percentage of total with same occupation	Unclear status	Percentage of total with same occupation
Day laborer	622	87.98	85	12.02
Sharecropper	221	88.05	30	11.95
Farmer/ property owner	183	91.04	18	8.96
Merchant	17	100	0	0

Sources: AHMC, SEC Secretaría, SSEC Archivo, SER Censos, SSER Habitantes, 1882–83, C26.
Note: The table does not include occupations with five or less workers.

and of fathers' recognition of their paternity suggests the acceptance of consensual unions among the majority of the people living in the countryside of Caguas. People's wide acceptance of consensual union forced authorities eventually to recognize its legal significance. Thus, in 1903 legal authorities in Puerto Rico recognized "common law marriages" that bestowed on couples had the same responsibilities and benefits as official marriages. Even though the law was described as a "great moral reform," it merely represented the legitimation of an old practice.[40]

The acceptance of consensual union also rejected elitist perceptions of illegitimacy, which were usually linked to notions of race and slavery. In Puerto Rico, as in the rest of Latin America, conventional thought assumed that people of mixed race were born "out of wedlock" because a white person would not willingly marry someone of a different race.[41] However, governmental reports indicate that people of color in Caguas married at a rate similar to that of whites. In 1879 racially mixed and black married couples outnumbered white couples by two to one. Ten years later the figure was much lower but still comparable to that of whites (see table 5.3).

Table 5.2.   Number of marriages by groom's occupation, 1880–1902

Occupation	Number	Percentage
Day laborer	156	60.23
Farmer/owner	55	21.24
Sharecropper	31	11.97
Merchant	5	1.93
Cashier	5	1.93
Other	7	2.7

Source: AHMC, SEC Secretaría, SSEC Archivo, SER Expedientes/Documentos, SSER Matrimonios, 1866–1933, C145–50.

Table 5.3. Number of marriages by race, 1879 and 1889

	1879	1889
White	21	36
People of color	45	21

Sources: AHMC, SEC Secretaría, SSEC Archivo, SER Expedientes/documentos, SSER Matrimonios, 1866–91, C145.

Marriage seemed to be the goal of most couples, white and non-white, who often resorted to consensual union as a transitional period. By first eloping, some couples found a mechanism to establish socially their love choices.[42] To elude parents' supervision, lovers often wrote letters to each other. In 1918, for example, Francisco Ramos, a resident of Barrio Toita, Cayey, declared his love for Leonor Rodríguez through letters (see appendix E), promising to marry her. The couple eloped and Rodríguez's father accused Ramos of seduction, but shortly thereafter they married. By eloping, young people challenged their parents but stressed their beliefs in and desire for a righteous sexual code as prescribed by marriage. As Guido Ruggiero suggests in his study of Renaissance Venice, "people often cross the boundaries of sexuality in sexual matters not to thwart the dominant culture but, with a paradoxical irony, to join it."[43] Elopement often represented a mechanism for achieving marriage sanctioned by the Catholic Church. In 1894, for example, Gumersindo Nieves y Alicea of Barrio Sábana del Palmar, Cidra, was in love with Evangelia Giménez and wanted to marry her, but Giménez's father did not approve the young couple's love and prohibited his daughter from seeing Nieves y Alicea again. On the morning of November 24, 1894, Nieves y Alicea saw his girlfriend on the road and asked her to elope with him. The couple lived for two days in a coffee-tree forest (*cafetal*), where they made love. After these two days, Nieves y Alicea brought his lover to her parents' house and left for downtown. The police arrested Nieves y Alicea, who claimed that he had gone to see the priest to make their union official.[44] Giménez's parents had no other choice but to accept Nieves y Alicea as their son-in-law because the young couple had been together sexually.

After elopement, parents sought the intervention of municipal authorities not to get their daughters back home but to guarantee that their daughters would marry legally. In 1880 Petrona Ortiz of Barrio Borinquen and Ramona Almelia and José Encarnación Delgado of Barrio Turabo independently asked for the intervention of the alcaldes de barrio because their daughters had eloped. Ortiz's daughter left at night with Jesús María Montañez.[45] According to Almelia, her daughter, Ursual López, had hidden her love affair with José Guzmán of Barrio Culebras for a while. The couple agreed to meet on the night of February 27, 1880, to escape and start living together. Amelia's neighbor warned her of the couple's plans, and the mother reported her daughter's lover to the alcalde de barrio.[46] Delgado accused young Pedro Correa of seducing his daughter and living with her in Barrio Tomás de Castro.[47] In spite of municipal intervention, there is no evidence that these young men received any legal punishment; they ended up marrying their lovers. Parents successfully used authorities to protect their daughters' reputations and futures by arranging legal marriages for them.

Parents feared most that unscrupulous men would seduce their daughters with no intention of ever marrying them. Often, men promised to marry women as proof of their sincere love, attempting to entice women into sexual relations before marriage. As Ann Twinam argues for colonial Latin America, sex did not threaten a woman's honor as long as it occurred within the context of a betrothal.[48] But men did not always keep their word, and when they did not, parents solicited the intervention of the municipal government. In 1915, for example, Gerardo Carattini seduced and deflowered Carmen Álvarez, promising marriage. Carattini was accused but set free because he presented evidence that Álvarez was not pure. Carattini's evidence referred to a couple of love letters between Álvarez and an ex-lover, declaring their desire to be together and to marry each other (see appendix F). Even though the letters did not make any reference to sexual love, they sufficed as proof of Carmen's loss of virginity. Like Carattini, other men were said to be provoked by a woman's reputation as non-pure. Some men abandoned women after having sexual relations with them. In 1880 Micaela Rosado wrote the mayor of Caguas, stating, "Simeon Estrella, who lives in this town or in Barrio Turabo, abandoned [my daughter] on the river shore after engaging in carnal acts with her. She took refuge in the house of Juana Mercado of that barrio."[49] Ultimately, parents asked the municipal government to support them in their duty to protect their own children, which often meant a forced Catholic marriage.

Suárez Findlay suggests that the ideals of an official marriage were more important for those of the peasant sectors living in the mountains than for coastal workers.[50] In Caguas similar numbers of consensual unions among all social sectors might suggest the same results. Consensual union is slightly higher for day laborers (12.02 percent) than for sharecroppers (11.95 percent), landowners (8.96 percent), and merchants (0 percent) (see table 5.1). However, the difference is too minor to draw any significant conclusion, and, more important, the people themselves did not make a distinction between official and consensual union. The context of some of the legal cases is more indicative of people's orientation than mere statistics. The ideal of marriage in the rural barrios of Caguas seemed to have equally great significance for day laborers, sharecroppers, peasants, and large landowners. The young men who freely married or were forced to marry their girlfriends were mostly day laborers. For example, a tobacco worker expressed in love letters his strong desire to marry his girlfriend Carmen Álvarez (see appendix F). Their acts and words expressed a strong belief and even commitment to official marriage.

Young people were also encouraged to marry in the Catholic Church by other social and religious movements, such as the millenarian movement Hermanos Cheo.[51] At the turn of the century, the Hermanos Cheo was particularly strong, commanding thousands of followers among residents of the rural barrios of Caguas. Some of its most important leaders settled in the rural barrios of Caguas: Brother Polo (Policarpo Rodríguez) lived in Barrio Borinquen, Eugenia Torres Soto preached in Barrio Borinquen, and the Mother Elenita lived in the nearby town of San Lorenzo and preached in the mountainous barrios of Caguas.[52] Millenarian leaders emphasized conforming to Church sacraments and sent dozens of country couples to be married by Catholic priests. People were receptive to their command as hundreds gathered to hear and participate in the prayers and ceremonies.

Protestants also served country people in achieving their ideal of marriage. In Caguas the U.S. Baptist Church established a mission in Barrio Río Cañas, where Baptist ministers celebrated marriages for couples that had been living together.[53] Missionaries felt that their work was a tremendous success, for they gave people an alternative to Catholic marriage without requirements or fees. In 1914 Mr. Freeman declared that "before baptizing these converts, he has married grandfather, father, and son."[54] However, the Catholic Church often dissolved Protestant unions and reestablished them again with a Catholic ceremony. In 1911, for example, the bishop of Puerto Rico authorized priests who encountered Protestant marriages in the countryside to annul them.[55] In May 1923 Father Lapsley, while in mission in Barrio Tomás de Castro, observed, "Not a few were reconciled to God and several marriages were righted."[56]

Whether through the Catholic or Protestant Church, love seems to have been the main reason for marriage among country people, who incorporated the code of a righteous sexuality when it enabled them to follow their choice of love. In most cases, marriage followed a period of courtship in which love and pain were often mingled. Countrymen seemed to follow a pattern of behavior to impress and gain the favor

6. A married couple in Barrio San Salvador, 1953 (Redemptorist Archives, San Juan, Puerto Rico)

of women. Men presented themselves as martyrs of love whose will and mental and physical health depended upon women's acceptance. In a love letter, Francisco Ramos wrote to his girlfriend, "Everything about you is attractive, inspiring so much attention that I have fallen at your feet to implore that sacred loved, those very sweet words pronounced only by a woman's heart that sublimely enchant everything your mouth says and your heart feels."[57] In 1900 Juan Rodríguez, a resident of Barrio Beatriz, told Moncerrate Losano that he would go to prison for her ("iba á coger el presidio por ella").[58] In another love letter, a man named Ceferino accused his co-worker Carmen of destroying him because his love for her was so immense. Ceferino confirmed his suffering by stating that he had lost fifteen pounds. Carmen claimed in response that she was the real sufferer because her father had prohibited from seeing him. Carmen swore that she would rather kill herself than live without seeing Ceferino:

> besides Dad told me that he talked to [Alonso] so he will not hire me any more, and if this is true I will kill myself before dying of suffering. Dad did this so I could not talk to you outside the house because he knew that we chat everyday in the warehouse. He told Mom and I told him that if I have to stop working in town because I talk to you that would be worse. I said that I always love you and

*the only way to force me to leave you is by killing me; otherwise
they can't.*[59]

Lack of mental control because of love also led to violence against
women. In 1897 a man killed Manuela Torres in Barrio Río Cañas after
being "lovesick" (*por mal de amores*).[60] Men argued that women were
to blame for rape and violence because they challenged their status as
males or provoked them. For instance, an interviewee who was living
with the love of his life, Petra, justified having sexual relations with another woman, Corintia, because Corintia provoked him.[61] He wanted
to demonstrate to Corintia that "a man has to be man, has to let the
woman know who is the man." The interviewee then brought Corintia
to his sister's house, where he lived with her for three months. He finally
abandoned Corintia, who was by then pregnant. Corintia's uncle tried to
force the interviewee to marry her but to no avail because he was living
with Petra after marrying her in the Catholic Church. He used marriage to
get rid of an unwanted lover and avoid paternal responsibility, marrying
instead the woman he loved.[62]

The harsh characterization of women in these cases is hard to believe,
considering that in general women must have entered into relationships of
inequality where they were on the subordinate end, judging from couples'
ages. Husbands for the most part were older than their wives, commanding respect and deference from their wives simply because in their pater-
nalistic society, people, women in particular, were brought up to respect
and obey their elders. In general, women were much younger than their
husbands; men were older in 85.03 percent of couples, whereas women
were older in 10.5 percent of the cases, and only 4.47 percent (fifty-four)
of the couples were the same age. The age difference was minimal (four
years or less) among couples where the woman was older than the man.
In sharp contrast, men were older than women by nine years or more in
43.92 percent of all couples (see table 5.4). The largest gap is fifty years;
Juan Clavijo (ninety years old), and Claudia Azuaga (forty years old), lived
in Barrio San Salvador with their eleven children.[63] The first male provider
in most women's lives was her father; her second often was her husband.
In the case of Claudia, her husband could easily have been her father.

Age differences was relevant in the ideals and practices of marriage,
whereby husbands provided for the wives and the whole family. In fact,
for both popular and elite sectors, the ideal of male providers was part of
the male honor code as well as of women's expectations of marriage.[64] Partially because of the economic difficulties of the period and because it was

Table 5.4. Age gap of couples in the rural barrios of Caguas by number of cases, 1882

Age Gap in Years	Man is Older	Percentage*	Woman is Older	Percentage
1–4	237	19.6	75	6.2
5–8	260	21.5	27	2.23
9–12	236	19.52	15	1.24
13–16	110	9.1	5	0.41
17–20	83	6.87	3	0.25
21–24	39	3.23	2	0.17
25–28	34	2.81	0	—
29 and over	29	2.4	0	—
Total	1028	85.03	127	10.5

Sources: AHMC, SEC Secretaría, SSEC Archivo, SER Censos, SSER Habitantes, 1882–83, C26.
*Percentage of total of 1,209 couples, including 54 couples who had the same age.

a matter of honor to provide for the family, many adult males lived with their parents until their late twenties and early thirties. In Barrio Turabo, for example, Inocencio Díaz y Báez was thirty, single, and living with his parents, like Martín León (thirty-five years old) and Eustaquio de Jesús (thirty-four) in Barrio Tomás de Castro.[65] There are abundant examples like these, suggesting that young men waited to amass some belongings, even the very few materials necessary to built a straw hut (*bohío*), before departing to live with a woman. Also, young men's work was valued by both families with farms and by those who depended on wage labor. It seems that families kept young men at home as long as possible, whereas women's work was not so valuable, and it was acceptable, even desirable, for them to depart from their family of origin in their teens.

Like age differences, having several children would have deepened women's dependence on men for a living. The median number of family members in Caguas was 5.2 in 1899, but many women had from 8 to 11 children.[66] Petronila Coris had 9 children living with her and her husband in Barrio Borinquen, and Petrona Claudio (thirty-eight years old) had 12 children and lived with her husband in Barrio San Salvador. Examples like these were abundant in the rural barrios of Caguas.[67] In general, children elevated the importance of male support for women's survival because women were the main child caretakers, which limited their options for other kinds of work. Petronila Sosa, for example, was a thirty-year-old widow with 9 children. Her eldest son, Jesús Carrasco y Sosa was only fourteen years old but became the main provider of the house, as he worked as a day laborer in Barrio Borinquen.[68] Petronila, like other women, could find some relief by finding another man who would support her and her numerous children, but this alternative also

Table 5.5.   Heads of co-residential households by gender, 1882

	Male	Female
Total	1,309	345
Percentage	79.14	20.86

Source: AHMC, SEC Secretaría, SSEC Archivo, SER Censos, SSER Habitantes, 1882–83, C26.
Note: These results do not include Barrio Cañabón because the census taker forgot or refused to number or mark residential patterns.

posed some challenges. While serial monogamy offered some freedom to women of the popular classes as Suárez Findlay argues, it also imposed some limitations.[69] Women and men of the popular classes practiced serial monogamy. Men could leave an unhappy relationship, leaving the woman without support for at least some time. In the probable case of children, the woman remained responsible without male support, urgently needing to find a substitute either through salaried labor or through another man who would support the family. In the nineteenth century, salaried female labor in the rural barrios of Caguas was almost non-existent. Therefore, women either moved to cities or found male support essential to their survival. In Caguas and San Juan, many women, particularly racially mixed, made a living by washing laundry, serving, or doing domestic work.[70]

Women ultimately searched for male support either through official marriage, consensual union, or serial monogamy, as shown by patterns of residential accommodations. Men headed most households (79.14 percent), while female heads represented only 20.86 percent. Women's headship decreases slightly (17.76 percent) when examining alternative households or co-residential families.[71] Women's dependence on men seemed higher in the rural barrios of Caguas than in the city. In contrast, Suárez Findlay found that women in Ponce headed about 26 percent of all households, while Kinsbruner shows that in San Juan white women represented 47 percent and free colored women 67.2 percent of the same in 1846.[72] In the rural barrios of Caguas there were fewer opportunities for women than in the cities to make a living on their own; therefore women reached out for any opportunity for male economic support. Heading families must have been extremely difficult for women since only a few of them had salaried labor or property. Of the 345 women who headed households in Caguas, only 24 had a remunerated occupation: 9 laundrywomen, 7 property owners, 2 day laborers, 2 sharecroppers, 1 maid, 1 cook, 1 seamstress, and 1 teacher. The rest did domestic work at home.[73] In order to survive, many must have worked in the fields, but their labor was not considered actual work, for they often were paid with food, accounting

Table 5.6. Heads of alternative households by gender, 1882

	Male	Female
Total	1,843	398
Percentage	82.24	17.76

Source: AHMC, SEC Secretaría, SSEC Archivo, SER Censos, SSER Habitantes, 1882–83, C26.

for their absence from the census. Others had children who worked daily for a salary. At least one woman depended on public charity; she was a beggar (*limosnera*) whose age (eighty-six years) kept her from working.[74]

For many women in the rural barrios of Caguas, headship came not as a choice but because their male partners died. Some 190, or 55.07 percent, of the women who headed households were widows. This strikingly high percentage of widows among female heads is easily explained with the wide age gap among couples. As discussed before, men were usually much older than their wives, so the chances of widowhood were also higher. The ages of widows heading households ranged from nineteen to eighty-five years old; older women, sixty years and older, accounted for slightly over a third (70 widows, or 36.84 percent).[75] Their chances to remarry or find another male partner were very slim because, in general, men looked for younger women. In sum, the practices of courtship, marriage, and consensual union in the rural barrios of Caguas reverberated with the sexual subordination of women of all social backgrounds. This subordination was replicated in civil life.

Women's Civil Status in Caguas

Women's unequal stand in sexual matters kept them from enjoying civil life to its fullest. Women were excluded from formal politics, specifically office holding and voting, until the late 1920s in Puerto Rico. In 1929 for the first time on the island the electoral law opened voting rights to literate women who were twenty-one years and older. Only few women, mostly from the wealthy classes, were able to vote. A few years later, universal suffrage was established on the island, and women of all classes participated in elections.[76] Women of all social classes were also under-represented in property ownership, education, and wage labor in the nineteenth century. However, despite unequal conditions, many women challenged the status quo, attaining some prerogatives traditionally reserved for men. In their challenges, women began to lessen inequality for the majority. After 1898 women's civil status benefited tremendously with U.S. reforms of marriage, property, and education. However, some of these changes had been put in motion before.

Table 5.7. Number of female landowners according to the size of the farm in Caguas, 1880–1900

Size of farms by cuerdas	1880		1890		1900	
	Number of farms	Percent	Number of farms	Percent	Number of farms	Percent
.25–30	30	7.48	31	9.12	98	16.17
31–70	19	4.74	16	4.71	30	4.95
71–199	14	3.49	8	2.35	22	3.63
200–400	2	0.50	2	0.59	3	0.50
401 and over	1	0.25	0	0	1	0.17
Total	66	16.46	57	16.76	154	25.41

Source: AHMC, SEC Finanzas, SSEC Contribuciones, SER Planillas de Riqueza, SSER Agrícola, 1880–1900, C81–100.

Because Spanish law considered married women incapable of administering property, men were sole representatives of the conjugal unit and marital property.[77] Even under these limiting circumstances, a number of women managed to own property, asserting their right to be full members of their communities. In the rural barrios of Caguas, a small minority of women in 1880 and 1890 held property. Women, single, married, and widowed, made up 16.46 percent of all the landowners in the rural barrios of Caguas in 1880, and 16.76 percent in 1890. By 1900 the number of female property owners had risen by about 10 percent (to 25.41 percent of all the landowners) (see table 5.7). This increase certainly suggests the political changes of the period. Women took advantage of the U.S. ordinances of 1899 that promoted individual property at every level.

Also, women benefited from the belief in natural law that facilitated a more equal inheritance among male and female heirs. Age differences among couples made widowhood a real possibility for many women in Caguas, as discussed previously. Widows had the right to represent their property, though they faced some obstacles, and a male relative represented some widows. But widowhood was not the only way in which women acquired title to land. Often men and women who owned property in the rural barrios of Caguas distributed their belongings equally among their children after death. In 1884 Teresa Guerra received part of her husband's estate, and the other part went to her stepdaughter, Avelina Burgos y Ramírez.[78] Property was sometimes distributed while the owner was still living as well. Marcos Ríos, for example, divided half of his estate in Barrio Tomás de Castro among his children and retained the other half for himself and his wife.[79] Daughters often inherited as much land as sons, an interesting interpretation of the Spanish law regarding inheritance. Spanish law established male prerogatives to represent and administer family property and provided for the protection of women, who were considered weak and vulnerable. These legal concepts were continued with the Spanish Civil Code of 1889, which applied in theory to Puerto Rico, and during the first years of U.S. government in the island. It was not until 1902 that women in Puerto Rico gained equal standing in administering the property of the family.[80]

Women's ownership of farm property seems to have been more feasible among the landed peasantry than among large landowners. That is, in general, women of the landed peasantry had a better chance than elite women to own farm property. In 1880 thirty women owned small farms, while only three had large farms. This trend continued in 1890, and accelerated after 1900, when ninety-eight women owned small farms and only four had large estates. Differences among the landed peasantry and the elite clearly point to the diverse values of property referred to in chapter 3. Elite women usually had a man representing their land, and their families were more likely to pass on their property to male heirs. In comparison, many families of the landed peasantry believed in natural law and were more prone than the landed elite to give women a fair share. Equal distribution favored women of the lower social classes, but its impact was limited to the possibilities of the period.

Women greatly depended on men in the rural barrios of Caguas because of their low levels of land ownership and, more important, because their access to wage labor was extremely limited. In 1882 women represented only 4.92 percent of the workforce, while men constituted 95.08 percent.[81] Only 108 women (4.43 percent) in the rural barrios of Caguas actually engaged in wage labor, excluding 2 beggars and 10 farmers or property owners. Most of these women did laundry and sharecropping (see table 5.8). By the end of the century, women's position in the labor force was basically unchanged, representing 9.69 percent of Caguas's labor force in 1899. While 49 women in 1882 engaged in agriculture (sharecroppers, farmers, and day laborers), in 1899 only 36 women were employed in agriculture (see tables 5.8 and 5.9). Even accounting for urban jobs, women constituted a small portion of the working labor force throughout the late nineteenth century.

In the twentieth century, however, women's position in wage labor changed dramatically with the introduction of U.S. capitalism to the island. By 1910 Puerto Rican women constituted close to a third of the labor force, and slightly more than half by 1920.[82] During this period, Caguas quickly became a center for tobacco manufacturing. In Barrio Turabo, for

Table 5.8. Women's occupations in the rural barrios of Caguas, 1882

Occupation	Number	Percentage
Laundry woman	37	30.83
Sharecropper	34	28.33
Seamstress	19	15.83
Farmer/Property Owner	10	8.33
Cook	8	6.66
Day Laborer	5	4.17
Maid	3	2.5
Beggar	2	1.66
Artisan	2	1.66

Source: AHMC, SEC Secretaría, SSEC Archivo, SER Censos, SSER Habitantes, 1882–83, C26.

example, only 1 woman worked as a day laborer in agriculture, and no women in the rural barrios of Caguas worked in any type of factory in 1882.[83] The picture changes dramatically after 1898. In Barrio Turabo 46 women worked in tobacco factories in 1910, whereas 201 women were so employed in 1920.[84] Women represented the majority of workers in the tobacco industry in Caguas and throughout Puerto Rico. They operated the cigar-making machines, the stampers, the labelers, and the packers. Hand-making cigar was considered a man's job, so few women were employed in hand plants; instead, they usually occupied less skilled jobs such as stripping the tobacco.[85]

Thus, after the 1910s women in Caguas were increasingly incorporated into the labor force, and almost simultaneously they began to enter trade unionism. If within the labor movement Caguas became the "cradle of the struggle," as was mentioned in the previous chapter, Caguas women were its front soldiers or avant-garde. The Puerto Rican Federation of Labor at first resisted recruiting women, and its male members portrayed women workers as detrimental to the struggle, believing that women's presence lowered wages and that women were too apathetic to

Table 5.9. Women's occupations in Caguas, 1899

	Number	Percentage
Domestic and personal services	500	84.03
Manufactures and mechanical industries	50	8.4
Agriculture, fishing and mining	36	6.05
Commerce and transportation	5	0.84
Professional services	4	0.67

Sources: Departamento de la Guerra, Dirección del Censo de Puerto Rico, *Informe sobre el censo de Puerto Rico, 1899*, 299–300.

organize. However, women workers challenged such perceptions by not only demanding membership in large numbers but also demonstrating their capacity for leadership. Slowly, women workers won the respect of male trade unionists even though men controlled the top leadership of the Free Federation of Workers.[86] In Caguas, women were the avant-garde of labor activism in the tobacco industry. In 1917–18, thirty-two female tobacco strippers and sixty-two men went on strike.[87] In June 1919 women tobacco workers led a strike that involved most factories in town. A newspaper reported that women workers protested by walking around the city at different times during the day, holding meetings at the main square in the downtown area (*la plaza*). The principal leader of the Socialist Party, Santiago Iglesias, participated in one of these meetings.[88] Women's struggle for better wages continued when, in October 1919, Caguas's female workers won a legal case against several employers for paying less than what was stipulated by the law.[89] A study about the tobacco industry in Caguas and its labor movement is surely needed, but the discussion of the labor movement is beyond the scope of this book. Nonetheless, it is clear that women workers were a competing social element that pushed the limits of what was permissible, demanding better wages and better living conditions throughout the twentieth century.

Similarly, women's opportunities in education began to improve after 1898. Under Spanish rule, public education was part of the legal system, as expressed in the Decree of Despujol of 1880, which mandated separate schools for girls and boys and organized an education board for each municipality.[90] Women's education was strongly supported by the liberal sector, particularly in the interest of forming productive mothers and wives in the countryside.[91] The municipal government of Caguas also agreed that educating women was a "very important factor for the development of nations as well as for their moral and material progress."[92] However, women's education in the rural barrios of Caguas was an ideal rather than a reality. In general, education in the countryside was in a precarious state, reaching only a minority of the people. There were only four schools in the rural barrios of Caguas by 1880 and five by 1898, and student absenteeism was widespread.[93] These schools served almost exclusively the male population. Most girls of school age were not in school, mainly because the municipal mayor saw no use in women's education.[94] In 1884 the mayor of Caguas tried to convince the governor that schools for girls in the countryside "will not give any result."[95] Accordingly, the mayor did not assign funds for a girls school, either to pay the teacher or to rent a place.[96] In 1896 the mayor again excused the lack of school for girls in the rural barrios of Caguas citing the scattered population.[97]

It was not until November 1898 that the U.S. military government opened a school for girls in Barrio Cañaboncito.[98] The liberal sector in Puerto Rico again applauded the merits of educating women. In 1899 Mariano Abril celebrated, "We belong to a progressive nation that has perfectly educated woman in such a way that is still an ideal for the rest of the countries."[99] However, the reluctance to educate women in the countryside of Caguas continued for many years. An interviewee recounted a story told by his father, Lino Carrasquillo. The comisario of Barrio Turabo used to advise his father as follows: "Lino, look, you don't send women to school because they'll learn to write and all they'll do is write letters to their boyfriends. Send the boys."[100] Nonetheless, women's education in the countryside was improving after 1898, albeit at a slow pace. The number of rural schools increased; by 1902 there were eight rural schools in Caguas, but their attendance was still mostly male.[101] In 1906 the commissioner of education stated, "in both the graded and the rural schools the number of boys is greater than the number of girls, though the difference is greater in the rural schools."[102]

Not only did popular attitudes affect women's chances of getting some schooling, but the role models also maintained a strictly male teacher figure in the countryside. Under Spanish rule the educational system mostly hired men who were between twenty-one and forty-eight years old.[103] U.S. authorities in the island began to change this hiring practice and, in fact, favored female teachers for the countryside.[104] The first female teacher to apply in Caguas was Doña América Duprey y Roqué, but the first woman to get the job was Doña Celia Concepción Rivera.[105] Afterward, more women became teachers, but men still dominated the profession.[106] By 1910 men represented more than half of the rural teachers.[107]

Despite all the disadvantages women confronted in the school system, they were not at great disadvantage with their male counterparts in terms of literacy rates. In 1882 women constituted 40.39 percent of the people in Caguas who were fully or somewhat literate, while men accounted for 59.61 percent (see table 5.10). While women were still at a disadvantage, the relatively slim gap seemed to belie the institutional obstacles of the period. How did 290 women manage to acquire some literacy skills when their society formally denied most of them schooling?

In general, literacy rates for both men and women were very low; only 718 people in the countryside of Caguas (or 8.31 percent of the population) had literacy skills (see table 5.9). Even within this very small group

Table 5.10. Literacy rates by gender in the rural barrios of Caguas, 1882

	Fully Literate	Read	Total	Percentage
Women	213	77	290	40.39
Men	344	84	428	59.61
Total	557	161	718	

Source: AHMC, SEC Secretaría, SSEC Archivo, SER Censos, SSER Habitantes, 1882–83, C26.

of literate people, women were at a disadvantage.[108] But how did women acquire literacy skills when the few schools in the rural areas almost exclusively taught boys? The census suggests that girls learned to read and write mostly from their mothers. In most cases in which girls and young woman had some literacy, their mothers were literate too. For example, Carmen Diepa Arroyo was a fully literate twenty-two-year-old widow in Barrio Tomás de Castro. Her five-year-old daughter also knew how to read and write. Likewise, the Vélez Delgado sisters, Petrona (fourteen), Teresa (thirteen), Librada (twelve), and María (six), were fully literate, as was their mother.[109]

Women's literacy levels improved after 1898 with the U.S. island-wide literacy campaign. After this period, girls were part of public education, and their literacy increased with the rest of the population. In Caguas literacy rates grew from 24.8 percent in 1899 to 32 percent in 1910.[110] However, these figures account for both the rural and urban population, so it is safe to estimate lower figures for the countryside because the majority of schools were in the city. Moreover, as the commissioner of education observed, more boys than girls attended schools, particularly in the rural areas. Nonetheless, during the nineteenth century, women began to spread literacy among their children, benefiting girls and boys equally. Women began to assert equal access to books inside their homes. Although, it would take a long time before women had equal access to education in Puerto Rico, they planted the seeds of a right to education in the most political sphere of all, their homes.

This chapter has demonstrated that the intervention of the municipal government allied with men in monitoring women's behavior, affirming Elizabeth Jelin's conclusion that "the dichotomization of life into public and private spheres leads to a mutilation of women's citizenship."[111] The government offered some protection to women as long as their behavior conformed to the ideals of good mothers and wives and as long as they accepted their exclusion from the public sphere, a subordination that was accepted and reinforced by men in all sectors of society.

Conclusion
Toward an Inclusive Citizenship

The Spanish colonial administration in the late nineteenth century developed an odd, backward, and inefficient system to govern the island of Puerto Rico. Some of the most important policies, the Municipal Law of 1878 and the Mortgage Law of 1880, which instituted land privatization, were issued with Cuba and its revolutionary, colored, rural population in mind but nonetheless applied to Puerto Rico. In Puerto Rico, where the most heated political debate did not include the possibility of independence but rather focused on which political wing was the most loyal to Spain, the policies fomented some resentment among local elites. With the Municipal Law of 1878 the Spanish Crown attempted to centralize political power, first by positioning a direct representative of the governor at the head of the municipal government and, second, by increasing the number of councilmen and restricting suffrage, thus limiting the participation of the rural poor. This law effectively changed the terms of the political game.

However, large landowners in Caguas soon learned to reshape the policies to fit their own interests in a context of peace and loyalty to the Crown. Local elites effectively controlled the council and later the office of the mayor from the late nineteenth century until the mid-1910s. Because they were so successful, the majority of the population, who were excluded from office and even from voting, developed a marginal citizenship based on a series of strategies to guarantee the survival of the majority outside the realm of formal politics. These strategies claimed access to resources based on mobility rights as well as work and land use, rather than on formal titles of ownership.

Formal landownership was, in theory and in practice, the prerequisite for office holding. There was a direct relationship between occupying a municipal office and the class background of the official; wealthy landowners dominated the council, while members of the landed peasantry were coerced into the positions of alcaldes and comisarios de barrio. A rural laborer had no chance to enter into office unless he was literate and there was no landed person in the barrio available to occupy the position.

The council and the municipal government delegated to alcaldes and comisarios de barrio multiple tasks of surveillance and administration that dealt with country people. Indeed, alcaldes and comisarios de barrio tied the rural population to the mayor and council of Caguas. Some men found in the positions of alcalde or comisario de barrio a path to acquire power. In general, however, people tried to avoid these positions, for they often represented a social and economic burden. The council named alcaldes and comisarios de barrio mostly from the landed peasantry. In addition, mediating between government officials and country people was a difficult task that could compromise the safety of alcaldes and comisarios de barrio. They became targets of protests against governmental orders, deeds, and ordinances. Many alcaldes and comisarios de barrio chose to neglect their municipal duties and responsibilities, allying instead with neighbors and friends, who often shared a similar class background.

The social background of municipal officials is also indicative of a power struggle over land privatization. The Mortgage Law of 1880 institutionalized private property by enhancing the benefits of legal land titles. Because land title was the sole basis of credit, title holders were able to finance increased agrarian production and, by cultivating a larger area, register more land in their names. Large landowners in particular used these tactics to acquire land that was originally used by country residents who were unable to register their land or to pay taxes. The municipal government legalized and enforced this process of land privatization mainly in two ways: first, they argued that progress depended directly on the development and growth of private property and that, therefore, the role of the government was to protect private property. Second, the ayuntamiento adopted this point of view in policy making and considered it a duty to protect private property. In protecting the rights of those with private property, the government favored cash crop production and large estates. The process of land privatization effectively and actively alienated a racially mixed peasantry, who increasingly lost land to white farmers and sharecroppers.

In this process, the poorest sectors of society—colored laborers, sharecroppers, and landed peasants—resuscitated the principles of natural law within the Spanish system in order to justify access to land and its resources with the right of use and labor. Their persistence was such that they effectively defied the law and the police, forcing the Spanish Crown eventually to recognize use as another form of legal land possession with the 1884 Regulations of Registry and Common Land. Natural law also served the poor as a code by which to measure the actions of the rich and the powerful, offering grounds to confront prominent figures in the courts.

The rural poor also used natural law to evaluate other legal measures that threatened their survival, in particular laws that restricted their mobility rights. In 1881 the municipal government institutionalized the cédulas de vecindad, a legal identification document that served as a mechanism to tax people without titles of property. The cédulas attempted to curtail laborers' mobility rights to guarantee a labor force for commercial agriculture, creating living conditions that were often difficult to escape. First, laborers were required to pay for the document; otherwise, they were fined or punished with forced labor. The costs of the cédulas and forced labor often condemned laborers and the landed peasantry to economic destitution, for they became indebted for life to the municipal government. Second, the employer held the cédulas, which multiplied the chances of the police finding laborers without their documentation in hand. Thus, the cédulas became a municipal mechanism to fund public work as well as a way to support private property by curtailing laborers' mobility rights. In Caguas laboring classes resisted both the cédulas and forced labor with open confrontation, evasion, and disobedience of authorities. In doing so, laborers, sharecroppers, and the landed peasantry set limits to the government's projects to advance commercial agriculture and contain people of color. In particular, people of color from the rural barrios of Caguas asserted their freedom by choosing the terms of employment and fleeing when faced with unfavorable conditions.

Another strategy to impose capitalist discipline upon laborers was the promotion of bourgeois family values among the rural population. The ayuntamiento and large landowners maintained that monogamous and heterosexual relations within legal marriage contributed to the proper ordering of society so that the rural poor would accept the moral guidance of the nation's self-proclaimed wealthy leaders. The fathers of the nation used elements of traditional and modern patriarchy, the authority of the father, and male fraternity in imagining the universal benefits of their leadership. They believed that by their monitoring of the work and culture, including bourgeois family values of the laboring classes, Puerto Rico would advance toward progress and civilization. Women, in their assigned roles as mothers and wives, were to guarantee a nest of comfort and culture for future generations; hence, their roles demanded their confinement within their homes.

These family ideas and values informed day-to-day execution of the law and governmental authority. The municipal government, as the forum that united the wealthiest men of Caguas, claimed the ultimate authority over patriarchal relations in the realms of politics and people's lives. By demanding governmental intervention to resolve family disputes and reinforce parental and marital authority, country people legitimated the municipal government as the prime source of patriarchal power. Women sought shelter against male abuse and abandonment by demanding protection from other family men and government officials. Thus, women relied on asserting their own dependency on men as a strategy to defend themselves against male abuse and abandonment.

Confining family roles for women undermined their civil rights and status. First, most women entered marriage or consensual unions at an early age with much older men, reinforcing patterns of deference and respect to men initiated by their fathers. Second, men headed the great majority of households in the rural barrios of Caguas mostly because of the very few salaried opportunities that existed for women. Finally, women of the rural barrios of Caguas were at a great educational disadvantage because the municipal government denied them formal education throughout the nineteenth century. However, despite this quasi-institutional ban on education, women and men had a similar literacy rate in the countryside, mostly because of the poor educational opportunities for both genders. Nonetheless, the census of 1882 suggests that women learned to read and write from their mothers. In this way, women began to lessen inequality in another political sphere—their homes—by offering literacy to both boys and girls.

In the end, the rural poor's claims for a more egalitarian society, or what I call here "marginal citizenship," could not successfully transform the political exclusion of the countryside and its racially mixed population because it borrowed too many elements from the Spanish legal system. In particular, marginal citizenship adopted patriarchy as a model to regulate social relations at home, failing to address gender inequalities and perpetuating class differences. However, marginal citizenship never sought to completely transform the legal system. The significance of those claims lay not on what they achieved but rather on the strategies and possibilities they created. Because increasingly formal politics became a prerogative of a white minority, the majority of the rural population sought alternatives outside governmental representation and voting. Using the courts and evading unfair laws, the rural poor created a political space that successfully challenged the established order by pushing the limits of what was permissible. Unlike their counterparts in Cuba who had weapons, the rural poor in Caguas stressed the natural rights of each man, white or colored, rich or poor, to enjoy the fruits of his labor, moving around freely to find the best conditions to work.

This is the context of the change of sovereignty brought by the U.S. occupation. By the time the U.S. colonial government officially eradicated the cédulas de vecindad, the law had lost its relevance because the racially mixed peasantry had abolished it already through their refusal to comply with it. The U.S. colonial administration, however, continued and protected the process of land privatization, further alienating people of color from the land. Once again, the right to work and live decently dominated the petitions of the laboring classes in the early years of the twentieth century. Under the U.S. colonial power, the strategies of the rural poor proved more resilient than those of the local elite.

The local elite attempted to maintain their class and political privileges based on landownership, when the relatively small size of the island converted them into an increasingly powerless landowning class. They were never a very powerful elite, but by insisting on landownership as the basis of privilege, they further undermined their own power since the size of the island did not allow for the large *latifundios* found in other areas of Latin America. Meanwhile, the mulatto laboring population of the rural barrios had no other recourse but to search for legal options outside landownership as a way to guarantee citizenship. They created a political space where a legal community could maintain a living without fences or handcuffs. This legal space was movable because the rural poor had constantly to move around to find better terms of employment or sharecropping. Before and after 1898, this legal community was always "on the move."[1] In this sense, the rural poor had created the possibility of a landless patria for all.

The idea of justice lived on among the laboring classes throughout the twentieth century, taking different shapes and expressions. After 1898 the massive capitalist injection by the United States created conditions of poverty, devastation, and general unemployment for many Puerto Ricans. But as in the rest of Puerto Rico, laboring classes in Caguas welcomed the new colonial regime because they believed that the United States would guarantee basic rights for the majority of the population, including the right to organize, which had been prohibited under Spanish rule but was established in 1902.[2] Nonetheless, the new regime also had a strong commitment to protecting private property and did not hesitate to use the police against organized labor.[3]

In this context, the U.S. tobacco industry established some of the largest manufacturers of Puerto Rico in Caguas. The industry became the main source of employment for the racially mixed majority. For the first time, rural workers, female and male, could be educated and organized en masse. Tobacco factories became a school for many who for the first time heard about socialism, anarchism, and workers' rights and struggles through the most influential writings of the period from Europe and Latin America. Some Caguas cigar makers developed a radical anarchist movement that was typical of those found in Spain and Latin America. Free labor and progress were the movement's most important goals. The U.S. government immediately suspected its radical nature and dismantled it through violent repression. But even before the repression, the anarchist movement attracted few rural workers in Puerto Rico.[4] In contrast to anarchism, trade unionism was very successful among rural workers in Caguas, recruiting hundreds of workers. In fact, Caguas became the "cradle of the struggle" between labor and capital in the first decades of the twentieth century, leading organized labor to impressive activism.[5] As in the nineteenth century, local working classes sought a decent living for the racially mixed majority. In the twentieth century, women tobacco workers helped to lead the struggle for social equality with their impressive activism.

Today, we can learn from their ideals and practices because Cagüeños curbed the most devastating effects of land privatization and the capitalization of labor by challenging openly or through civil disobedience any law that seemed unjust. This simple and wise action established a legacy of civil culture that anyone, including the poor and uneducated, could participate in and understand, and it made the role of the government certain and specific. Within marginal citizenship, the government's only function is to guarantee that each social being has nourishment, a place to live, and the right to work and move freely. In this sense, the claims of Caguas's laboring classes innately had a universal character that elevated the well-being of the individual, regardless of social and racial differences, over the constraints of power achieved through wealth or politics. Today, that legacy is not just part of the history of Cagüeños and Puerto Ricans, it is also part of our human race.

Appendix A
Comparison of Farm Sizes in the Barrios of Caguas, 1880–1900

Farm Sizes in Caguas by Barrio, 1880

Barrio	Number of cuerdas[a]				
	0.25–30	31–70	71–199	200–400	401 & over
Bairoa	5	5	6	1	0
Beatriz[b]	10	6	11	3	1
Borinquen	17	12	7	2	1
Cañabón	21	8	0	2	2
Cañaboncito	22	13	6	1	2
Culebras	20	16	15	2	1
Quebrada Puercos	19	6	1	0	0
Río Cañas	14	10	5	1	0
Tomás de Castro	34	13	15	0	0
Turabo	41	10	8	3	3

Notes

[a] Because some residents owned land in more than one barrio, the total number of farms in this table is larger than the total number of farms in the table in appendix B ("Land Distribution by Farm Size in Caguas, 1880–1910").

[b] Figure is from 1881 because there was not enough information for Beatriz in 1880.

Source: AHMC, SEC Finanzas, SSEC Contribuciones, SER Planillas de Riqueza, SSER Agrícola, 1880–81, C81.

Farm Sizes in Caguas by Barrio, 1890

Barrio	Number of cuerdas				
	0.25–30	31–70	71–199	200–400	401 & over
Bairoa	3	2	5	2	0
Beatriz	12	7	6	2	1
Borinquen	16	5	4	1	2
Cañabón	14	5	4	2	2
Cañaboncito	17	9	6	1	0
Culebras	20	18	9	0	1
Quebrada Puercos	19	7	2	0	0
Río Cañas	15	10	6	0	1
Tomás de Castro	43	10	8	1	1
Turabo	22	9	7	1	2

Source: AHMC, SEC Finanzas, SSEC Contribuciones, SER Planillas de Riqueza, SSER Agrícola, 1890–91, C89.

Farm Sizes in Caguas by Barrio, 1900

Barrio	Number of cuerdas				
	0.25–30	31–70	71–199	200–400	401 & over
Bairoa	18	8	20	2	2
Beatriz	25	6	10	3	1
Borinquen	32	11	12	3	3
Cañabón	20	6	5	2	2
Cañaboncito	43	20	14	1	0
Culebras	34	17	13	3	0
Quebrada Puercos	46	9	0	0	0
Río Cañas	41	11	5	3	0
Tomás de Castro	52	20	12	4	0
Turabo	40	11	13	2	1

Source: AHMC, SEC Finanzas, SSEC Contribuciones, SER Planillas de Riqueza, SSER Agrícola, 1900, C99–100.

Appendix B
Land Distribution by Farm Size
in Caguas, 1880–1910

Year	Number of cuerdas (percentage of total)				
	0.25–30	31–70	71–199	200–400	401 & over
1880	196 (52.12)	96 (25.53)	64 (17.02)	14 (3.72)	6 (1.6)
1881	210 (53.03)	97 (24.49)	66 (16.66)	13 (3.28)	10 (2.52)
1882	235 (61.35)	79 (20.62)	58 (15.14)	3 (.78)	8 (2.08)
1883	180 (62.06)	60 (20.68)	40 (13.79)	5 (1.72)	5 (1.72)
1884[a]					
1885	185 (57.63)	73 (22.74)	50 (15.57)	3 (.93)	10 (3.11)
1886	186 (59.42)	58 (18.53)	50 (15.97)	12 (3.83)	7 (2.23)
1887	341 (58.49)	133 (22.81)	78 (13.37)	17 (2.91)	14 (2.4)
1888	111 (54.14)	57 (27.8)	28 (13.65)	3 (1.46)	6 (2.92)
1889	145 (52.53)	73 (26.44)	44 (15.94)	7 (2.53)	7 (2.53)
1890	184 (53.95)	80 (23.46)	55 (16.12)	12 (3.51)	10 (2.93)
1891	158 (54.10)	73 (25)	41 (14.04)	11 (3.76)	9 (3.08)
1892	148 (53.04)	70 (25.08)	39 (13.97)	10 (3.58)	12 (4.3)
1893	243 (52.71)	104 (22.55)	82 (17.78)	19 (4.12)	13 (2.81)
1894	259 (62.4)	80 (19.27)	56 (13.49)	12 (2.89)	8 (1.92)
1895	60 (54.54)	23 (20.9)	17 (15.45)	6 (5.45)	4 (3.63)
1896	331 (58.27)	118 (20.77)	88 (15.49)	22 (3.87)	9 (1.58)
1897	266 (57.7)	100 (21.69)	70 (15.18)	16 (3.47)	7 (1.52)
1898	198 (51.29)	98 (25.38)	67 (17.35)	15 (3.88)	8 (2.07)
1899	337 (62.75)	103 (19.18)	74 (13.78)	17 (3.16)	6 (1.11)
1900	341 (58.19)	114 (19.45)	97 (16.55)	23 (3.92)	11 (1.87)

Year	Number of acres (percentage of total)				
	0.25–49	50–99	100–174	175–499	500 & over
1910	698 (78.25)	93 (10.42)	52 (5.82)	37 (4.14)	12 (1.34)

[a] The financial records for 1884 are very incomplete and therefore not conclusive.

Sources: AHMC, SEC Finanzas, SSEC Contribuciones, SER Planillas de Riqueza, SSER Agrícola, 1880–1900, C81–100; U.S. Bureau of the Census, *Thirteenth Census of the United States*, 2:995.

Appendix C
Municipal Government
of Caguas, 1880–1903

1877

Mayor: Odón Somonte

Councilmen: Miguel Muñoz, Juan Méndez, Juan Isern, Benito Polo, and Ramón Vilar

Caballeros síndicos: José Martí y Bonet, Gerardo Puig

1880

Mayor: José María de la Vega

Tenientes alcaldes (lieutenant mayors): Juan Isern, Landelino Aponte, Francisco Méndez, and Tomás López

Councilmen: Basilio Fernando Aguirre, Manuel Joaquín Caballero, Francisco Fernández, Pedro Grillo, Felipe Jiménez, Manuel Jiménez Sicardó, Diego Lizardi y Echevarría, Marcelino López y Aponte, Salvador Más, Nicolás Morera, Vicente R. Muñoz Barros, Rafael Polo, Rafael Ramos, Celestino Solá, and Ramón Vilar

1881

Mayor: José María de la Vega

Tenientes alcaldes: Juan Isern, Landelino Aponte, Francisco Méndez, and Tomás López

Councilmen: Basilio Fernando Aguirre, Manuel Joaquín Caballero, Ramón Catá, Pedro P. Grillo, Francisco Fernández, Felipe Jiménez, Manuel Jiménez Sicardó, Diego Lizardi y Echevarría, Marcelino López y Aponte, Salvador Más, Vicente R. Muñoz Barros, Rafael Polo, Rafael Ramos, Celestino Solá, and Ramón Vilar

1882

Mayor: José María de la Vega

Tenientes alcaldes: Basilio Fernando Aguirre, Rafael Polo, Landelino Aponte, and Francisco Méndez

Councilmen: Bartolomé Borrás, Ramón Catá, Francisco Fernández, José Fernández, Santiago Franqui, Pedro P. Grillo, Juan Isern, Manuel Jiménez Sicardó, Diego Lizardi y Echevarría, Eduardo López y Caballero, Augusto Muñoz, Vicente R. Muñoz Barros, Celestino Solá, Marcelino Solá, Odón Somonte, and Ramón Vilar

1883

Mayor: José María de la Vega

Tenientes alcaldes: Basilio Fernando Aguirre, Rafael Polo, Landelino Aponte, and Francisco Méndez

Councilmen: Joaquín Aponte, Bartolomé Borrás, Pascual Borrás, Ramón Catá, Gabriel Dalmau, Francisco Fernández, José Fernández, Santiago Franqui, Pedro P. Grillo, Aniceto Guzmán, Manuel Jiménez Sicardó, Gerónimo Matanzos, Augusto Muñoz, Vicente R. Muñoz Barros, Celestino Solá, Marcelino Solá, and Odón Somonte

1884

Mayor: José María de la Vega

Tenientes alcaldes: Basilio Fernando Aguirre, Rafael Polo, Aniceto Guzmán, Francisco
    Méndez
Councilmen: Joaquín Aponte, Pascual Borrás, Ramón Catá, Gabriel Dalmau, José Fernán-
    dez, Santiago Franqui, Manuel Jiménez Sicardó, Gerónimo Matanzos, Augusto
    Muñoz, Vicente R. Muñoz Barros, Marcelino Solá, Odón Somonte, and Ramón
    Vilar

1885

Mayor: José María de la Vega
Tenientes alcaldes: Basilio Fernando Aguirre, Francisco Méndez, Ramón Catá, and Rafael
    Polo
Councilmen: Joaquín Aponte, Pascual Borrás, Gabriel Dalmau, José Fernández, Santiago
    Franqui, Manuel Jiménez Sicardó, Celestino López, Gerónimo Matanzos, Vicente R.
    Muñoz Barros, Gerardo Puig, Nicolás Quiñonez Cabezudo, Marcelino Solá, Odón
    Somonte, and Ramón Vilar

1886

Mayor: Pedro Pastor y Egea
Tenientes alcaldes: Basilio Fernando Aguirre, Francisco Méndez, Pascual Borrás, and Odón
    Somonte
Councilmen: Ramón Catá, José Fernández, Santiago Franqui, Manuel Jiménez Sicardó,
    Venancio Lasa, Salvador Más, Gerónimo Matanzos, Vicente R. Muñoz Barros, Rafael
    Polo, José Ramírez de Arellano, Celestino Solá, Modesto Solá, José María Solís, Odón
    Suárez, and Ramón Vilar

1887

Mayor: Pedro Pastor y Egea
Tenientes alcaldes: Basilio Fernando Aguirre, Francisco Méndez, Pascual Borrás, and Odón
    Somonte
Councilmen: Joaquín Aponte, Gabriel Dalmau, Federico Diez y López, José Fernández,
    Víctor Fernández, Venancio Lasa, Gerónimo Matanzos, Vicente R. Muñoz Barros,
    Agustín Plá, Gerardo Puig, José Ramírez de Arellano, Celestino Solá, Modesto Solá,
    José María Solís, and Ramón Vilar

1888

Mayor: Pedro Pastor y Egea
Tenientes alcaldes: Arturo Más, Francisco Méndez, Víctor Fernández, and Odón
    Somonte
Councilmen: Pascual Borrás, Federico Diez y López, José Fernández, Víctor Fernández, Ve-
    nancio Lasa, Ignacio Lizardi Delgado, Vicente R. Muñoz Barros, Agustín Plá, Gerardo
    Puig, José Ramírez de Arellano, Rafael Rodríguez, Celestino Solá, Modesto Solá, José
    María Solís, and Ramón Vilar

1889

Mayor: Pedro Pastor y Egea
Tenientes alcaldes: Arturo Más, Francisco Méndez, Odón Somonte, and Víctor
    Fernández

Councilmen: Pascual Borrás, Silverio Campos, Federico Diez y López, Víctor Fernández, Antonio Jiménez Sicardó, Venancio Lasa, Vicente R. Muñoz Barros, Agustín Plá, Rafael Polo, Gerardo Puig, Miguel Puig, José Ramírez de Arellano, Rafael Rodríguez, Celestino Solá, Modesto Solá, José María Solís, Pedro Eduardo Vidal y Ríos, and Ramón Vilar

1890

Mayor: Eduardo Vidal y Ríos
Tenientes alcaldes: Miguel Puig, Rafael Polo
Councilmen: Pascual Borrás, Silverio Campos, Federico Diez y López, Santiago Franqui, Antonio Jiménez Sicardó, Venancio Lasa, Francisco Méndez, Vicente R. Muñoz Barros, Agustín Plá, Gerardo Puig, Rafael Rodríguez, Celestino Solá, and Ramón Vilar

1891

Mayor: Rafael Polo
Tenientes alcaldes: Antonio Jiménez Sicardó, Miguel Puig, Víctor Fernández
Councilmen: Landelino Aponte, Bartolomé Borrás, Pascual Borrás, Silverio Campos, Federico Diez y López, Víctor Fernández , Santiago Franqui, Venancio Lasa, Francisco Méndez, Vicente R. Muñoz Barros, Agustín Plá, Gerardo Puig, Rafael Rodríguez, Avelino Saurí, Celestino Solá, and Ramón Vilar

1892

Mayor: Rafael Polo
Tenientes alcaldes: Antonio Jiménez Sicardó, Miguel Puig, Víctor Fernández
Councilmen: Landelino Aponte, Bartolomé Borrás, Silverio Campos, Santiago Franqui, José Garriga, Venancio Lasa, Gerónimo Matanzos, Francisco Méndez, Vicente R. Muñoz Barros, Agustín Plá, Gerardo Puig, Avelino Saurí, and Celestino Solá

1893

Mayor: Rafael Polo
Tenientes alcaldes: Antonio Jiménez Sicardó, Miguel Puig, Agustín Plá
Councilmen: Bartolomé Borrás, Pascual Borrás, Silverio Campos, Víctor Fernández, Arturo Más, Gerónimo Matanzos, Francisco Méndez, Vicente R. Muñoz Barros, Agustín Plá, Miguel Puig, Regis Ramos, and José María Solís

1894

Mayor: Francisco Méndez
Tenientes alcaldes: Antonio Jiménez Sicardó, Víctor Fernández, and Silverio Campos
Councilmen: Bartolomé Borrás, Pascual Borrás, Silverio Campos, Víctor Fernández, Antonio Jiménez Sicardó, Arturo Más, Gerónimo Matanzos, Vicente R. Muñoz Barros, Agustín Plá, Rafael Polo, Miguel Puig, José Ramírez de Arellano, and Regis Ramos

1895

Mayor: Francisco Méndez
Tenientes alcaldes: Antonio Jiménez Sicardó, Víctor Fernández, and Silverio Campos
Councilmen: Landelino Aponte, Bartolomé Borrás, Pascual Borrás, Silverio Campos, Federico Diez y López, Víctor Fernández, Santiago Franqui, José Garriga, Antonio

Jiménez Sicardó, Arturo Más, Salvador Más, Gerónimo Matanzos, Agustín Plá, Rafael Polo, Miguel Puig, José Ramírez de Arellano, Regis Ramos, Rafael Rodríguez, Marcelino Solá, and Odón Somonte

1896

Mayor: Arturo Más

Tenientes alcaldes: Antonio Jiménez Sicardó, José Garriga, Miguel Puig, and Silverio Campos

Councilmen: Bartolomé Borrás, Pascual Borrás , Víctor Fernández , Santiago Franqui, Salvador Más, Gerónimo Matanzos, Agustín Plá, Rafael Polo, Gerardo Puig, Regis Ramos, Rafael Rodríguez, and Marcelino Solá

1897

Mayor: Arturo Más

Tenientes alcaldes: Antonio Jiménez Sicardó, José Garriga, Miguel Puig, and Silverio Campos

Councilmen: Bartolomé Borrás, Pascual Borrás, Silverio Campos, Víctor Fernández, Santiago Franqui, Manuel García, José Garriga, Antonio Jiménez Sicardó, Salvador Más, Gerónimo Matanzos, Manuel Muñoz, Vicente R. Muñoz Barros, Agustín Plá, Gerardo Puig, Miguel Puig, Nicolás Quiñonez Cabezudo, José Ramírez de Arellano, Regis Ramos, Marcelino Solá, Modesto Solá, Odón Somonte, and Ramón Sotomayor

1898

Mayor: Vicente R. Muñoz Barros, Celestino Solá, Antonio Jiménez Sicardó, Gervasio García, and Ramón Sotomayor

Tenientes alcaldes: Antonio Jiménez Sicardó, Ramón Sotomayor, Gerardo Puig

Councilmen: Bartolomé Borrás, Pascual Borrás, Pedro Cardona, Víctor Fernández, Santiago Franqui, Gervasio García, Manuel García, Antonio Jiménez, Arturo Más, Gerónimo Matanzos, Enrique Moreno, Manuel Muñoz, Agustín Plá, Gerardo Puig, Nicolás Quiñonez Cabezudo, José Ramírez de Arellano, Celestino Solá, Marcelino Solá, Modesto Solá, José María Solís, and Ramón Sotomayor

1899

Mayor: Vicente R. Muñoz Barros, Celestino Solá, Antonio Jiménez Sicardó, Gervasio García, and Ramón Sotomayor

Tenientes alcaldes: Antonio Jiménez Sicardó, Ramón Sotomayor, Pedro Cardona, Gervasio García

Councilmen: Francisco Aacutelvarez, Mauricio Aacutelvarez, Ramón Aacutelvarez, Benito Aponte, Pedro Cardona, Raimundo Faura, Santiago Franqui, Gervasio García, Antonio Jiménez, Juan Isern Jiménez, Pedro Jiménez Sicardó, Vicente R. Muñoz Barros, Miguel Quiñonez Cabezudo, Nicolás Quiñonez Cabezudo, José Puig Morales, José Ramírez de Arellano, Marcelino Solá, Modesto Solá, and Ramón Sotomayor

1900

Mayor: Gervasio García

Councilmen: Ramón Aacutelvarez, Landelino Aponte, Santiago Franqui, Pablo Hereter, Enrique Moreno, Manuel Muñoz Delgado, Vicente R. Muñoz Barros, Francisco Nicolau, José Puig, Bernardino Román, José Rosario Santiago, Acisclo Sánchez, Ramón Santos, Marcelino Solá, Modesto Solá, and Ramón Sotomayor

1901

Mayor: Gervasio García

Councilmen: Ramón Aacutelvarez, Benito Aponte, Landelino Aponte, Pablo Hereter, Juan Isern Sánchez, José Molina Muñoz, Enrique Moreno, Manuel Muñoz Delgado, Vicente R. Muñoz Barros, Francisco Nicolau, José Puig, Regis Ramos, Bernardino Román, José Rosario Santiago, Acisclo Sánchez, Ramón Santos, Marcelino Solá, Modesto Solá, and Ramón Sotomayor

1902

Mayor: Gervasio García

Councilmen: Benito Aponte, Landelino Aponte, Pablo Hereter, Juan Isern Jiménez, José Molina Muñoz, Enrique Moreno, Vicente R. Muñoz Barros, Francisco Nicolau, José Puig, Regis Ramos, Bernardino Román, José Rosario Santiago, Julio Santana, Marcelino Solá, and Modesto Solá

1903

Mayor: Gervasio García

Councilmen: Nicolás J. Aguayo, Landelino Aponte, Juan Díaz Hernández, Federico Diez y López, Rufo J. González, Pablo Hereter, Juan Isern Jiménez, Antonio de Jesús, Enrique Moreno, Vicente R. Muñoz Barros, Francisco Nicolau, José Puig, Juan Ramón Quiñonez, Regis Ramos, Bernardino Román, José Rosario Santiago, Julio Santana, Celestino Solá, Marcelino Solá, and Modesto Solá

Sources: AHMC, SEC Gobierno, SSEC Asamblea Municipal, SER Actas del Cabildo, 1880–1903, C13–34.

Appendix D
Ordinance for the Comisarios of Caguas's Rural Barrios

Ordenanza de los Comisarios de los Barrio rurales de Caguas
Deberes de los Comisarios de los Barrios Rurales:
Se decreta por el Concejo Municipal de Caguas

Sección 1a

En cada barrio rural de esta jurisdicción habrá un Comisario que nombrará libremente el Alcalde.

Sección 2a

El comisario, con arreglo á la Ley, desempeñará su cargo sin remuneración, y, como agente de la autoridad, merecerá la consideración y el respeto de los vecinos del barrio.

Sección 3a

Los comisarios desempeñarán sus cargos por un año, á menos que no se imposibiliten por enfermedad, que acreditarán debidamente, ó sean separados por el Alcalde.

Sección 4a

Será obligación de los comisarios:

Primero. Vigilar para que se cumplan las leyes y disposiciones vigentes sobre sanidad.

Segundo. Dar cuenta al Alcalde cuando notare que exista en su barrio algún foco de infección, que pueda ser causa de que se altere la salud pública.

Tercero. Cumplir las órdenes que la Autoridad municipal dicte, fijar los avisos que le remitiere y hacer las citaciones que se le ordenare por dicha Autoridad ó por el Juez de paz.

Cuarto. Auxiliar la acción del Comisionado ó Ejecutor de apremios, cuando pasare al barrio á asuntos de su cometido.

Quinto. Dar cuenta al Alcalde de todo aquello que crea punible y que por su naturaleza merezca ser conocido por dicha Autoridad.

Sección 5a

No permitirán los comisarios que ningún animal que padezca de escoriaciones y úlceras, cuando se consideren contagiosas á juicio de persona perita, paste libremente. Cuando esto suceda, deberán inmediatamente tomar las medidad necesarias para que el animal enfermo quede absolutamente aislado de otros animales.

Sección 6a

Tampoco permitirán que los caballos enfermos pasten en ningún sitio que no esté cercado en debida forma, á fin de evitar que se pongan en contacto con otros animales.

Sección 7a

Tendrán especial cuidado de que los animales muertos sean enterrados á cuatro piés bajo tierra, contados desde la parte posterior del cuerpo del animal hasta la superficie del terreno, y á gran distancia de cualquier corriente de agua.

Sección 8a

Además de lo expuesto, los comisarios de los barrios estarán obligados á cumplir las indicaciones que les haga el Alcalde, y á auxiliar debidamente la acción de los Tribunales de Justicia si necesitaren de su concurso.

Caguas, Agosto 12 de 1902.
G. García
Alcalde Municipal

Source: Caguas: Establecimiento Tip. "La Democracia," 1902, AHMC, SEC Secretaría, SSEC Seguridad Pública, SER Correspondencia, SSER Comisario de Barrio, 1880–1906, C24.

Appendix E
Love Letters

Distinguida Señorita:

Le dirijo ésta con el premeditado fin de abrirle todos los secretos de mi corazón y toda la pasión de una alma.

A primera vista quedé enamorado de usted y ahí resulta el que le escriba esta donde le explique todas mis ideas y pensamientos.

Sabrá usted que ante el amor nada se resiste y si es en la mujer donde mejor se desarrolla esa tan sublime pasión, de ahí resulta que el hombre se declare a la mujer que ya ha abierto sitio en el alma y en la mente de aquel que quiere poseer las miradas tiernas y puras de una joven.

Yo, por medio de esta le expongo este pensamiento, que al mismo tiempo es el sentimiento que dicta mi corazón:

Usted me ha gustado y a usted me dirijo manifestándole que será usted quien guarde en su corazón todo mi amor.

Usted sabrá que yo tengo un permiso concedido por usted y aprovecho esta tan grata oportunidad para decirle a su oido las ternezas de un amor que no morirá, pero si vivirá eternamente en mi corazón.

Yo espero que usted accederá a mi súplica y sabrá corresponder a mi amor llevando así mis aspiraciones y deseos nobles que hacia usted siento y que será uno de mis momentos más dichosos experimetados en esta vida.

> Esperando su grata contesta quedo su amante en el porvenir,
> Francisco Ramos

Cayey, P.R.
Mayo 20–18
Srta. . . . .
Estimada Srta.

Le he dirigido la primera carta que es el primer mensaje enviado a usted.

Como es mi amor tan ferviente hacia usted, quiero oir su voz y sus frases retratadas en una cartita suya y que sea fiel reflejo de su amor hacia mí.

Verá por las lineas que ya usted ha leído todo mi pensamiento llevado a lo más recondito de su corazón y a lo más sublime de su alma.

Todo en usted es atractivo e inspira tanta atención que yo he caído rendido a sus plantas para implorar ese santo amor, esas palabras tan dulces que solo pueden salir de un corazon de mujer que encanta y sublimiza todo cuanto su boca dice y su corazón siente.

Esperando su contesta que satisfara mi humilde ofrenda de amor.

> Quedo de usted para siempre, su amante,
> Francisco Ramos

Source: AGPR, F Judicial, SF Tribunal General de Justicia, SEC Tribunal Superior de Guayama, SER Exp. Civiles, SSER Cayey, C45.

Appendix F
Love Letters

Cayey
Marzo 9 de 1915
Miss Carmen

La presente es para haserte Algunas Referncia sobre de lo que Emos hablado anterior Pues tu sabes que yo te jurado no mirar para otra mugel jamas En la bida y hasi deseo cumplirte yo te ofresi casamiento deseo poderte cumplir y a llegado el momento que me as obligado quererte demaciado. y creo que si tu Me obligaras ha dejarnos arias mi desgracia Por completo. porque no queria [Two pages of the original letter have disappeared.] tu si tienes conzienzia y sabel querel beras como yo te querido. Pero tu sabes que el publico habla lo que no le en porta y por Ese momento me an metido en mil duda por que tu sabes to do lo que me an contado y yo deseo casarme contigo lo mas pronto posible Pero si es berda que me quieres tienes que conplaserme y aserme conbensel que lo que dise el publico Es mentira y si tu me complase y ases lo que yo te digo te juro por mi alma que baya a un lago de fuego casarme con tigo y si es belda. [The rest of the original letter has disappeared.]

Señor Don Ceferino

Mi apreciado amigo que gusto [unclear] el lapiz para contestarte tu atenta carta y al mismo tiempo decirte esto papa a mi no me regaña por que tu bayas a casa hasta la fecha no me he dicho nada. Ceferino yo no me apuro porque la jente hable de mi ya tu comprenderas que lo que hablan nada es y yo no me apuro por eso por que el publico le de gusto de hablar lo que no es pero eso ami me causa sufri miento [Pages have disappeared from the original letter.] mi arma tuya C. en ver que el publico dice lo que no es. Ceferino cuenta con migo que aunque te bayas te te [aprores?] que yo ati te quiero con todo mi amor nunca te olvidare menos que tu no me olvides y siempre estoy pensando en ti te quiero mas de lo demostrado y quisas tu ami no me quieras tanto como yo ati yo ati ni muerta te olvido siempre pienso en ti despues de que tu te bayas yo no me boy a costunbrar por que te quiero con to.

Cayey P.R. Julio 1 de 1915
Señor D. Ceferino Dueño

Mi apreciado Ceferino Con mucho gusto tomo el lapiz para contestarte tu atenta carta que en la cual e recibido el gran cariño tengo. Ceferino vd cree que yo á vd no lo quiera como vd me quiere ami y yo creo que vd lo dira a lo contrario por que segun vd me dice que me quiere con todo su amor igual digo yo si mucho vd. me quiere mas lo quiero yo y amas con lo que vd. me dice que sufre mucho por mí que entre un mes atras ha rebajado 15 libras y yo contesto eso sufro mas con lo que vd me dice que yo no le he demostrado nada. ningun cariño de que yo estoy arepentida de lo he dicho de que yo tal ves tenga ideas para otro de que cuando vd se vaya yo no me ocupo de contestarle las cartas ay lo que vd hace con eso es hacer me sufril mas de lo que sufro en vel que vd. me dice lo contrario. Segun vd. me dice de que yo no le quiero tal ves tenga ideas para otro.

Si yo no lo quisiera como vd. me dice yo no sufriria por vd.

Ceferino yo te quiero con toda mi arma no creas que por que yo no te he demostrado de que te quiero tenga ideas para otro o que este arrepentida de lo e dicho no yo siempre te quiero si mucho te queria mas te quiero. no creas que por que te vea to dos los dias te odie no asi yo veo que me quieres. Segun me demuestras no queremos mucho de parte á parte y yo tengo un solo pensamiento que es en ti mientras no me hagas por que no creas que yo te olvido nunca he pensado eso ni lo pensare no valdran consejos para que yo te deje de lo mucho que te quiero yo si algun dia te olvidara sera muerta y con todo eso no te olvido lo que yo no quiero es que hables con esas mujeres que tanto se han ocupado de hablar mal de nosotros Sin mas nada tuya Carmen. [The original letter has a note that reads, "en la otra sera mas era poco papel."]

Señor Don Ceferino Dueño

Mi apreciado amigo con gran placer tomo el lapiz para contestarte la tuya y al mismo tiempo decirte esto ayer despues de que tu te viniste papa dijo que á lo que te hablo y que no le habias dado ni siquiera contesta y tambien que menos que no fuera en las con di cio nes de que te dijo y que tambien que si estas con vencido en estas condiciones que se lo digas para saberlo.

Ceferino tu crees que yo no sufro yo sufro mas de lo que sufre cuarquiera mujer.

lo que tiene que yo no doy a demostrarlo.

yo me encuentro sufril mas que tu por que tu sufriras por mi y yo sufro por ti y por muchas cosas que hablan y no lo son. y amas papa me dijo que habia hablado con el mayor [Alonso?] para que no me diera mas trabajo y si asi resultare yo me mato antes de moril asufrimentos por que papa lo hace por que yo no hable con tigo fuera de casa y amas supo hablabamos to dos los dias en el almacen. el se lo dijo á mama y yo le dije que si por causa de el dejaria yo de ir á trabajar [sic] a al pueblo y hablaba siempre con tigo que si por eso lo hacia lo haria peor por que yo á ti siempre te quiero e obligarian á dejarte matandome de lo contrario no pueden.

Ceferino te quiero con todo el corazon siempre tengo las mismas ideas para ti siempre soy la misma.

cada dia mas te quiero aunque lejos te bayes siempre estare pensando en ti y nunca te olvido como yo me acostumbrare despues de te bayes tan lejos de aqui que estaremos dias sin vernos seran los dias que mas distranquila estoy sufriendo antes de irte quiero de todo el corazon nunca te olvido y amas te encargo que un día antes de irte vengas a dispedirte de mi que despues seran mas sufrimientos

Sin mas nada cuenta con tu apreciada

Carmen que nunca te olvida recibe un b[eso] y un abraso de tu C.

Source: "El pueblo de Puerto Rico contra Gerardo Carattini por seduccion," AGPR, F Judicial de Guayama, SF Tribunal General de Justicia, SEC Tribunal Superior de Guayama, SER Expedientes Criminales, SSER Cayey, C757 (November 30, 1915).

Notes

During the period of my research, the Archivo Histórico Municipal de Caguas (AHMC) opened for the first time to the public and underwent a series of reorganizations, which are reflected in the references and citations.

Introduction

1. Pantaleón María Colón to Ruperto Caballero (comisario of Barrio Borinquen), August 10, 1881, Archivo Histórico Municipal de Caguas (AHMC), Sección Secretaría, Subsección Seguridad Pública, Serie Correspondencia, Subserie Comisario de Barrio, 1880–1906, Caja 24 (I hereafter cite this collection as "AHMC," where SEC=Sección, SSEC=Subsección, SER=Serie, SSER=Subserie, and C=Caja).

2. AHMC, SEC Secretaría, SSEC Archivo, SER Censos, SSER Habitantes, 1882–83, C26. It is difficult to document the cases of those who lost access to land because of their inability to formalize ownership, as often no public record is left. The process of land privatization affected many people, like Tirado, who, after losing access to land, hired their labor for a wage. Thus, the number of laborers throughout the years serves as one indication of land privatization in the rural areas of Caguas.

3. For a depiction of the Puerto Rican elites' obsessive and contradictory attempts to define a nation by land ownership, see Rosario Ferré's wonderful novel *Maldito Amor*.

4. The case of Puerto Rican landed elites contrasts also with that of Latin American elites because most countries in Latin America, particularly continental, have ample land resources. José Martí makes reference to the vast territory of Latin America in the chapter "Madre América" in *Nuestra América*.

5. Peter Guardino defines political culture as the set of practices and discourses through which groups and individuals in any society articulate, negotiate, enforce, and implement the competing claims that they make upon one another (*Peasants*, 10–11 and 24). See also Baver, *The Political Economy of Colonialism*, 4–5.

6. See, for example, Mallon, *Peasant and Nation*, 220; Alonso, *Thread of Blood*, 48; Becker, *Setting the Virgin on Fire*; and Guardino, *Peasants*, 10–11 and 24.

7. Such juxtaposition has developed as an interdisciplinary enterprise, drawing upon many ethnographies dealing with peasants around the world, particularly in Africa and India.

8. For recent studies of popular liberalism in Latin America, see Sanders, " 'Citizens of a Free People' " and *Contentious Republicans*. Also see Chambers, *From Subjects to Citizens*; Appelbaum, Macpherson, and Rosemblatt, *Race and Nation in Modern Latin America*; Appelbaum, "Whitening the Region" and *Muddied Waters*; and Thurner, *From Two Republics to One Divided*.

9. Here peasants are defined as a group whose social reproduction was structured around agrarian production but whose political identity was also expressed through agricultural activities. For instance, San José rural producers in Nicaragua adopted the term *campesino* to describe agrarian protest organizations that struggled for land, higher wages, and improved working conditions on cotton and sugar plantations. See Gould, *To Lead as Equals*, 7 and 140.

In Dominica, British authorities refused to call small rural producers a "peasantry"; instead, officials called them "ex-slaves" and "former apprentices." It was not until the 1870s that the peasantry was mentioned, in part because of its proven resilience. See Trouillot, "Discourses of Rule," 709–12, and *Peasants and Capital*, chapter 5.

In Namiquipa, Mexico, rural producers fought with the state for their identity as *agricultores* rather than *campesinos*, since the latter term carried social connotations of larger exploitation (Nugent, *Spent Cartridges of Revolution*, 74).

10. See Mallon, *Peasant and Nation*; Becker, *Setting the Virgin on Fire*; Alonso, *Thread of Blood*; Nugent, *Spent Cartridges of Revolution*; and Guardino, *Peasants*.

11. Anthony Giddens's concept of unconscious consequences is helpful. The idea of unconscious consequences refers to the lack of awareness of the results of social activities—more specifically, to a lack of awareness that stresses historical agency (*The Constitution of Society*, 9–14 and 294).

12. See, for example, Baud, *Peasants and Tobacco*; Trouillot, *Peasants and Capital*; Clark, *My Mother Who Fathered Me*; Black, "My Mother Never Fathered Me"; Smith, *The Negro Family in British Guiana*; Wilson, *Crab Antics*; Beckford and Witter, *Small Garden*; Thomas, *Plantations, Peasants, and State*; Mandle, *The Plantation Economy*; Momsen and Besson, *Land and Development in the Caribbean*; Sharpe, *Peasant Politics*; Mintz, "The Rural Proletariat"; Mintz and Wolf, "An Analysis of Ritual Co-Parenthood"; Gómes, *Rural Development in the Caribbean*; León and Deere, *Debate sobre la mujer*; and Deere, *The Peasantry in Political Economy*.

Pedro L. San Miguel's work treats the relations of power between peasants and Trujillo's state in the Dominican Republic as well as the forms of peasant resistance under the U.S. occupation. See San Miguel, "Peasant Resistance to State Demands" and *Los campesinos del Cibao*.

13. Quintero Rivera, "La ideología populista," 139 and 141.

14. Rosario, *The Development of the Puerto Rican Jíbaro*; Enrique Bird-Piñero, in "The Politics of Puerto Rican Land Reform," studies land tenure in Puerto Rico from the 1900s to the 1940s and confirms the political manipulations of land reform and the political struggle for self-government. John P. Angelli, in "San Lorenzo," analyzes the pattern of rural migration from San Lorenzo to Caguas, San Juan, Harlem, and agrarian areas of the United States. He concludes that the people driven off the land by the decline of tobacco represent the poorest emigrant element. Charles C. Rogler developed a community study emphasizing civic and state institutions and the way people understood them. The most influential work of this generation was the landmark book *The People of Puerto Rico*, published under the direction of Julian H. Steward (1972). This project sought to analyze the experiences of Puerto Rican peoples in diverse environmental and cultural settings that included the coasts and the mountains. Conrad Seipp and Annete B. Ramírez suggest that by 1946–47 Puerto Rico had become a laboratory for demographers and other social scientists (*Colonialism, Catholicism, and Contraception*, 94 and 175).

15. Angel G. Quintero Rivera studies the formation of the working class during the first five decades of American rule. He explains that the hacienda system progressively dissolved in favor of the sugar cane plantation system and its rural proletariat ("la clase obrera"). See Quintero Rivera, *Patricios y plebeyos*, and González Velez, "Tenencia de tierra."

Fernando Picó documents the process of peonization and rural forms of resistance during the latter half of the nineteenth century in Utuado, Puerto Rico, as well as the co-existence and persistence of small and mid-size farmers in the coffee economy during the late nineteenth and early twentieth centuries, in *Libertad y servidumbre* and *Amargo café*. See also Bergard, "Agrarian History of Puerto Rico" and *Coffee and the Growth of Agrarian Capitalism*; Cabrera Collazo, "Los peninsulares y la transición hacia el siglo XX"; Casanova, "Propiedad agrícola y poder"; Gavillán Rivera, "Gobierno y justicia en Juncos"; González

Libra, "Agricultores y comerciantes"; Rodríguez Nieves, "Las fluctuaciones en la población de Cayey"; Santiago González, "El régimen de la propiedad rural"; and Seda Prado, *El campesinado en Puerto Rico*.

The preferred crop to combine with coffee in the early twentieth century was tobacco. This combination occurred most often after World War I, especially in the mountainous fields in the east-central part of the island where tobacco production was more conspicuous after the introduction of North American capitalism. Unfortunately, the "Nueva Historia" scholarship has largely ignored tobacco and the central-eastern region of the island. Nonetheless, within the almost invisible historiography on tobacco, Juan José Baldrich undoubtedly stands as a pioneer among the practitioners of the Nueva Historia. He studied the 1930 peasant boycott, which was opposed the commercial and industrial interests of the tobacco manufacturing sector then attacking their way of life (Baldrich, *Sembraron la no siembra.*)

16. Baldrich, *Sembraron la no siembra*; Álvarez Curbelo, "La patria agrícola" and "Un discurso ideológico olvidado"; and Seda, "Participación gubernamental en el desarrollo del cooperativismo agrícola." There are some exceptions that attempt to study the lives of rural subalterns in their "autonomous spaces" or in moments of resistance. See, for example, Picó, "Fuentes para la historia de las comunidades rurales," "Las trabajadoras del tabaco," and *Los gallos peleados*.

17. The only studies that directly address rural women are Jiménez-Muñoz, "'A Storm Dressed in Skirt,'" and Bonilla, "Kinship and Household." Jiménez-Muñoz analyzes rural women's lives in the late nineteenth and early twentieth centuries based solely on anthropological work of the 1940s without questioning its possible bias, and Bonilla focuses on rural women within the institution of the family.

18. Scarano, "The Jíbaro Masquerade."

19. Guerra, *Popular Expression and National Identity*.

20. For a critique of the new cultural history in Latin America, see, for example, Haber, "The Worst of Both Worlds" and "Anything Goes," and Socolow, "Putting the 'Cult' in Culture." Another trend is the tendency to use amorphous categories such as "elite" and "masses." I contextualize these categories by studying individuals within these social groups.

21. Vaughan, "Cultural Approaches to Peasant Politics," 302.

22. Lovejoy, *Transformations in Slavery*, xx.

23. Kearny, *Reconceptualizing the Peasantry*, 1, 62.

24. Jelin, "Citizenship Revisited," 107–8.

25. Cutter, "The Legal System as a Touchstone of Identity," 67.

26. Kinsbruner, *Not of Pure Blood*, 43–44.

27. In Saint-Domingue and Haiti, free non-whites relied heavily on the legal system as interpreted by the metropolitan center. See Trouillot, "The Inconvenience of Freedom," 151.

28. Díaz, *Female Citizens, Patriarchs, and the Law*, 43–59, 190–92.

29. "Annual Report of the Governor of Porto Rico for the Fiscal Year Ended June 30, 1908," Washington DC: Government Printing Office, 1909, 18.

30. See, for example, Beiner, *Theorizing Citizenship*, and Turner, *Citizenship and Social Theory*.

31. J. M. Barbalet's summary of T. H. Marshall's thesis in "Citizenship, Class Inequality, and Resentment" (37).

32. Flathman, "Citizenship and Authority," 111.

33. Low citizenship is also used to describe political withdrawal (Flathman, "Citizenship and Authority," 105–51).

34. Blanca Silvestrini and Luis Figueroa in personal conversation.

35. Adas, "From Avoidance to Confrontation," 89.

36. Feinberg and Rosenberg, *Civil Society and the Summit of the Americas*.

37. See, for example, Jelin and Hershberg, *Constructing Democracy*; Fitzsimmons, *Beyond the Barricades*; and Roniger and Herzog, *The Collective and the Public*.

38. See, for example, Ryan, *Civic Wars*, and Schudson, *The Good Citizen*.

39. Dore, "One Step Forward, Two Steps Back," 9.

40. I do not use the phrase "popular liberalism" as was the case in Columbia or Peru because in Puerto Rico the type of liberalism was closer to the one described by Dore. See note 7.

41. Jelin, "Citizenship Revisited," 106.

42. Weinreb, *Natural Law and Justice*, 79–81.

43. Pocock, "The Ideal of Citizenship," 45–46.

44. Vassberg, *Land and Society*, 41, 54–56, and 86–87.

45. For a discussion on how gender inequalities create class differences in an empirical context, see Nash, *We Eat the Mines*.

1. Mapping Caguas, Mapping the Country

1. For a discussion about Caguax's resistance to the Spaniards, see Juan David Hernández, "Reflexiones sobre Caguax."

2. Bunker, *Historia de Caguas*, 48–53.

3. Bunker, *Historia de Caguas*, 72–74 and 83.

4. This estimate includes the municipality of Gurabo, which was part of Caguas at the time (Juan David Hernández, "Orígenes y fundamentos del criollo").

5. See appendix 4 in Rosario Rivera, *La Real Cédula de Gracias*, 143–235.

6. Bunker, *Historia de Caguas*, 98 and 246–47.

7. Bunker, *Historia de Caguas*, 135, 170, 266, and 268; AHMC, SEC Secretaría, SSEC Archivo, SER Censo, SSER Habitantes, 1882–83, C26; Departamento de la Guerra, *Informe sobre el censo de Puerto Rico, 1899*, 162.

8. Bunker, *Historia de Caguas*, 277–78.

9. Bunker, *Historia de Caguas*, 135, 170, 266, and 268; AHMC, SEC Secretaría, SSEC Archivo, SER Censo, SSER Habitantes, 1882–83, C26; Departamento de la Guerra, *Informe sobre el censo de Puerto Rico, 1899*, 162.

10. Brockmann, "Land Types and Land Utilization," 297, 300, and 319. Soil productivity has changed because since the 1950s the valley has been extremely dense with houses and cement buildings.

11. The municipality of Caguas was divided among urban and rural barrios. The municipal government recognized at least ten different rural barrios in the period under study: Bairoa, Borinquen, Cañabón, Cañaboncito, Beatriz, Río Cañas, San Antonio (formerly Quebrada Puercos), San Salvador (formerly Culebras), Turabo, and Tomás de Castro. In addition, Barrios La Mesa, Barra y Jagua, and Cagüitas were often listed separately but formed part of the territory of the ten previously mentioned rural barrios.

12. These hills are scientifically known as the Humid Northeastern Cretaceous Foothills, and the mountains as the Humid East Central Mountains (Brockmann, "Land Types and Land Utilization," 298–300 and 319).

13. Bunker, *Historia de Caguas*, 268–69.

14. Cuerda is a measure of land area. One cuerda is equivalent to 0.9712 acres.

15. AHMC, SEC Finanzas, SSEC Contribuciones, SER Planillas de Riqueza, SSER Agrícola, 1880–81, C81.

16. Luciano Santos to Sr. Presidente y Concejales del Ilustre Ayuntamiento, July 4, 1887, AHMC, SEC Gobierno, SSEC Asamblea Municipal, SER Correspondencia, 1886–87, C83. See also José G. Esterás to the Ilustre Ayuntamiento, June 27, 1888, AHMC, SEC Gobierno, SSEC Asamblea Municipal, SER Correspondencia, 1888–89, C85.

17. Bunker, *Historia de Caguas*, 268–69.

18. The Solá family established a cigar factory called Solá, Cadiz y Co. ("La industria tabacalera en Caguas," *La Democracia*, October 9, 1901, 4).

19. Acosta Lespier, *Santa Juana y Mano Manca*.

20. Puerto Rico Reconstruction Administration, *Puerto Rico*, 277–78.

21. Brockmann, "Land Types and Land Utilization," 302.

22. Picó, *Los gallos peleados*. Laird W. Bergard states that the change in sovereignty in 1898 resulted in a complete reorganization of Puerto Rican agrarian structure ("Agrarian History of Puerto Rico," 85).

23. Baldrich, *Sembraron la no siembra*.

24. Glasser, *Aquí me quedo*, 21–23.

25. For a history of Operation Bootstrap, see Dietz, *Economic History of Puerto Rico*, 200–257.

26. The development of Caribbean peasantries is directly related to the rise of capitalism. See Trouillot, *Peasants and Capital*, 21, and Roseberry, *Coffee and Capitalism*.

27. Momsen and Besson, *Land and Development in the Caribbean*, 1.

28. Raymond Williams developed the concept of "structural feelings" to describe principles and assumptions of social groups that escape formal ideological expression but that define a particular quality of social experience and relationship (*Marxism and Literature*, 130).

29. Rama, *The Lettered City*.

30. Raymond Williams, *The Country and the City*, 48. But, as Williams states, imperialism imposed the country-city order in other faraway places, in the colonies, as part of their capitalist exploitation (*The Country and the City*, 279). For a revision of Williams's paradigm see Maclean, Landry, and Ward, *The Country and the City Revisited*.

31. See Dávila Santiago, *El derribo de las murallas*.

32. Brockmann, "Land Types and Land Utilization," 302.

33. See Bergard, "Agrarian History of Puerto Rico."

34. Seda Prado, *El campesinado en Puerto Rico*, 21–24. The municipality of Corozal also followed this pattern of small-size farms throughout the nineteenth century. In Corozal subsistence agriculture and cattle raising dominated (see Cabrera Collazo, "Los peninsulares y la transición hacia el siglo XX," 202). Cattle raising constituted the major economic activity of the municipality of Aibonito throughout the nineteenth century, where large farms were scarce (see Santiago González, "El régimen de la propiedad rural," 157–62).

35. "Land tenure" refers here to the structuring or organizing of people's access to land, which after 1880 is closely linked to a title of ownership. Land tenure in Caguas demonstrated a rich diversity, where peasants, large landowners, and middling sectors shared land resources with day laborers and sharecroppers.

36. Torrech San Inocencio, "Los Barrios de Caguas," 106. In 1882, 3,197 Cagüeños

(27.01 percent) lived in urban areas, while 8,638 (72.99 percent) lived in the countryside. (AHMC, SEC Secretaría, SSEC Archivo, SER censo, SSER Habitantes, 1882–83, C26).

37. The Spanish state defined these categories. State officials consistently described farms with 30 cuerdas or less as *parcelas* or "pieces of land." They also named *estancia* those farms with 70 or more cuerdas of land. Thus, farms of 30 cuerdas or less were considered small, while medium farms consisted of land estates of 70 or more. Historians of Puerto Rico have consistently used these categories, and they serve as a basis for comparison between the land pattern of Caguas and those of other municipalities. Farms of 401 cuerdas or more are considered *latifundia*, and large farms are those with 200 to 400 cuerdas of land (Seda Prado, *El campesinado en Puerto Rico*, 31n35 and 32). In order to avoid confusion, I will use only the term "large farms" to refer both to farms with 200 to 400 cuerdas and to farms with 401 cuerdas or more.

38. Nazario Velasco, *Discurso legal y orden poscolonial*, 184–91.

39. Marcus, "Labor Conditions in Porto Rico," 13.

40. The percentages are calculated with the total rural population in 1882 (8,638 inhabitants) and 1899 (14,407 inhabitants) (AHMC, SEC Secretaría, SSEC Archivo, SER Censos, SSER Habitantes, 1882–83, C26; see also table 1.2).

41. AHMC, SEC Secretaría, SSEC Archivo, SER Censos, SSER Habitantes, 1882–83, C26; see also table 1.5.

42. AHMC, SEC Gobierno, SSEC Asamblea Municipal, SER Actas del Cabildo, 1886, 1888, C19, 21, February 17, 1886, and August 1, 1888. In Barrio Borinquen, Francisco Díaz Rojo was fined five pesos for killing a cow (Dionisio Álvarez to the mayor of Caguas, January 20, 1887, AHMC, SEC Secretaría, SSEC Seguridad Pública, SER Multas, 1884–1901, C65). Don José Antonio Ramírez sold meat without a permit in Barrio Río Cañas and was brought to justice (Víctor Fernández to the juez municipal, October 8, 1890, AHMC, SEC Secretaría, SSEC Judicial, SER Libro Copiador, SSER Juzgados, 1883–89, C27).

43. AHMC, SEC Gobierno, SSEC Asamblea Municipal, SER Actas del Cabildo, 1882, C15, October 12, 1882.

44. Pedro Z. Solá was an official meat supplier in 1891 ("Declaración jurada," April 25, 1891, AHMC, SEC Secretaría, SSEC Judicial, SER Expedientes/Documentos, SER Expedientes/Documentos, 1860–1917, C9). He brought to justice to Francisco Álvarez (Pedro Z. Solá to the mayor of Caguas, August 12, 1893, AHMC, SEC Gobierno, SSEC Alcalde, SER Correspondencia, 1893, C97). He also accused Don Antonio Orta of killing a pig without a license ("Expediente contra D. Antonio Orta por matanza clandestina de un cerdo," 1893, AHMC, SEC Secretaría, SSEC Seguridad Pública, SER Expedientes/Documentos, SSER depósito de animales, 1848–99, C51). Solá also accused Joaquín Giménez Saurí of killing a pig without permission ("Expediente contra D. Joaquín Giménez por matanza clandestina de un cerdo," 1894, AHMC, SEC Secretaría, SSEC Seguridad Pública, SER Expedientes/Documentos, SSER depósito de animales, 1848–99, C51). In 1897 *La Democracia* denounced the monopoly of meat and bread as scandalous ("De *La Correspondencia*," October 29, 1897, 3).

45. There is one large landowner missing in the 1896 tax records, explaining the apparent decrease.

46. In Andalusia, for example, tenants who controlled a large area of land were called labradores (Herr, *Rural Change and Royal Finances*, 29–30, 184–85).

47. Vassberg, *Land and Society*, 142–43. According to the census of 1882, there were 542 labradores in the rural barrios of Caguas, constituting 22.21 percent of the working population. Rural laborers and sharecroppers undoubtedly constituted an important sector

in the development of agriculture, as suggested by their numbers, but information about the percentage of the territory under their control is not available.

48. U.S. Bureau of the Census, *Thirteenth Census of the United States*, 7:1001.

49. In 1897 there were 17,820 inhabitants in Caguas, of whom 1,156 were peninsulares (Coll y Toste, *Reseña del estado social, económico, e industrial*, 28, 90, and 367). Despite the marginal political representation, the Spanish Republic had positive effects in Puerto Rico, such as the abolition of slavery in 1873 and the formation of the first political parties in 1869 and 1871. For a discussion of liberal measures in Puerto Rico and the effects of the Spanish Revolution of 1868, see Díaz Soler, *Puerto Rico*, chapters 20 to 23, and Lalinde Abadía, *La administración española*. On the role of the abolition of slavery on the politics of Spain and Puerto Rico in the nineteenth century, see Schmidt-Nowara, "The Problem of Slavery," and Navarro Azcue, *La abolición de la esclavitud negra*. Finally, on the formation of political parties in Puerto Rico, see Bothwell, *Orígenes y desarrollo*; Quiñones Calderón, *Trayectoria política de Puerto Rico*; and Dapena, *Trayectoria del pensamiento liberal puertorriqueño*.

50. Schmidt-Nowara, "The Problem of Slavery."

51. See Cruz Monclova, *Historia de Puerto Rico*, and García Ochoa, *La política española en Puerto Rico*.

52. Cubano-Iguina, "Political Culture," 632.

53. See chapter 2.

54. Barbosa de Rosario, *Historia del autonomismo puertorriqueño*, 183.

55. Celestino Solá to the mayor of Caguas, December 29, 1897, AHMC, SEC Gobierno, SSEC Alcalde de Barrio, SER Correspondencia, 1897, C117. In this letter, Celestino Solá informs the mayor about a future meeting in Don Manuel Lizardi's house in Barrio Turabo, where they intend to register followers of the Liberal Party.

56. Cubano-Iguina, "Political Culture," 635 and 655–56, and Henry B. Burch quoted in Cabán, *Constructing a Colonial People*, 179–80.

57. War Department, "Annual Reports for the Fiscal Year Ended June 30, 1900," 116.

58. See chapter 2.

59. Cabán, *Constructing a Colonial People*, 185.

60. Cabán, *Constructing a Colonial People*, 173–77.

61. For an excellent discussion of classical liberal ideology see Holt, "The Essence of the Contract." See also Peloso and Tenenbaum, *Liberals, Politics, and Power*.

62. Álvarez Curbelo, "El afán de la modernidad," chapter 6, p. 1.

63. Martínez-Vergne, *Shaping the Discourse on Space*, 61 and 70.

64. Álvarez Curbelo, "El afán de la modernidad," chapter 5, p. 16.

65. Sklar, *The Corporate Reconstruction*, 51–52. See also Lustig, *Corporate Liberalism*.

66. Sklar, *The Corporate Reconstruction*, 81–82.

67. See Salvatore, "The Enterprise of Knowledge."

68. In this sense, the Puerto Rican case is similar to that of India, as Guha states: "India figured almost obsessively in the metropolitan discourse on Improvement, precisely because of its importance as a limiting case" (*Dominance without Hegemony*, 31).

69. Rivera Ramos, *The Legal Construction of Identity*, 113.

70. For a discussion of the contradictions between colonialism and human rights see Conklin, "Colonialism and Human Rights."

71. Scarano, *Sugar and Slavery in Puerto Rico*, 162.

72. Morelli, "Territorial Hierarchies," 41.

73. Bunker, *Historia de Caguas,* 145 and 220, and Celestino Solá to the mayor of Caguas, March 6, 1884, AHMC, SEC Alcalde de Barrio, SSEC Correspondencia, 1884, C74.

74. Martínez-Vergne, *Shaping the Discourse on Space,* 2, 22–23.

75. Duany, "Ethnicity in the Spanish Caribbean," 32.

76. Eric Williams, *From Columbus to Castro,* 111–35; Lewis, *Puerto Rico,* 29–31; Mintz, "The Caribbean as a Socio-cultural Area"; Ayala, *American Sugar Kingdom,* 5–22; and for a provocative discussion of the cultural consequences of the plantation see Benítez-Rojo, *The Repeating Island,* particularly chapter 1, "From the Plantation to the Plantation," 33–81.

77. Dore, "One Step Forward, Two Steps Back," 9. Classic liberalism, as opposed to popular liberalism, did not incorporate in practice the demands of the racially mixed population.

78. Cubano-Iguina, "Political Culture," 643–44.

2. From Crown to Citizen

1. Ferrer, *Insurgent Cuba,* 16.

2. Ferrer, *Insurgent Cuba,* 99, 103–4, 109 (quote from p. 103).

3. Morelli, "Territorial Hierarchies," 45.

4. Caro Costas, *Legislación municipal puertorriqueña,* vii–viii.

5. In colonial Latin America, the municipal government served both judicial and administrative functions (Morelli, "Territorial Hierarchies," 46).

6. Martínez-Vergne, *Shaping the Discourse on Space,* 45.

7. The governor of the island, not the audiencia, had the right to veto any aspect of municipal administration in the nineteenth century (Trías Monge, *Historia constitucional,* 26).

8. From 1825 to 1869 the governor had explicit dictatorial powers to administer the island (Trías Monge, *Historia constitucional,* 19).

9. On April 1, 1871, the Crown created an advisory board for Puerto Rico (Diputación Provincial de Puerto Rico). The board, composed of members elected by property holders, was expected to advise the governor in the areas of education, public charity, local administration, finances, and ecclesiastical and civil matters. Presided over by the governor of Puerto Rico, the board oversaw the effectiveness of Spanish laws on the island and supervised all the municipal governments of the island. However, Spanish law permitted the governor to ignore or even abolish the board at will. In 1874 the governor, Gen. Laureano Sanz, dissolved the board. The board was reestablished in 1878, but it increasingly became the executor of the governor's orders (Lalinde Abadía, *La administración española,* 150). The number of elected members was reduced from twenty-four to seven, and the board became an instrument of the office of the governor and voice of the colonial official position. Thus, given the effective identity of the governor and the advisory board, the ayuntamiento, in practice, responded directly to the authority of the governor. When the United States assumed control of Puerto Rico in November 1898, Gen. John R. Brooke disbanded the board forever (Trías Monge, *Historia constitucional,* 27, 165; Cruz Monclova, *Historia de Puerto Rico,* vol. 3, part 2, p. 229).

10. Barceló Miller, *Política ultramarina,* 61.

11. Barceló Miller states that two hundred vecinos sufficed to establish a municipality, but it seems that there is a typographical error in her book because the municipal law of 1878 reads two thousand vecinos (Barceló Miller, *Política ultramarina,* 24n17; *Leyes provincial y municipal de 24 de mayo de 1878,* 33).

12. Trías Monge, *Historia constitucional,* 26.

13. In Spain, any man who paid 25 pesetas to the state was allowed to vote, but in Puerto Rico the Municipal Law of 1878 required 125 pesetas (Barceló Miller, *Política ultramarina,* 53n104).

14. *Leyes provincial y municipal de 24 de mayo de 1878,* 36–37; Trías Monge, *Historia constitucional,* 26.

15. Most of the lists of voters for the last two decades of the nineteenth century have been lost. From the available information, there were 84 voters in Caguas in 1879 and 165 in 1880. The lists are better for 1873, and a newspaper listed the number of voters for 1899. These results are more reliable. In 1873 Caguas had 727 voters, and in 1899, 953 men voted in Caguas (AHMC, SEC Secretaría, SSEC Archivo, SER Cédulas Electorales, 1873–91, C6–11; AHMC, SEC Secretaría, SSEC Archivo, SER Censos, SSER Electorales, 1873–97, C16–18; and "Triunfo Federal en Caguas," *La Democracia,* December 27, 1899).

16. Trías Monge, *Historia constitucional,* 26.

17. Guillermo Céspedes quoted in Martínez-Vergne, *Shaping the Discourse on Space,* 45.

18. Lalinde Abadía, *La administración española,* 157.

19. After the mid-1870s the council of Caguas met regularly because Caguas had become an official municipality.

20. Pedro and Marcelino were farmers who owned 140 cuerdas in Barrio Cañaboncito and 156 cuerdas in Barrio Beatriz respectively.

21. Bunker, *Historia de Caguas,* 21 and 31; *La Correspondencia,* March 15, 1891, 2; "De Caguas," *La Democracia,* June 13, 1899; "Adhesiones. Caguas," *La Democracia,* November 5, 1899, 2; *La Democracia,* November 1, 1899, August 13, 1902, 1, August 7, 1902, 3; "Más federales en Caguas," *La Democracia,* October 9, 1902, 1; and "'Unión Club' de Caguas," *La Democracia,* December 6, 1904, 1.

22. In 1880 Landelino Aponte maintained a large farm of 800 cuerdas in Barrio Borinquen. However, he resided with his family on Turabo Street in downtown Caguas (Mayor of Caguas to the alcaldes of Barrios Turabo, Borinquen, Culebras, and Beatriz, April 23, 1881, AHMC, SEC Secretaría, SSEC Seguridad Pública, SER Correspondencia, SSER Alcalde de Barrio, 1880–81, C8). On his farm Aponte cultivated sugar and tobacco to sell in the market. In 1888 his land estate increased considerably to 2,464 cuerdas of land, and Aponte produced rum as well. After 1888, however, Aponte sold land year after year and in 1900 registered "only" 684 cuerdas of land in Barrio Borinquen (AHMC, SEC Finanzas, SSEC Contribuciones, SER Planillas de Riqueza, SSER Agrícola, 1880–1900, C81–100).

23. "Don Landelino Aponte," *La Democracia,* September 28, 1904, 1.

24. Muñoz Barros in 1881 paid taxes for 700 cuerdas of land in Barrio Beatriz. His estate increased to 1,000 cuerdas in 1887, and to 1,300 cuerdas in 1896. Muñoz Barros added 100 cuerdas more in the next year, and 40 cuerdas in 1899. In 1900 Muñoz Barros owned 1,453 cuerdas of land in Barrios Beatriz, Cañaboncito, and Turabo (AHMC, SEC Finanzas, SSEC Contribuciones, SER Planillas de Riqueza, SSER Agrícola, 1880–1900, C81–100).

25. Negrón Sanjurjo, *Los primeros treinta años,* 19, 53, and 88. Muñoz Barros's father, Luis Muñoz Iglesias, came from Spain as a military official and later settled down in the interior and served as the mayor of Cidra. His brother Luis (father of Luis Muñoz Rivera) became the mayor of Barranquitas (1855–65) and Bayamón (1865) and was his commercial partner from 1866 to 1874.

Muñoz Barros served in the liberal party assemblies from 1887 (in Ponce) to 1900 (in

Caguas) and died on May 8, 1909. *La Democracia* described him as a patriotic fighter, a writer, and an exemplary man ("Vicente Muñoz Barrios," May 10, 1909, 1).

26. Negrón Sanjurjo, *Los primeros treinta años*, 43, 78, and 85.

27. Negrón Sanjurjo, *Los primeros treinta años*, 53.

28. Celestino was already a councilor in 1880 and was still a councilor in 1898 when the governor, Gen. John R. Brooke, named him mayor of Caguas. He stayed in office only a couple of months but for the rest of the decade was a member of the municipal council of Caguas. In 1907 Celestino was a deputy in the Union Party ("Notas de Caguas," *La Democracia*, November 2, 1907).

Celestino's son, Juan Mauricio, was a member of the legislature in 1906. In 1908 he was also a member of the local Masonic League of Caguas. The following year, Juan Mauricio was president of the Union Club, the local board of the Union Party in Caguas ("J. M. Solá," *La Democracia*, February 22, 1906, 1; "Notas de Caguas," *La Democracia*, February 5, 1908, 5; and "El temporal. Caguas," *La Democracia*, August 28, 1899).

Marcelino started his political career as an alcalde of Barrio Borinquen. From 1881 to 1911 he was a councilman in Caguas. In January 1907 Marcelino was the vice-president of the Union Club in Caguas ("Notas de Caguas," *La Democracia*, January 23, 1907, 2; "Desde Caguas," *La Democracia*, January 4, 1907, 2).

Modesto became a councilor in 1886 and in 1898 was the vice president of the Local Board of Education of Caguas. He became vice president of the council in 1902 and held that office until 1904 (Modesto Solá, "Aviso Importante," *La Democracia*, September 4, 1902, 3; Bunker, *Historia de Caguas*, 39). In 1907 Modesto was named president of the local board of the Union Party and was also an active member of the Masonic League of Caguas ("Notas de Caguas," *La Democracia*, May 8 and October 24, 1907, 3).

In 1907 Muñoz Rivera, along with his wife and son, visited Modesto's residence in Caguas for the baptism of Modesto's grandson. Muñoz Rivera was the child's godfather ("Un día en Caguas," *La Democracia*, February 4, 1907, 1).

29. Cubano-Iguina, "Political Culture," 661.

30. Pateman, *The Sexual Contract*, 23–25.

31. Dore, "One Step Forward, Two Steps Back," 9. The notion of broker clientelism does not apply here because the number of voters was too small. The ultimate goal of party politics was not to amass extraordinary numbers of voters, as in broker clientelism, but to influence those few people with property who could vote and, more important, who could occupy a position on the council. Cristina Escobar analyzes broker clientelism for Northern Colombia in "Bullfighting Fiestas" (183–84). For the same reason, popular liberalism was not part of nineteenth-century politics in Puerto Rico as it was in Columbia (see Introduction, note 8).

32. Rivera to the ayuntamiento, December 31, 1883, AHMC, SEC Gobierno, SSEC Asamblea Municipal, SER Correspondencia, 1883–86, [c80].

33. Bunker, *Historia de Caguas*, 145, 163, and 266–67.

34. For instance, in July 1880 the mayor of Caguas ordered the alcaldes de barrio to capture Nicómedes Soler and Esteban Félix Baños (Mayor of Caguas to the alcaldes de barrio, July 17, 1880, AHMC, SEC Secretaría, SSEC Seguridad Pública, SER Correspondencia, SSER Alcalde de Barrio, 1880, C6).

35. See, for example, Comisario of Barrio Borinquen to the mayor of Caguas, December 31, 1896, AHMC, SEC Gobierno, SSEC Alcalde de Barrio, SER Correspondencia, 1896, C111.

36. For instance, two councilors were assigned to rectify the census of Barrio Beatriz.

On December 13, 1880, the mayor wrote to the alcalde of Barrio Bairoa ordering him to meet the councilmen on December 17 and to act as their auxiliary (Mayor of Caguas to the alcalde of Barrio Bairoa, December 13, 1880, AHMC, SEC Secretaría, SSEC Seguridad Pública, SER Correspondencia, SSER Alcalde de Barrio, 1880, C5).

37. For instance, in 1896 the mayor of Caguas ordered all the alcaldes de barrio to find the most frequented place in the barrios and post an ad for monetary exchanging (Arturo Más [mayor of Caguas] to Manuel Solá Prado [alcalde of Barrio Beatriz], March 26, 1896, AHMC, SEC Secretaría, SSEC Seguridad Pública, SER Correspondencia, SSER Alcalde de Barrio, 1896, C17. See also Arturo Más to the comisarios de barrio, April 7, 1903, AHMC, SEC Secretaría, SSEC Seguridad Pública, SER Correspondencia, SSER Comisario de Barrio, 1880–1906, C24).

38. For example, the alcalde of Barrio Bairoa grouped neighbors in the house of Miguel Muñoz (Alcalde of Barrio Bairoa to the mayor of Caguas, December 7, 1880, AHMC, SEC Gobierno, SSEC Alcalde, SER Correspondencia, 1880, C67). Other state authorities, such as the local board of sanitation, education, and the judge, also used them as intermediaries between themselves and the rural population.

39. "Sandalio Ortiz está enfermo de un golpe que le ha dado un buey en el testiculo derecho, el cual tiene como dos pulgadas la herida y en mi concepto es de gravedad" (Alcalde of Barrio Turabo to the mayor of Caguas, January 25, 1880, AHMC, SEC Gobierno, SSEC Alcalde, SER Correspondencia, 1880, C65).

40. "Paltisipo a ustes el indibido Catalino donis está Enterado del abiso como ustes le rreclama y el dise que no se presenta y no tiene que bel con el abiso para que uste sepa que llo cumplo con abisallo" (Alcalde of Barrio San Antonio to the mayor of Caguas, November 29, 1897, AHMC, SEC Secretaría, SSEC Seguridad Pública, SER Correspondencia, SSER Alcalde de Barrio, 1897, C18). Ironically, judging by his grammar, Rodríguez's education was that of basic literacy.

41. "No sabiendo leer ni escribir ni tener en mi casa persona alguna que sepa hacerlo quizas por ignorancia pudiera incurrir en alguna responsabilidad y entorpecer la marcha administrativa" (Luterio Núñez [written by S. Martínez] to the mayor of Caguas, August 3, 1895, AHMC, SEC Gobierno, SSEC Alcalde, SER Correspondencia, 1895, C104). Likewise, Claudio Velázquez, interim alcalde of Barrio Cañabón in 1880, did not know how to write or read, but he served until the official alcalde de barrio, Tiburcio Negrón, recovered from his illness (Claudio Velázquez [signed by Jaime Barety] to the mayor of Caguas, November 8, 1880, AHMC, SEC Secretaría, SSEC Personal, SER Expedientes/Documentos, SSER Renuncias, 1861–99, C12).

42. After losing thirty cuerdas of land in 1881, Mangual sharecropped on his father's farm for six years. It seems that Mangual was a successful farmer and saved enough money in this period to buy land again. He bought a farm of fifty-five cuerdas in Barrio Turabo in 1887, where he cultivated tobacco for cash, fruits, and vegetables. However, he was unable to keep the farm at its original size and sold twenty-five cuerdas of land. In 1896 Mangual owned a farm of thirty cuerdas (AHMC, SEC Finanzas, SSEC Contribuciones, SER Planillas de Riqueza, SSER Agrícola, 1880–1900, C 81–100). In April 1882 Mangual moved to Barrio Borinquen and refused to serve once again (Mangual to the president of the ayuntamiento, April 27, 1882, AHMC, SEC Gobierno, SSEC Asamblea Municipal, SER Correspondencia, 1882–83, C5).

43. "Vivo agregado con mi padre, caresco hasta de un caballo en que salir á cumplimentar las órdenes de la Alcaldía" (Cesareo Mangual to the Ilustre Ayuntamiento, February 8, 1882, AHMC, SEC Gobierno, SSEC Asamblea Municipal, SER Correspondencia, 1882–83, C5).

44. Some examples are Manuel Aponte (alcalde of Barrio Tomás de Castro) to the mayor of Caguas, June 15, 1891, AHMC, SEC Gobierno, SSEC Alcalde de Barrio, SER Correspondencia, 1891, C91, and Alcalde of Barrio San Salvador to the mayor of Caguas, June 22, 1891, AHMC, SEC Gobierno, SSEC Alcalde de Barrio, SER Correspondencia, 1891, C91.

45. "Yo me mejoro ó bengo de los baños que por necesidad tengo que hacerlo" (Francisco Grillo [alcalde of Barrio Cañaboncito] to the mayor of Caguas, AHMC, SEC Gobierno, SSEC Alcalde de Barrio, SER Correspondencia, 1893, C97). Narciso Solá, alcalde of Barrio Borinquen, assigned Eleuterio Caballero as substitute, as he needed to leave the barrio for some days (Narciso Solá to the mayor of Caguas, June 17, 1893, AHMC, SEC Secretaría, SSEC Seguridad Pública, SER Correspondencia, SSER Comisario de Barrio, 1893, C24).

46. Francisco Ramos (alcalde of Barrio Tomás de Castro) to the ayuntamiento, March 31, 1880, AHMC, SEC Gobierno, SSEC Asamblea Municipal, SER Correspondencia, 1879–81, C4; AHMC, SEC Gobierno, SSEC Asamblea Municipal, SER Actas del Cabildo, 1880–82, C13, 15, August 21, 1880, February 4 and May 4, 1882; Acisclo Lizardi (alcalde of Barrio Cañabón) to the mayor of Caguas, July 18, 1881, AHMC, SEC Gobierno, SSEC Alcalde de Barrio, SER Correspondencia, 1881, C69.

47. Medical certification written by Dr. Gabriel Giménez, July 6, 1883, AHMC, SEC Secretaría, SSEC Beneficiencia, SER Expedientes/Documentos, SSER Enfermos, 1858–1947, C8.

48. These offices resembled the *jefaturas políticas* in Mexico. See Falcón, "Force and the Search for Consent," 110, 112, and 127.

49. It seems that the alcaldes de barrio received a small amount of money for their services that depended directly on the municipal budget. After revising the municipal budget of 1890, the ayuntamiento informed the alcaldes de barrio in Caguas that due to the ayuntamiento's precarious conditions, their "gratification" would end. The term "gratification" suggests that the ayuntamiento considered any monetary remuneration to the alcaldes de barrio more as a supplement than a wage. In 1900 Demetrio López heard for the first time that the ayuntamiento paid "desk costs" to the alcaldes de barrio (José Quesada [mayor of Caguas] to the alcaldes de barrio, July 16, 1890, AHMC, SEC Secretaría, SSEC Judicial, SER Libro Copiador, SSER Juzgados, 1890–1902, C28; Demetrio López (alcalde of Barrio Beatriz) to the mayor of Caguas, December 26, 1900, AHMC, SEC Gobierno, SSEC Alcalde de Barrio, SER Correspondencia, 1900, C127).

50. Narciso Solá was a businessman and part of a close social group of men of power in Caguas. He practiced freemasonry and was a member of the Logia Unión Amparo of Caguas in the twentieth century ("Fiesta masónica en Caguas," *La Democracia*, February 6, 1908, 5; "Notas de Caguas," *La Democracia*, May 26, 1908, 2).

51. Leopoldo Cano (Secretaría del Gobernador General de la Isla de Puerto Rico) to the mayor of Caguas, November 5, 1892, AHMC, SEC Gobierno, SSEC Alcalde de Barrio, SER Correspondencia, 1892, C95.

52. These were Heraclio Lizardi, alcalde of Barrio Turabo (1881–82, 1890–92), who registered no property before 1887 and 72 cuerdas by 1891; José Santos y Rodríguez, comisario (1881) and alcalde of Barrio Turabo (1881, 1883, 1898, 1901), whose farm increased from 14 cuerdas in 1880 to 130 cuerdas by 1898; Juan Jiménez Saurí, comisario and alcalde of Barrio Culebras (1885–86, 1889, 1899, and 1903), whose farm increased from 30 cuerdas in 1886 to 369 cuerdas in 1900; Juan Jiménez, alcalde of Barrio Quebrada Puercos (Barrio San Antonio; 1885, 1891) and comisario of Barrio San Salvador (1890), whose farm increased from 16 cuerdas in 1886 to 62 cuerdas in 1894 (decreasing to 30 cuerdas in 1899); José María Rodríguez, alcalde of Barrio San Antonio (1897–1901), whose

farm increased from 14.5 cuerdas in 1897–98 to 38 cuerdas by 1900; Demetrio López, alcalde and comisario of Barrio Beatriz (1889, 1896–1900), whose estate increased from 49.5 cuerdas in 1890 to 187 cuerdas in 1900; and José M. Caballero, comisario and alcalde of Barrio Borinquen (1897–99), whose land holdings increased from 1.5 cuerdas in 1897 to 100 cuerdas in 1898 (AHMC, SEC Finanzas, SSEC Contribuciones, SER Planillas de Riqueza, SSER Agrícola, 1880–1900, C81–100).

53. These were Cesareo Mangual; Francisco Grillo, alcalde of Barrios Cañabón and Cañaboncito (1893–94), whose land holdings fluctuated from 30 cuerdas (1889) to 81 cuerdas (1893) to 64 cuerdas (after 1893); Antonio H. Grillo, alcalde and comisario of Barrio Cañaboncito (1883, 1885, 1895, 1897, 1899, 1903), whose farm was reduced from 411 cuerdas in 1886 to only 30 cuerdas in 1900; and Francisco Rodríguez, alcalde of Barrios Culebras (1881), Bairoa (1893–95), and Río Cañas (1897–99), whose land in Barrio Culebras decreased from 100 cuerdas in 1880 to 12 cuerdas in 1887, the last year he appeared in the tax records (AHMC, SEC Finanzas, SSEC Contribuciones, SER Planillas de Riqueza, SSER Agrícola, 1880–1900, C81–100).

54. For Francisco Ramos, alcalde of Barrio Tomás de Castro, the duties represented an impediment to his economic activities, which demanded his continuous presence (AHMC, SEC Gobierno, SSEC Asamblea Municipal, SER Actas del Cabildo, 1880, C13, April 1, 1880). In 1880 José Y. Esterás, who owned thirty-two cuerdas of land, was named temporary alcalde of Barrio Cañabón. He attempted to refuse the appointment, arguing that he confronted problems with his new business (AHMC, SEC Finanzas, SSEC Contribuciones, SER Planillas de Riqueza, SSER Agrícola, 1880–81, C81; J. Y. Esterás to the mayor of Caguas, April 24, 1880, AHMC, SEC Gobierno, SSEC Alcalde de Barrio, SER Correspondencia, 1880, C66).

55. "El nombramiento de Alcalde de barrio recaído en mí, es injusto á todas luces y perjudicial á la admin., lo primero porque me arruinaría y dejaría sin pan á mí familia que la constituyen mí muger y cuatro niños, de los que la mayor á penas cuenta siete años, y lo segundo, porque un hombre pobre y que no sabe leer ní escribir, por mas que quiéra servir bien, nunca podrá conseguirlo" (Alberto Torres y López [written by R. A. Grillo] to the Ilustre Ayuntamiento, June 28, 1880, AHMC, SEC Gobierno, SSEC Asamblea Municipal, SER Correspondencia, 1879–81, C4).

56. Certification written by Ferardo Darder, July 3, 1880, attached to letter to the Ilustre Ayuntamiento from Alberto Torres y López (see note 56; AHMC, SEC Gobierno, SSEC Asamblea Municipal, SER Correspondencia, 1879–81, C4; see also AHMC, SEC Gobierno, SSEC Asamblea Municipal, SER Actas del Cabildo, 1880, C13, July 1, 1880). Torres y López served as alcalde of Barrio Cañabón in 1880 and again in 1895. Happily, despite his fears of economic bankruptcy, he increased the size of his estate—in 1880 he owned thirteen cuerdas of land, which increased to twenty in 1882, to twenty-seven in 1885, to twenty-eight in 1893, and to fifty-three in 1896; in 1899 Torres y López owned sixty-five cuerdas of land (AHMC, SEC Finanzas, SSEC Contribuciones, SER Planillas de Riqueza, SSER Agrícola, 1880–1900, C81–100).

57. "El que espone no tiene mas para ganarse su subsistencia, que un bentorillo y como no puede ganar un dependiente tiene que estar al frente de el y si se ausentara tendria que cerrarlo. . . . no querrá causar perjuicios tal vez irrreparables á un padre de familia que tiene que vivir de su Industria, que exige continuamente su trabajo personal" (Antonio Ramírez de Arellano [comisario of Barrio Río Cañas and La Mesa] to the mayor of Caguas, December 17, 1883, AHMC, SEC Gobierno, SSEC Alcalde de Barrio, SER Correspondencia, 1884, C73).

58. Mayor of Dorado to the mayor of Caguas, April 15, 1880, AHMC, SEC Gobierno,

SSEC Alcalde de Barrio, SER Correspondencia, 1880, C66. Like Ramírez de Arellano, other officials sometimes did not respond to the mayor's or judge's order to capture an outlaw (AHMC, August 14, 1884, SEC Secretaría, SSEC Judicial, SER Libro Copiador, SSER Juzgados, 1883–89, C27).

59. "Que mi fortuna ó sea el capital que poseo, es tan insignificante que solo se compone de doce cuerdas de terrenos, no de muy buena calidad; una yunta de bueyes, destinada á las labores y dos bestias, teniendo con ellos y mi trabajo personal, que atender al sostenimiento y demas necesidades de mi esposa con cinco hijos pequeños, mis suegros y mi madre, ancianos septayenarios, formando incluso yo, un total de diez de familia. . . . De obligarme á desempeñar la comisaría se me conduce indudablemente a la total ruina y por consiguiente á mi familia á la miseria, y antes que esto suceda y para evitarlo se me pondría en la imprescindible necesidad de enagenar el pedacito de terreno y cambio de domicilio, cáso que no creo que llegue, por que siendo U. padre de familia, ilustrado y adornado de sentimientos humanitarios, hijos de un sencible corazón no pretenderá la completa ruina de uno de sus gobernados y su numerosa familia" (Regino García [written by Diego Lizardi y Sosa] to the mayor of Caguas, April 17, 1883, AHMC, SEC Gobierno, SSEC Asamblea Municipal, SER Correspondencia, 1882–83, C5).

60. "Lla ha cumplido los dos años en el servicio de comisario 2do y desea se nombre otro en su lugar" (Juan Solana [written by Nicanor Esteves] to Gerardo Daldel, September 31, 1885. AHMC, SEC Gobierno, SSEC Asamblea Municipal, SER Correspondencia, 1884–86, C82).

Mateo Fonseca, comisario of Barrio Borinquen, and Demetrio López, comisario of Barrio Beatriz, demanded the same in 1895 and 1900 respectively, but the ayuntamiento ignored López's resignation. Two weeks later, he resigned again and demanded remuneration for his service, specifically for the cost of paper. López emphasized that in order to fulfill his responsibilities as a comisario he was forced to spend his own money. Again the ayuntamiento did not respond, and López wrote once more, claiming that he needed money for stationery in order to pay his municipal taxes (Mateo Fonseca [comisario of Barrio Borinquen] to the mayor of Caguas, June 30, 1895, AHMC, SEC Gobierno, SSEC Alcalde de Barrio, SER Correspondencia, 1895, C103; Demetrio López [comisario of Barrio Beatriz] to the mayor of Caguas, November 30 and December 12 and 26, 1900, AHMC, SEC Gobierno, SSEC Alcalde de Barrio, SER Correspondencia, 1900, C127).

Vicente Ramos emphasized in his resignation as alcalde of Barrio Cañaboncito in 1900 that he had already served the period required by the ayuntamiento. Therefore, Ramos added, it was time to nominate another alcalde for Barrio Cañaboncito ("Expediente sobre renuncia de D. Vicente Santos del cargo de Alcalde de Barrio Cañaboncito y nombramiento de D. Andrés González para sustituirle"). (Ciudad de Caguas, 1900, AHMC, SEC Secretaría, SSEC Empleados Municipales, SER Expedientes/Documentos, SSER Nombramientos, 1900–1901, C8).

61. Mayor of Caguas to the alcaldes of Barrios Borinquen and Culebras, August 30, 1880, AHMC, SEC Secretaría, SSEC Seguridad Pública, SER Correspondencia, SSER Alcalde de Barrio, 1880, C5; Mayor of Caguas to the alcalde of Barrio Turabo, December 15, 1884, AHMC, SEC Secretaría, SSEC Seguridad Pública, SER Correspondencia, SSER Alcalde de Barrio, 1883–85, C11.

62. Mayor of Caguas to Luis Acosta (alcalde of Barrio Turabo), December 22 and 27, 1884, and January 2, 1885, AHMC, SEC Secretaría, SSEC Seguridad Pública, SER Correspondencia, SSER Alcalde de Barrio, 1883–85, C11; Mayor of Caguas to the alcalde of

Barrio Borinquen, September 7, 1898, AHMC, SEC Secretaría, SSEC Seguridad Pública, SER Correspondencia, SSER Alcalde de Barrio, 1898, C19; Mayor of Caguas to the alcalde of Barrio Borinquen, September 6, 1880, AHMC, SEC Secretaría, SSEC Seguridad Pública, SER Correspondencia, SSER Alcalde de Barrio, 1880, C6.

63. Mayor of Caguas to the alcalde of Barrio Borinquen, March 8, 1881, AHMC, SEC Secretaría, SSEC Seguridad Pública, SER Correspondencia, SSER Alcalde de Barrio, 1880–81, C8.

64. Mayor of Caguas to the alcalde of Barrio Borinquen, August 30, 1881, AHMC, SEC Secretaría, SSEC Seguridad Pública, SER Correspondencia, SSER Alcalde de Barrio, 1880–81, C8.

65. "La necesidad de que sean avisados dichos vecinos, pues sucede con frecuencia que muchos recurren en los recargos y apremios, por no tener conocimiento de las épocas en que deben proveerse de dicho documento, debido á que los comisarios no se toman el trabajo de avisarles" ([Fermín] López to the alcalde of Barrio Cañabón, August 16, 1895, AHMC, SEC Secretaría, SSEC Seguridad Pública, SER Correspondencia, SSER Comisario de Barrio, 1880–1906, C24).

66. In February 1880, the mayor of Caguas accused Salvador López, alcalde of Barrio Beatriz, of failing to cite some individuals under his jurisdiction. The mayor ordered him to fulfill his responsibilities and threatened to fine him if he "vuelve a desobedecer" (Mayor of Caguas to Salvador López [alcalde of Barrio Beatriz], February 16, 1880, AHMC, SEC Secretaría, SSEC Seguridad Pública, SER Correspondencia, SSER Alcalde de Barrio, 1880–81, C8). Likewise, the comisario of Barrio Beatriz, José López, even went to court (*juicio oral*) for disobedience (Gerardo Puig [representative of the municipal court] to the mayor of Caguas, May 22, 1894, AHMC, SEC Gobierno, SSEC Alcalde de Barrio, SER Correspondencia, 1894, C99).

67. "Sucede con bastante frecuencia que algunos de los Alcaldes de los barrios de esta jurisdicción, no devuelven diligenciadas las órdenes que les dirigen, lo cual redunda en daño del mejor servicio público" (Mayor of Caguas to the alcalde of Barrio Bairoa, September 28, 1897, AHMC, SEC Secretaría, SSEC Seguridad Pública, SER Correspondencia, SSER Alcalde de Barrio, 1897, C18).

68. C. Solá (mayor of Caguas) to the alcalde of Barrio San Salvador, April 15, 1899, AHMC, SEC Secretaría, SSEC Seguridad Pública, SER Correspondencia, SSER Alcalde de Barrio, 1899, C20; G. García (mayor of Caguas) to the comisario of Barrio San Antonio, April 17, 1903, AHMC, SEC Secretaría, SSEC Seguridad Pública, SER Correspondencia, SSER Comisario de Barrio, 1880–1906, C24.

69. Mayor of Caguas to the Juez Municipal, January 9, [?], AHMC, SEC Secretaría, SSEC Judicial, SER Libro Copiador, SSER Juzgados, 1890–1902, C28.

70. J. Garriga (of the juzgado municipal) to the mayor of Caguas, August 22, 1885, AHMC, SEC Gobierno, SSEC Asamblea Municipal, SER Correspondencia, 1884–86, C82.

71. "Citar á su vecino Don Ramon Lopez á ser notificado de una providencia en juicio de faltas, cuya órden ha sido devuelta ayer dies y ocho por el citado Alcalde de barrio Don Juan Portela sin cumplimentar y puesto á su calce lo siguiente = 'El comisario del barrio de Bairoa no es Portero' " (J. Garriga [of the juzgado municipal] to the mayor of Caguas, October 19, 1885, AHMC, SEC Gobierno, SSEC Alcalde de Barrio, SER Correspondencia, 1885, C79).

72. Portela acted as alcalde de barrio in 1880 and again in 1885. In 1882 he was forty-four years old and a literate man. Portela raised cattle in Barrio Bairoa in addition to working as an "*industrial*," which in his case meant meat supplier. He lived with his wife and two

children in Barrio Bairoa. After 1885 Portela did not represent the state again but remained in Caguas (AHMC, SEC Secretaría, SSEC Archivo, SER Censos, SSER Habitantes, 1882–83, C26; Juan Portela to the alcalde delegado, April 22, 1886, AHMC, SEC Gobierno, SSEC Alcalde de Barrio, SER Correspondencia, 1886, C80; Felipe Muñoz to the mayor of Caguas, October 15, 1884 and November 21, 22, and 23, 1884, AHMC, SEC Gobierno, SSEC Alcalde de Barrio, SER Correspondencia, 1884, C76; Juan Portela to the ayuntamiento, October 11, 1882, August 12, 1883, and August 11, 1886, AHMC, SEC Gobierno, SSEC Asamblea Municipal, SER Correspondencia, 1882–83, 1886, C5, 19).

Portela was a liberal, and Garriga was part of the opposite party, but in the twentieth century both men found themselves in the same wing. Garriga became a follower of Muñoz Rivera. In 1909 both men, Portela and Garriga, signed letters congratulating Muñoz Rivera for his "virile and patriotic speech" ("La opinión de Caguas se muestra de una manera patriótica y terminante," *La Democracia*, January 18, 1909, 4).

73. Gregorio Arroyo (alcalde of Barrio Tomás de Castro) to the mayor of Caguas, June 1, 1899, AHMC, SEC Gobierno, SSEC Alcalde de Barrio, SER Correspondencia, 1899, C122.

74. AHMC, SEC Gobierno, SSEC Asamblea Municipal, SER Actas del Cabildo, 1898–99, C29–30, June 7, 1899.

75. "No ignorará que el vecindario no ve con gusto algunas de sus cosas, pués al salir una vez de comisario le gopearon é hirieron teniendo que ir al hospital" (Francisco Díaz Rezino [teacher at the rural school in Tomás de Castro] to the mayor of Caguas and the local board of education, June 30, 1899, in "Expediente sobre esclarecimiento de hechos imputados al Profesor Rural del barrio de Tomas de Castro Don Francisco Díaz Resino," AHMC, SEC Secretaría, SSEC Judicial, SER Investigaciones, 1899–1933, C14).

76. In 1884 Eugenio Lebrón wounded the alcalde of Barrio Quebrada Puercos with a machete (Mayor of Caguas to the juez municipal, July 25, 1884, AHMC, SEC Secretaría, SSEC Judicial, SER Libro Copiador, SSER Juzgados, 1883–87, C27). In 1886 the ex-slave Ancermo Acosta insulted and mocked Francisco Acosta, comisario of Barrio Turabo (Francisco Acosta [comisario of Barrio Turabo] to the mayor of Caguas, October 10, 1886, AHMC, SEC Gobierno, SSEC Alcalde de Barrio, SER Correspondencia, 1886, C81). In 1889 Ceferino Ocasio, resident of Barrio Borinquen insulted the alcalde de barrio, failing "to demonstrate respect to the authority" (Mayor of Caguas to the juez municipal, May 26, 1889, AHMC, SEC Secretaría, SSEC Judicial, SER Libro Copiador, SSER Juzgados, 1883–87, C27).

77. Mayor of Caguas to Serafín Acosta, Benito Polo, and José Santos, December 19, 1898, AHMC, SEC Secretaría, SSEC Seguridad Pública, SER Correspondencia, SSER Alcalde de Barrio, 1898, C19.

78. For example, when Henry Carroll visited Caguas, the alcaldes de barrio gathered farmers in their jurisdiction together to be interviewed by Carroll (Mayor of Caguas to the alcalde of Barrio Cañabón, February 25, 1899, AHMC, SEC Secretaría, SSEC Seguridad Pública, SER Correspondencia, SSER Alcalde de Barrio, 1899, C20).

79. Nazario Velasco, "Negociación en la tradición legal", 173–74; El Capitán Franqueza, "Los tribunales de policía," *La Democracia*, January 5, 1901.

80. Carlos Harrell (secretary of Porto Rico) to the mayor of Caguas, July 16, 1902, AHMC, SEC Gobierno, SSEC Alcalde, SER Correspondencia, 1902, C131.

81. Trías Monge, *Historia constitucional*, 1:281.

82. In fact, there are many examples of comisarios and alcaldes who held office for over a decade. For instance, Francisco Rivera occupied the offices of comisario and alcalde of Barrio Bairoa from 1882 to 1908, almost consecutively. Bunker states that in 1902 the

comisarios de barrio received $300 annually, but my data shows that they did not receive any money for their public service (Bunker, *Historia de Caguas*, 268; Secretary of Porto Rico to the mayor of Caguas, July 16, 1902, AHMC, SEC Gobierno, SSEC Alcalde de Barrio, SER Correspondencia, 1902, C131).

83. "Notas de Caguas," *La Democracia*, October 15, 1908, 3. Enrique Fernández, comisario of Barrio Turabo, also belonged to the Union Party ("Desde Caguas," *La Democracia*, January 4, 1907, 2, and December 30, 1908, 3).

84. For a detailed survey on Puerto Ricans' attitudes toward the U.S. invasion see Luque, *La ocupación y la Ley Foraker.*

85. The political advantages were mostly theoretical because the autonomy status lasted only one week. The United States invaded exactly seven days after the inauguration of the Autonomous Charter (Trías Monge, *El sistema judicial de Puerto Rico*, 45).

86. Cabán, *Constructing a Colonial People*, 174, 185.

87. "Triunfo Federal en Caguas," *La Democracia*, December 27, 1899. In May 1906, 660 Cagüeños filed their affiliation with the Union Party, while the opposition merely gained 36. In the next two months, the Union Party received 203 new inscriptions while the opposition got 5 ("Desde Caguas," *La Democracia*, May 26, 1906, 2, and July 18, 1906, 1).

88. One example is Raimundo Faura, who had been born in Cataluña, Spain, and started as an alcalde of Barrio Río Cañas in 1895. He moved to the council in 1897 and continued in office until the following year. After the U.S. occupation, Faura stayed on the island, and in 1901 the governor of Puerto Rico named him municipal judge (juez de policía). After 1899 Faura belonged to the Republican Party. Even though Faura stayed in local politics as a public figure, he did not return to the council of Caguas (Bunker, *Historia de Caguas*, 190).

Likewise, the Cataluñan Agustín Plá; the Mallorcan brothers Bartolomé and Pascual Borrás; and the Asturian councilors Odón Somonte, Gerónimo Matanzo, Silverio Campos, and Víctor Fernández never returned to the council after 1898. Plá, Pascual Borrás, Campos, and Fernández had just started their political career in 1897. However, Bartolomé Borrás, Matanzo, and Somonte formed part of the old guard in Caguas. Bartolomé Borrás and Somonte served as municipal councilors for the first time in 1881, and Matanzo in 1883. During the 1880s and 1890s, they were members of the municipal council of Caguas. The brothers Borrás dedicated themselves to sugar production; in 1905 they announced major improvements to the buildings in their Hacienda Santa Catalina. Pascual also owned cattle ("Correo de Caguas," *La Democracia*, November 23, 1905, 2; and "Desde Caguas," *La Democracia*, February 27, 1906, 3).

Somonte died on December 20, 1906 ("Desde Caguas," *La Democracia*, December 20, 1906, 3). Fernández died on October 4, 1906 (Franca Mar, "Desde Caguas," *La Democracia*, October 5, 1906, 2).

Bartolomé Borrás was the owner of one of the largest land estate in Caguas, the Hacienda Santa Catalina. In 1880 his estate registered 1,400 cuerdas in Barrio Cañabón (AHMC, SEC Finanzas, SSEC Contribuciones, SER Planillas de Riqueza, SSER Agrícola, 1880–81, C81).

89. Bunker, *Historia de Caguas*, 152 and 156.

90. Aguayo was a member of the Union Club. In 1909 he was secretary of both the Union Club and of the municipal court of Caguas ("Desde Caguas," *La Democracia*, December 30, 1908, 4; "Notas de Caguas," *La Democracia*, January 4, 1909, 1). In 1907 Aguayo was municipal secretary and a businessman who directed the commercial house Aguayo

Hermanos. He also owned buildings in the downtown of Caguas, one of which he rented out as a government office ("Desde Caguas," *La Democracia*, August 1, 1906, 1). In 1909 he took control of the commercial house of Don José R. Santiago, former councilman ("Caguas," *La Democracia*, February 19, 1909, 2).

Johnson established links of friendship and business with the Solá family (Bunker, *Historia de Caguas*, 239–40.) In 1907 he married a Cagüeña. In their new home in Barrio Turabo, this couple offered numerous parties for the high society of Caguas at which they served luxurious items such as ice cream, candies, and liquors ("Notas de Caguas," *La Democracia*, October 24, 1907, 3, and July 15, 1908, 3). Johnson was a vocal member of the Director Board of the Local Committee of the Union in 1907 ("Notas de Caguas," *La Democracia*, January 7, 1907, 2).

Moreno was a member of the Union Club. He entered the council of Caguas in 1898 and served almost continuously until 1912. He became the mayor of Caguas in 1914. In 1906 he constructed a house facing the plaza in Caguas, which was used by the Union Club. Moreno also offered parties for the high society of Puerto Rico. Don Mariano Abril, a prominent politician in Puerto Rico, attended to the celebration of the Morenos' daughter's baptism ("Una fiesta en Caguas," *La Democracia*, January 17, 1906, 1; "Correo de Caguas," *La Democracia*, January 23, 1906, 3). In 1909 he was vice president of the Union Club ("Desde Caguas," *La Democracia*, December 30, 1908, 3). In 1909 the governor named Moreno mayor of Caguas, but Moreno declined the position in order to protest the lack of municipal autonomy (E. Moreno, "La terna de Caguas," *La Democracia*, January 19, 1909, 1; "Renuncia del Sr. Moreno," *La Democracia*, January 20, 1909, 1).

91. Bunker, *Historia de Caguas*, 80–82 and 146.

92. In 1907 the Ayuntamiento de Caguas publicly declared García "Hijo Adoptivo de Caguas" (Adoptive son of Caguas), for his excellent service as mayor. This title was published in the paper again in 1909 ("Ese es el hombre," *La Democracia*, January 21, 1909, 3).

García began his public career in 1885, working as an alcalde of Barrio Beatriz during that year. In 1898–99, he served as a municipal councilor. While he was living in Barrio Beatriz, García collaborated in the foundation of the Casino de Caguas, a social and cultural club for well-to-do Cagüeños (AHMC, Gervasio Garcia's manuscript). García was also a good friend of Don Herminio Díaz Navarro, the most influential judge in Puerto Rico from the late nineteenth century to the twentieth (*La Correspondencia*, March 15, 1891, 2; Bunker, *Historia de Caguas*, 234).

93. Jiménez Sanjurjo studied medicine in Spain, France, England, and the United States and started practicing in 1879. He cared for patients who came from other islands in the Caribbean, and his medical reputation was known throughout the Antilles ("De Caguas: muerte y entierro del Doctor Jiménez Sanjurjo," *La Democracia*, January 7, 1909, 3). In 1880 Jiménez Sanjurjo owned a farm of 380 cuerdas in Barrio Cagüitas, and after this year there is no land property registered under his name (AHMC, SEC Finanzas, SSEC Contribuciones, SER Planillas de Riqueza, SSER Agrícola, 1881–82, C82).

94. Negrón Sanjurjo, *Los primeros treinta años*, 166–67; "El doctor Jiménez Sanjurjo," *La Democracia*, January 5, 1909, 1. Jiménez Sanjurjo became a prominent liberal until his death on January 4, 1909. He was one of the founders and president of the local committee of the liberal Union Party ("Es escandaloso lo que viene sucediendo en Caguas, *La Democracia*, July 11, 1904, 3; "Correo de Caguas," *La Democracia*, January 23, 1906, 3; "Desde Caguas," *La Democracia*, August 18, 1906, 2).

95. Johnson was a successful businessman, who established his residency in Caguas in

1901. He was born in Chicago and came to Puerto Rico to work with the U.S. military government in San Juan. In 1906 Johnson funded the construction of a building outside the plaza of Caguas to be used for the manufacture of tobacco ("Desde Caguas," *La Democracia*, May 8, 1906, 2).

96. Bunker, *Historia de Caguas*, 264.

97. "Correo de Caguas," *La Democracia*, October 24, 1905, 2; "Notas de Caguas. El teatro 'Manrique' capacidad para 700 expectadadores," *La Democracia*, April 8, 1908, 2; "Desde Caguas," *La Democracia*, November 2, 1906, August 16 and 21, 1907, December 21, 1907, and May 22, 1908.

3. In the Face of Inequality

1. Godreau and Giusti, "Las concesiones de la Corona," 363, 355, 483, 487.

2. Rosario Rivera, *La Real Cédula de Gracias*, 21, 26. Rosario Rivera challenges the idea of the cédula as an attempt to whiten the population of the island. She states that early in the nineteenth century there was neither a numerically important population of color nor a preference for a white population in the island. Francisco A. Scarano questions the success of the cédula in the development of agrarian wealth in Puerto Rico (*Sugar and Slavery in Puerto Rico*, 18–19).

3. Godreau and Giusti, "Las concesiones de la Corona," 497–500, 502, and 515.

4. Godreau and Giusti, "Las concesiones de la Corona," 363, 516, and 537.

5. Mayor of Caguas to the alcalde of Barrio Turabo, April 1, 1880, AHMC, SEC Secretaría, SSEC Seguridad Pública, SER Correspondencia, SSER Alcalde de Barrio, 1880, C6.

6. The board also attempted to protect state forests with the specific purpose of having wood available for the construction of navy ships and of preserving soil quality (Godreau and Giusti, "Las concesiones de la Corona," 427, 429, 517–20, and 522).

7. Vassberg, *Land and Society*, 41, 54–56, and 86–87.

8. Godreau and Giusti, "Las concesiones de la Corona," 363.

9. Nazario Velasco, *Discurso legal y orden poscolonial*, 182–84. "Science" in this context refers to the best methods to make the land produce commercially. In this sense, land privatization was understood as the most scientifically viable way to achieve economic growth.

10. Telésfora García vs. Emilio Fernández, 1929, AHMC, SEC Secretaría, SSEC Judicial, SER Expedientes/Documentos, SSER Demandas, 1824–1946, C11.

11. Godreau and Giusti, "Las concesiones de la Corona," 539, 558–59, and 566.

12. *Leyes provincial y municipal de 24 de mayo de 1878*, 74–89.

13. Mayor of Caguas to the alcaldes of Barrio B. y Jagua and Cañaboncito, August 3, 1880, AHMC, SEC Secretaría, SSEC Seguridad Pública, SER Correspondencia, SSER Alcalde de Barrio, 1880–81, C7–8.

14. Angel Lozano, "Circular. Administración Central de Contribuciones y Rentas de la Isla de Puerto Rico," May 2, 1880, AHMC, SEC Gobierno, SSEC Asamblea Municipal, SER Correspondencia, 1879–81, C4.

15. Landelino Aponte (August 8, 1880), Francisco Delgado (April 26, 1880) Pedro García (August 10, 1880), José María Lasanta (October 5, 1880), Eduardo López (October 5, 1880), Manuel Joaquín Caballero (October 5, 1880), Evangelista González (October 5, 1880), Manuel Correa (October 5, 1880), Lorenzo Vélez (August 10, 1880), Pedro Pablo Grillo (November 10, 1880), Eusebio Montañez (December 14, 1881) to the ayuntamiento, AHMC, SEC Gobierno, SSEC Asamblea Municipal, SER Correspondencia, 1879–81, C4; Dionisio Alamo y Vargas (July 1, 1882), Grau and nephew (July 14, 1882), Leocadio Correa

(July 14, 1882), Regino de León (July 12, 1882) to the ayuntamiento, AHMC, SEC Gobierno, SSEC Asamblea Municipal, SER Correspondencia, 1882–83, C5.

16. "Debe desde luego adoptar otro sistema para que a la propiedad se respete, y no esté al capricho y voluntad de los ejecutores de apremio para que sin atender á razones ni documentos que se les exiban, continuen cometiendo aquellos actos, en gran manera odiosos, viniendo como es consiguiente á dejar en total ruina á los pobres vecinos que por carecer de medios con que alzar su voz, no tienen mas remedio que dejar pregonar sus bienes sin ser deudores al Estado ni al Municipio"

(Leonor Donis [signed by Federico Diez y López] to the Ilustre Ayuntamiento, April 12, 1882, AHMC, SEC Gobierno, SSEC Asamblea Municipal, SER Correspondencia, 1882–83, C5).

17. Mercedes Rodríguez de Negrón (written by Avelino Saurí) to the Ilustre Ayuntamiento (its responses and documents attached), October 2, 1883, AHMC, SEC Gobierno, SSEC Asamblea Municipal, SER Correspondencia, 1883–86, C80.

18. "Repartimiento de Contribuciones," *El Buscapié*, December 4, 1881, 1; see also "La contribución territorial en Puerto-Rico," *El Buscapié*, April 16, 1882, 1.

19. "El repartimiento de las contribuciones," *El Buscapié*, September 29, 1889. See also "Artículos coloniales: La cuchara y el sable," *El Buscapié*, April 9, 1882, 1, and "El nuevo proyecto de contribución municipal," *El Buscapié*, March 28, 1886, 1.

20. Pedro Garay y Sosa to the Ilustre Ayuntamiento, July 4, 1887, AHMC, SEC Gobierno, SSEC Asamblea Municipal, SER Correspondencia, 1887–88, C84.

21. "La propiedad de Don Nicolás Quiñonez, de Cagüitas, otra sin duda de las más valiosas que aquí existen y que tambien se encuentra un gran número de cuerdas de cañas magníficas y produce además un gran número de quintales de café. Tiene este mismo Señor, otra propiedad en la Jagua de muy buenas condiciones y extension, por estas dos propiedades se le reduce á setecientos pesos de productos menos de la *mitad de lo que le habian señalado los peritos*. ¿Es equidad, esto, Señores? Como repartidor no puedo conformarme, y como contribuyente me quejo" (Miguel Puig to the mayor and council, July 11, 1887, AHMC, SEC Gobierno, SSEC Asamblea Municipal, SER Correspondencia, 1887–88, C84).

22. "Como consecuencia de las rebajas hechas, ó sea, de las gracias concedidas, han tenido que aumentarse los productos á muchas propiedades que ni remotamente pueden darlos" (Miguel Puig to the mayor and council, July 11, 1887, AHMC, SEC Gobierno, SSEC Asamblea Municipal, SER Correspondencia, 1887–88, C84).

23. "Relación de los individuos que han presentado quejas á este Ayuntamiento y Junta repartidora, en solicitud de rebaja en la riqueza territorial del corriente año ecco, con expresión de lo resuelto sobre cada una de ellas," September 20, 1884, AHMC, SEC Gobierno, SSEC Asamblea Municipal, SER Correspondencia, 1884–86, C82. In 1891, the municipal government reduced the taxes of five individuals (1,930 pesos), which were redistributed among six individuals ("Relación de los individuos que han presentado quejas contra el reparto territorial del expresado año económico, con expresión de lo resuelto por este Ayuntamiento en cada una de ellas," July 20, 1891, AHMC, SEC Gobierno, SSEC Asamblea Municipal, SER Correspondencia, 1890–1893, C86).

24. Gerardo Puig to Señores Pte. Y Concejales de este Ilustre Ayto., July 11, 1887, AHMC, SEC Gobierno, SSEC Asamblea Municipal, SER Correspondencia, 1886–87, C83.

25. Jaime Vilá to the mayor of Caguas, August 1, 1887, AHMC, SEC Gobierno, SSEC Asamblea Municipal, SER Correspondencia, 1887–88, C84. In 1886 Vilá filed an affidavit protesting the high taxes (eight hundred pesos) on his farm in Barrio Tomás de Castro, and

asking a reduction of 50 percent (Jaime Vilá to the ayuntamiento, July 13, 1886, AHMC, SEC Gobierno, SSEC Asamblea Municipal, SER Correspondencia, 1886–1887, C83).

26. Investigator to the Ilustre Ayuntamiento, November 29, 1887, AHMC, SEC Gobierno, SSEC Asamblea Municipal, SER Correspondencia, 1887–88, C84.

27. Felicita Santos de Amalbert to the president and councilors of the ayuntamiento, June 14, 1885, AHMC, SEC Gobierno, SSEC Asamblea Municipal, SER Correspondencia, 1884–86, C82.

28. Pedro Pablo Grillo to the ayuntamiento, October 29, 1884, AHMC, SEC Gobierno, SSEC Asamblea Municipal, SER Correspondencia, 1884–86, C82. This is the only example I found in which an alcalde de barrio took advantage of his position to lower his taxes.

29. Domingo Fuentes y Aponte, through the alcalde of Barrio Borinquen, asked the mayor for an extension because his family was sick (Marcelino Solá [alcalde of Barrio Borinquen] to the mayor of Caguas, August 31, 1880, AHMC, SEC Gobierno, SSEC Alcalde de Barrio, SER Correspondencia, 1880, C67). The mayor of Caguas sent long lists to the alcaldes de barrio with the debtors' names, urging them to pay taxes (Mayor of Caguas to the alcaldes de barrio January 17, 1880, and April 23, 1880, AHMC, SEC Secretaría, SSEC Seguridad Pública, SER Correspondencia, SSER Alcalde de Barrio, 1880, C6).

30. Carmen Reyes Luna protested the seizure of one cow on her property. Her mother had died and left seven cuerdas of land to each of her four children. Because Carmen was the only child with cattle, the government confiscated a cow to pay for the four children's taxes (Carmen Reyes Luna [signed by José García] to the Ilustre Ayuntamiento, August 30, 1886, AHMC, SEC Gobierno, SSEC Asamblea Municipal, SER Correspondencia, 1886–87, C83). The alcalde of Barrio Cañaboncito reported that the farms of Blas Cedeño, Juan de Paz Pagán, Juan Gregorio Coto, and Saturnino Sánchez had no fruits to confiscate (Mayor of Caguas to the alcalde of Barrio Cañaboncito, May 20, 1897, AHMC, SEC Secretaría, SSEC Seguridad Pública, SER Correspondencia, SSER Alcalde de Barrio, 1897, C18). Likewise, the alcalde of Barrio Beatriz informed the mayor that José María Pérez Arroyo had an insignificant amount of crops on his farm (Mayor of Caguas to the alcalde of Barrio Beatriz, May 12, 1897, AHMC, SEC Secretaría, SSEC Seguridad Pública, SER Correspondencia, SSER Alcalde de Barrio, 1897, C18).

31. In Barrio Turabo, Felix Ríos lost 40 cuerdas of land as a result of a municipal confiscation (Mayor of Caguas to the Juez de Primera Instancia, November 5, 1887, AHMC, SEC Secretaría, SSEC Judicial, SER Libro Copiador, SSER Juzgados, 1883–89, C27). In 1898 the mayor of Caguas warned Nicanor Esteves, Claudiano Solano, and Francisco Rodríguez of a possible property confiscation for not paying taxes (Mayor of Caguas to the alcalde of Barrio Río Cañas, October 17, 1898, AHMC, SEC Secretaría, SSEC Seguridad Pública, SER Correspondencia, SSER Alcalde de Barrio, 1898, C19). In Barrio Tomás de Castro, Antonio Cruz Alicea had a farm of 140 cuerdas. He was forced to give 100 cuerdas to his creditor Sebastián Mons, and in subsequent years the municipal government confiscated the rest of the farm (Antonio Cruz Alicea to the Ilustre Ayuntamiento, July 4, 1887, AHMC, SEC Gobierno, SSEC Asamblea Municipal, SER Correspondencia, 1886–87, C83).

32. Rufino Díaz to the president and the ayuntamiento, April 22, 1885, AHMC, SEC Gobierno, SSEC Asamblea Municipal, SER Correspondencia, 1884–86, C82.

33. Ramón Villafañe to the Ilustre Ayuntamiento, July 19, 1886, AHMC, SEC Gobierno, SSEC Asamblea Municipal, SER Correspondencia, 1886–87, C83.

34. Rafael Ramos (tax commissioner) to the Ilustre Ayuntamiento, December 22, 1892, AHMC, SEC Gobierno, SSEC Asamblea Municipal, SER Correspondencia, 1894–1898, C87.

Don José S. Solá bought land in this way (M. Solá y Compañía to the Ilustre Ayuntamiento; July 27, 1897, AHMC, SEC Gobierno, SSEC Asamblea Municipal, SER Correspondencia, 1894–98, C87).

35. Mayor of Caguas to the alcaldes of Barrios Beatriz and Turabo (June 20, 1898), alcalde of Barrio San Salvador (July 5, 1898), and alcalde of Barrio Tomás de Castro (July 11, 1898), AHMC, SEC Secretaría, SSEC Seguridad Pública, SER Correspondencia, SSER Alcalde de Barrio, 1898, C19; "Reparto Municipal," La Democracia, February 14, 1899, 2.

36. Cabán, Constructing a Colonial People, 76.

37. Nazario Velasco, Discurso legal y orden poscolonial, 184–91.

38. Mayor of Caguas to the alcaldes of Barrios Turabo and Cañaboncito, April 11, 1899, AHMC, SEC Secretaría, SSEC Seguridad Pública, SER Correspondencia, SSER Alcalde de Barrio, 1899, C20.

39. Cabán, Constructing a Colonial People, 76.

40. "Todo el mundo sabe lo que ha ocurrido en esta isla con la contribución territorial; que los pequeños propietarios han llevado siempre la carga de las contribuciones, mientras los caciques, los que influían en el gobierno y en la política, los grandes propietarios, con raras excepciones, figuran siempre con menor riqueza de la que en realidad poseían" ("Tributación territorial," La Democracia, February 1, 1899, 2).

41. "Tributación Territorial," parts 2 and 3, La Democracia, February 2 and 3, 1899, 2.

42. Secretary William F. Willoughby cited in Cabán, Constructing a Colonial People, 171.

43. Nazario Velasco, Discurso legal y orden poscolonial, 191–98. The following articles are from La Democracia: "Contribuyentes: defendeos" (February 5, 1901, 1); "¡Propietarios a Defenderse!" (I and II, January 16 and 17, 1901, 2); "Los nuevos impuestos municipales" (July 1, 1901, 3); M. Buxeda, "Las contribuciones y el hambre: Estudiando para pájaros" (September 11, 1901, 2); "A la junta revisadora de tasación de la propiedad de Puerto-Rico" (June 11, 1902, 2).

44. Mayor of Caguas to the comisarios of Barrios Beatriz and San Antonio from the mayor of Caguas, October 22, 1903. AHMC, SEC Secretaría, SSEC Seguridad Pública, SER Correspondencia, SSER Comisario de Barrio, 1880–1906, C24.

45. Cabán, Constructing a Colonial People, 172–73.

46. "Siempre el otro," La Democracia, February 14, 1901, 1; "Lo que pasa en los municipios: situación crítica," La Democracia, October 2, 1901, 3. Liberals protested the appointment of Don Severo Abella Bastón to the Office of Property Registry in Caguas ("Manifestación de Caguas," La Democracia, May 1, 1899; "¡Abella Bastón a Caguas!" La Democracia, May 2, 1899).

47. "Los tasadores," La Democracia, February 15, 1901, 2.

48. Quoted in Nazario Velasco, Discurso legal y orden poscolonial, 196, and in Cabán, Constructing a Colonial People, 67–68.

49. See Acosta Lespier, Santa Juana y Mano Manca.

50. After 1898 U.S. state officials in Puerto Rico also valued the scientific, positivist, and modern character of such Spanish property laws, leaving them intact at least in the first decades of the twentieth century (Nazario Velasco, "Negociación en la tradición legal," 62, 213, 218, 358).

51. Álvarez Curbelo, "El afán de la modernidad," chapter 3, pp. 71–72 and chapter 4, p. 69.

52. López Tuero's position reverberated in many social forums in Puerto Rico. In the late nineteenth century, many Puerto Rican intellectuals believed in the power of positive progress for societies. Political economy represented not only a field of study but also a morality by which to judge societies and individuals. Salvador Brau, for instance, found in Henry George's and Federico Bastiat's work a model for understanding Puerto Rican society. Brau, like many other Puerto Ricans, believed that political economy constituted a medium for studying the whole society (Álvarez Curbelo, "El afán de la modernidad," chapter 4, pp. 2–3 and 8, and chapter 5, p. 91).

53. In 1878 the civil guard became an integral part of the Spanish army in all the national territory of Spain, including its colonies. The civil guard (guardia civil) under Spanish rule intended to police the countryside. Created in 1844 the civil guard served in Spain as a mechanism to support the central state. Diego López Garrido describes it as a true exercise of bureaucratization ("ejercicio de burocratización") because its principally rural character forced its members to live and interact among commoners in a very intimate way (López Garrido, *La Guardia Civil*, 9–10 and 113). This institution was transported to Puerto Rico but remained an urban force.

54. "Las ordenanzas municipales," *El Buscapié*, June 29, 1884, 1.

55. For instance, as soon as a farmer knew about the loss of an animal, she or he reported it to the legal authorities. The mayor of Caguas then sent a report to all the comisarios and alcaldes de barrio ordering the search for a "blond chicken," a "black mare," or a "marked horse"; the list of examples is endless (AHMC, SEC Secretaría, SSEC Seguridad Pública, SER Correspondencia, SSER Alcalde de Barrio, 1880–99, C6–8, 12–14, and 18–20; AHMC, SEC Secretaría, SSEC Seguridad Pública, SER Correspondencia, SSER Comisario de Barrio, 1880–1906, C24; Rafael Díaz to the mayor of Caguas, January 9, 1885, AHMC, SEC Gobierno, SSEC Alcalde de Barrio, SER Correspondencia, 1885, C77; Cesareo Mangual [alcalde of Barrio Turabo] to the mayor of Caguas, February 12, 1894, AHMC, SEC Gobierno, SSEC Alcalde de Barrio, SER Correspondencia, 1894, C98).

56. The following are in AHMC, SEC Secretaría, SSEC Personal, SER Expedientes/Documentos, SSER Nombramientos, 1837–99, C7: "Nombramiento de guardia jurado á favor de D. Salvador Biosca y Just para custodiar las propiedades de Don Rafael Rodríguez, sitas en el barrio de Turabo" (1890), "Expediente sobre nombramiento de un guardia jurado particular p. la propiedad de D. Victor Fernandez" (1890), "Nombramiento de guarda jurado á favor de D. Salvador Biosca y Yust pa. Custodiar las propiedades de Don Landelino Aponte y de D. Víctor Fernández" (1890), "Nombramiento del guarda jurado á favor de Don Juan Aruejo y Gontón para custodiar las propiedades de la sucn. de D. Bartolomé Borrás sitas en el barrio de Cagüitas" (1890), "Nombramiento de guarda jurado á favor de D. Salvador Biosca y Yust para custodiar una finca, arrendada por D. Nicolás Quiñonez Cabezudo, y la Had. Santa Bárbara" (1892).

57. "Sentencia número 573," December 31, 1891, AHMC, SEC Secretaría, SSEC Judicial, SER Testimonios, SSER Condenas, 1891–92, C48. Landowners continued to employ private guards after U.S. rule began. For instance, Don Rafael Rodríguez, a large landowner and ex-councilor, hired Jesús María Ramos to herd his cattle. On the afternoon of March 23, 1899, Ramos, as usual, conducted his rounds on Rodríguez's farm and found that someone tied a female calf with a "good rope." Ramos immediately suspected that the rope represented the first step to steal the calf. He reported the incident to the comisario de barrio, who asked the help of the police "with the intent of catching such a bad deed" ("con el fin de ver si podemos sorprender semejante fechoría") (AHMC, SEC Finanzas, SSEC Contribuciones,

SER Planillas de Riqueza, SSER Agrícola, 1899, C98; Salvador Sánchez [comisario of Barrio Turabo] to the mayor of Caguas, March 2, 1899, AHMC, SEC Gobierno, SSEC Alcalde de Barrio, SER Correspondencia, 1899, C121).

58. "Se acabarán los alborotos de los turbulentos: los hurtos y los robos en los poblados y los campos; las jugadas y toda clase de vagabunderías, y el pueblo de Puerto-Rico, será felíz en esa parte, entregado al trabajo, en los brazos de un orden perfecto" (Vecinet, "La policía insular y el pueblo puertorriqueño," *La Democracia*, June 8, 1901, 2; see also same author and title, August 1, 1901, 5, and August 16, 1901, 1).

59. "Verdadera y única garantía de los hombres honrados que residen en los campos" ("La Guardia Civil," *La Correspondencia*, May 23, 1892, 3).

60. Silvestrini de Pacheco, *Violencia y criminalidad*, 24; Fuente, *A Nation for All*, 132.

61. Cabán, *Constructing a Colonial People*, 155.

62. "Ordenanza de los Comisarios de los Barrio rurales de Caguas: Deberes de los Comisarios de los Barrios Rurales Caguas," Establecimiento Tipografía, pamphlet published by *La Democracia*, 1902, AHMC, SEC Secretaría, SSEC Seguridad Pública, SER Correspondencia, SSER Comisario de Barrio, 1880–1906, C24.

63. "La Policía Insular," *La Democracia*, August 28, 1899; José Ataño, "En La Muda. Un atropello," *La Democracia*, October 25, 1900, 1; "En Caguas: Otro escándalo electoral," *La Democracia*, October 31, 1900; "Caguas. Detenciones ilegales," *La Democracia*, April 24, 1901, 2; "Ilegalidades cometidas por el Juez de Policía de Caguas," *La Democracia*, July 15, 1901, 4; "Una circular del gobernador sobre la policía," *La Democracia*, August 15, 1902, 2.

64. "El Juez Bazán inicia sus funciones en Caguas," *La Democracia*, June 4, 1904, 3; "La policía en Caguas," *La Democracia*, July 19, 1904, 1; "Interesantes noticias de Caguas," La Democracia, September 10, 1904, 2.

65. "Ni en los tiempos más turbulentos se presenciaron en Caguas los atropellos que realiza hoy la Policía, y de todo estos hacemos responsables á los jefes del puesto, . . . Sólo deseamos probar una vez más que la Policía Insular de hoy es aquí la misma de 1902, y que si no hace más, es porque no cuenta con aquellos jueces que no sólo aprobaban todos sus desmanes sino que los fomentaban" (Dr. Plicke, "Desde Caguas. Atropellos bochornosos cometidos por la policía en este pueblo," *La Democracia*, September 23, 1907, 2. See also "Notas de Caguas," *La Democracia*, December 27, 1906, 2).

66. "Guardia Nacional," *La Democracia*, April 23, 1907, 3.

67. Cubano-Iguina, "El autonomismo en Puerto Rico."

68. "La cuestión de subsistencias," *El Buscapié*, September 13, 1885, 1; Bernardino Vásquez (secretary of the ayuntamiento de Isabela) to the ayuntamiento de Caguas, September 9, 1884, AHMC, SEC Gobierno, SSEC Asamblea Municipal, SER Correspondencia, 1884–86, C82.

69. AHMC, SEC Gobierno, SSEC Asamblea Municipal, SER Actas del Cabildo, 1884–85, C17, January 14, 1885.

70. Frank H. Hitchcock cited in Cabán, *Constructing a Colonial People*, 69.

71. Thompson, *Customs in Common*, 1.

72. "Un jíbaro no cree violar ningún derecho cuando se apropia un ave de corral, un racimo de plátanos ú otra pequeñez, que no por serlo deja, sin embargo, de ser propiedad ajena y por lo tanto nos está vedado utilizarla sin consentimiento de su dueño, ó si lo cree, no es porque esté convencido de que practica un acto reprobado, sino porque sabe que si le sorprenden le castigan. Seguramente no todos los jíbaros profesan este comunismo, pero

sí hay muchos que no muestran escrúpulo en practicarlo" (del Valle Atiles, *El campesino puertorriqueño*, 131).

73. Hobsbawn, *Primitive Rebels*, 15 and 24.

74. This type of redistribution has been historically echoed in other areas of the Caribbean. For instance, in a study of rural people in Providence Island, Peter J. Wilson argues that predial larceny, as well as trespassing on private property, constitutes a way of nibbling at the inequities. It helps maintain a social balance (*Crab Antics*, 67). In a study of northeast Brazil, Nancy Scheper-Hughes documents the acceptance of stealing from the rich among poor inhabitants of the region. One of the principal informants, a woman, recalled:

Well, Mama stayed with her rich old man for five years, and during this whole time she gradually gave away his belongings—food, clothing, money, even his silverware—to her friends and neighbors. She robbed the old man blind! . . . She's not the least bit ashamed of it. You might call it "stealing," but that's not how Mae looked at it at all. To her way of thinking it was just that the old man had so much of everything and her neighbors had so little that it was right and just to share some of it around. (Scheper-Hughes, *Death without Weeping*, 453, 464, 506)

María de los Reyes Castillo Bueno, a black woman from Santiago de Cuba, narrated how she entered a fabric store that had been broken into by "thieves." She helped herself to all the fabrics and materials she needed and then reflected, "In the end, what the thieves did was open the door and leave alms for me. I went back to bed, thinking how uneven the world was, some with so much, others with little or nothing" (Castillo Bueno, *Reyita*, 153–54).

75. Even in New Jersey, insecurity over property rights united farmers of different social strata (McConville, *These Daring Disturbers*, 65).

76. "Hase el espacio de tres ó cuatro años que no me dedico á los trabajos de agricultura, en virtud de que estos en aquellos terrenos no dan resultados satisfactorios ningunos" (Francisco Osuna to the Ilustre Ayuntamiento, June 16, 1885, AHMC, SEC Gobierno, SSEC Asamblea Municipal, SER Correspondencia, 1884–86, C82).

77. "Sobre diez años que me encuentro enferma que para comer tiene otro que darme la comida porque no puedo haser uso de mis manos y tengo un pedacito de tierra que no me produce nada." (Mercedes Negrón to the Sres. Presidente y Vocales del Ilustre Ayuntamiento, June 30, 1887, AHMC, SEC Gobierno, SSEC Asamblea Municipal, SER Correspondencia, 1887–88, C84).

78. AHMC, SEC Finanzas, SSEC Contribuciones, SER Planillas de Riqueza, SSER Agrícola, 1887, C87. Likewise, Dionisio Fontánez explained his incapacity to pay taxes due to his old age and illnesses (Dionisio Fontánez to the Sres. Presidente y Vocales del Ilustre Ayuntamiento, June 30, 1887, AHMC, SEC Gobierno, SSEC Asamblea Municipal, SER Correspondencia, 1887–88, C84). Fontánez had a farm of thirty-eight cuerdas in Barrio Borinquen, where he cultivated some tubers (sweet potato, malanga, and yautía) (AHMC, SEC Finanzas, SSEC Contribuciones, SER Planillas de Riqueza, SSER Agrícola, 1887, C87).

Similarly, María del Rosario Claudio had some rice and coffee on her sixty cuerdas of land in Barrio Tomás de Castro but felt she could not exploit her farm because she was "alone" (María del Rosario Claudio to the Ilustre Ayuntamiento, July 4, 1887, AHMC, SEC Gobierno, SSEC Asamblea Municipal, SER Correspondencia, 1887–88, C84; AHMC, SEC Finanzas, SSEC Contribuciones, SER Planillas de Riqueza, SSER Agrícola, 1887, C87).

79. Vassberg, *Land and Society*, 41, 54–56, 86–87; Nazario Velasco, *Discurso legal y orden poscolonial*, 197.

80. José G. Esterás to the Ilustre Ayuntamiento, June 27, 1888, AHMC, SEC Gobierno, SSEC Asamblea Municipal, SER Correspondencia, 1888–89, C85.

81. Luis Acosta (alcalde of Barrio Turabo) to the mayor of Caguas, January 9, 1880, AHMC, SEC Gobierno, SSEC Alcalde de Barrio, SER Correspondencia, 1880, C65.

82. Dionisio Martínez (comisario of Barrio Cañabón) to the mayor of Caguas, November 2, 1900, AHMC, SEC Secretaría, SSEC Seguridad Pública, SER Expedientes/Documentos, SSER Tribunal de Policía, 1900–1901, C60; G. García (mayor of Caguas) to Dionisio Martínez (alcalde of Barrio Cañabón), November 3 and 5, 1900, AHMC, SEC Secretaría, SSEC Seguridad Pública, SER Correspondencia, SSER Alcalde de Barrio, 1900–1909, C21. Lope Muñiz owned twelve cuerdas of land in Barrio Cañabón in 1900 (AHMC, SEC Finanzas, SSEC Contribuciones, SER Planillas de Riqueza, SSER Agrícola, 1900, C99).

83. Salvador Sánchez (comisario of Barrio Turabo) to the mayor of Caguas, March 2, 1899, AHMC, SEC Gobierno, SSEC Alcalde de Barrio, SER Correspondencia, 1899, C121.

84. Jesús Pereira (municipal police) to the mayor of Caguas, July 23, 1885, AHMC, SEC Gobierno, SSEC Alcalde de Barrio, SER Correspondencia, 1885, C78.

85. Gregorio Arroyo (alcalde of Barrio Tomás de Castro) to the mayor of Caguas, July 9, 1895, AHMC, SEC Gobierno, SSEC Alcalde de Barrio, SER Correspondencia, 1895, C104.

86. In the eighteenth century, English farmers also agreed on customary rights for the poor in order to guarantee a labor force in the area (Thompson, *Customs in Common*, 150–51).

87. Ignacio Lizardi Delgado to the tribunal de policía, June 9, 1900, AHMC, SEC Secretaría, SSEC Seguridad Pública, SER Expedientes/Documentos, SSER Tribunal de Policía, 1899–1900, C59.

88. In 1900 Don Marcos Estrada owned forty cuerdas of land in Barrio San Antonio (AHMC, SEC Finanzas, SSEC Contribuciones, SER Planillas de Riqueza, SSER Agrícola, 1900, C99).

89. José María Rodríguez (alcalde of Barrio San Antonio) to the juez municipal, October 18, 1900, AHMC, SEC Secretaría, SSEC Seguridad Pública, SER Expedientes/Documentos, SSER Tribunal de Policía, 1900–1901, C60.

90. Jesús Cortés to the comandante de la policía, September 7, 1900, AHMC, SEC Secretaría, SSEC Seguridad Pública, SER Expedientes/Documentos, SSER Tribunal de Policía, 1900–1901, C60.

91. In 1896 Morales was accused of robbery, and in May 1900 he stole from the farm of Pedro José de León, a small farmer in Barrio Tomás de Castro who raised chickens, turkeys, and other farm animals (José Ramírez to the mayor of Caguas, June 9, 1896, AHMC, SEC Gobierno, SSEC Alcalde de Barrio, SER Correspondencia, 1896, C108). Pedro José de León owned four cuerdas of land in Barrio Tomás de Castro in 1900 (AHMC, SEC Finanzas, SSEC Contribuciones, SER Planillas de Riqueza, SSER Agrícola, 1900, C99).

92. Gregorio Arroyo (alcalde of Barrio Tomás de Castro) to the mayor of Caguas, May 30, 1900, AHMC, SEC Secretaría, SSEC Seguridad Pública, SER Expedientes/Documentos, SSER Tribunal de Policía, 1899–1900, C59; G. García (mayor of Caguas) to the alcalde of Barrio Tomás de Castro, May 31, 1900, AHMC, SEC Secretaría, SSEC Seguridad Pública, SER Correspondencia, SSER Alcalde de Barrio, 1900–1909, C21.

93. Gregorio Arroyo (alcalde of Barrio Tomás de Castro) to the mayor of Caguas, April 23, 1900, AHMC, SEC Secretaría, SSEC Seguridad Pública, SER Expedientes/Documentos, SSER Tribunal de Policía, 1899–1900, C59. Neither Colón nor Rodríguez appeared in the tax records of Caguas, but Arroyo owned thirty-two cuerdas of land. Probably, Colón and

Rodríguez were rural laborers (AHMC, SEC Finanzas, SSEC Contribuciones, SER Planillas de Riqueza, SSER Agrícola, 1900, C99).

94. There are other examples of recurrent thieves. In February 1880 Juan José Negrón, a rural worker of Don Bartolomé Borrás's, stole ten *reales* worth of milk from his boss and a month later stole some more milk from Ramón Carrasquillo (José Martí [February 5, 1880] and Ramón Carrasquillo [March 10, 1880] to the mayor of Caguas, AHMC, SEC Gobierno, SSEC Alcalde de Barrio, SER Correspondencia, 1880, C65). The second example is Ecudemio Caez, who stole some sugar cane from Bartolomé Borrás in October and December 1900 in Barrio Cañabón (Bartolomé Borrás to the juez municipal, October 16, 1900, AHMC, SEC Secretaría, SSEC Seguridad Pública, SER Expedientes/Documentos, SSER Tribunal de Policía, 1900–1901, C60; Bartolomé Borrás to the mayor of Caguas, December 20, 1900, AHMC, SEC Gobierno, SSEC Alcalde de Barrio, SER Correspondencia [in box to be archived]). In 1906 Ramón González, who lived in Barrio Río Cañas, was in jail for six cases of robbery perpetrated a short period of time ("Desde Caguas," *La Democracia*, July 13, 1906, 2).

95. "En este barrio nó se puede trabajar, pues, casi todas las noches ai robos—de serdas—gallinas pabos sogas i frutas pues el que suscribe le an llebado en estos dias las sogas del ganado, i otras cosas" (Reportes de Policía, September 7, 1900, AHMC [in box to be organized]).

96. Yeomen's actions were accepted by their community within the legal realm (McConville, *These Daring Disturbers*, 96, 152).

97. Luis Acosta (alcalde of Barrio Turabo) to the mayor of Caguas, January 9, 1880, AHMC, SEC Gobierno, SSEC Alcalde de Barrio, SER Correspondencia, 1880, C65). (Luis Flores, peón caminero 39, Reporte, May 14, 1885, AHMC [in box to be organized]).

98. Ramón Grillo (alcalde of Barrio Cañaboncito) to the juez municipal, and other attached materials, January 8, 1900, AHMC, SEC Secretaría, SSEC Seguridad Pública, SER Expedientes/Documentos, SSER Tribunal de Policía, 1899–1900, C59.

99. See Picó, *1898*, and Negrón Portillo, *Cuadrillas anexionistas y revueltas campesinas*.

100. Modesto Solá y Rodríguez to the Ilustre Ayuntamiento, July 29, 1897, AHMC, SEC Gobierno, SSEC Asamblea Municipal, SER Correspondencia, 1894–98, C87.

101. Similarly, New Jersey gentry in the eighteenth century understood that in order to obtain economic autonomy, it was necessary to surrender some to the community (McConville, *These Daring Disturbers*, 92).

102. Interview with Ramón Fabres of Yauco by Alicia Suárez Fajardo, CHO, Expediente 1120; interview with Domitila Rodríguez, CHO, Expediente 925; interview with Margaro Falcón by Miguel Marrero, CHO, 1985; interview with Lorenzo Melecio Ortiz by Ivette Reyes Lebrón, CHO, Expediente 1427. Problems and sorrows were also shared by all. According to Ramona Cruz López, born in Cidra, when something bad happened to someone in the barrio, people rallied to help (interview with by Elizabeth Pérez Torres, CHO).

103. Guerra, *Popular Expression and National Identity*, 142.

104. Kinsbruner, *Not of Pure Blood*; Paquette, *Sugar Is Made with Blood*, part I.

105. Scott, *Slave Emancipation*, 123–24.

106. In 1866 there were 41,600 slaves in Puerto Rico, out of a total population of 600,000 inhabitants (H. Augustus Cowper, qtd. in Camuñas, *Hacendados y comerciantes en Puerto Rico*, 160).

107. Bolland, "Systems of Domination after Slavery," 591 and 619; Trouillot, "Discourses of Rule," "The Inconvenience of Freedom," and *Peasants and Capital*, chapter 5; and Holt, "The Essence of the Contract," 48.

108. AHMC, SEC Secretaría, SSEC Archivo, SER Censos, SSER Habitantes, 1882–83, C26.

109. AHMC, SEC Secretaría, SSEC Archivo, SER Censos, SSER Habitantes, 1882–83, C26.

110. By 1900 Francisco Díaz owned 160 cuerdas of land. However, most of his land was dedicated to woods and not production (AHMC, SEC Finanzas, SSEC Contribuciones, SER Padrones de Riqueza, SSER Agrícola, 1880–1900, C81–100).

111. Francisco Díaz to the Ilustre Ayuntamiento, July 3, 1887, AHMC, SEC Gobierno, SSEC Asamblea Municipal, SER Correspondencia, 1887–88, C84. Regino de León, for instance, describing his poor living conditions described himself as a *labriego*, a word like *labrador* that was often used to describe sharecropping. Nevertheless, de León owned a farm of thirty-five cuerdas of land in Barrio Cañaboncito (Regino De León to the Ilustre Ayuntamiento, July 12, 1882, AHMC, SEC Gobierno, SSEC Asamblea Municipal, SER Correspondencia, 1882–83, C5; AHMC, SEC Finanzas, SSEC Contribuciones, SER Planillas de Riqueza, SSER Agrícola, 1881–82, C82).

112. AHMC, SEC Finanzas, SSEC Contribuciones, SER Planillas de Riqueza, SSER Agrícola, 1887, C87.

113. AHMC, SEC Finanzas, SSEC Contribuciones, SER Padrones de Riqueza, SSER Agrícola, 1880–1900, C81–100.

114. In Bahia, Stuart B. Schwartz found that with time people of color became cane farmers (*Sugar Plantation*, 312).

115. AHMC, SEC Finanzas, SSEC Contribuciones, SER Padrones de Riqueza, SSER Agrícola, 1880–1900, C81–100.

116. AHMC, SEC Secretaría, SSEC Archivo, SER Censos, SSER Habitantes, 1882–83, C26.

117. In Cienfuegos, Cuba, former slaves did not automatically become "independent farmers," as feared by ex-slave owners (Sartorious, "Conucos y subsistencia," 121). In Havana and Matanzas, Cuba, former slaves also had very few opportunities to own land (Scott, *Slave Emancipation*, 262–63). The Puerto Rican and Cuban cases contrast with that of the British Caribbean, where small holdings increased as a direct result of emancipation (Blackburn, *The Overthrow of Colonial Slavery*, 464).

118. Departamento de la Guerra, *Dirección del Censo de Puerto Rico*, 298–300.

119. AHMC, SEC Finanzas, SSEC Contribuciones, SER Planillas de Riqueza, SSER Agrícola, 1882–83, C83.

120. AHMC, SEC Finanzas, SSEC Contribuciones, SER Planillas de Riqueza, SSER Agrícola, 1885–86, C86.

121. AHMC, SEC Finanzas, SSEC Contribuciones, SER Planillas de Riqueza, SSER Agrícola, 1890–91, C89.

122. In Cuba, Alejandro de la Fuente documents that in the first decades of the twentieth century, blacks' control over land decreased 50 percent (Fuente, *A Nation for All*, 106).

4. Stepping toward Liberation

1. McCurdy, *The Anti-Rent Era*, 70.

2. Suárez Findlay, *Imposing Decency*, 58.

3. Smith, "Race, Class, and Gender," 272.

4. Schmidt-Nowara discusses the position of José Julián Acosta in detail. Acosta claimed that the "lazyness of workers" was a direct consequence of the lack of "civilizing institutions" in Puerto Rico, representing tremendous barriers to progress (see Schmidt-Nowara, "The Problem of Slavery," 130).

5. "El obrero, salvo numerosas excepciones, que honran por cierto á la clase, no tiene

afición al trabajo ni á la buena educación laboriosa; no quiere sufrir el menor accidente que contraríe su modo de ser; basta que se le dirija la más leve corrección para que deje el trabajo y se marche; no tiene estímulo, emplea á veces su inteligencia, que no es poca, en conspirar contra los intereses del amo; efectúa en frecuentes ocasiones mal el trabajo intencionalmente, confiado en que pasará por bueno, se burla del dueño y cuando ha ganado la cantidad suficiente para satisfacer, no sus necesidades, sino sus caprichos, le importa poco el trabajo ni sus compromisos; deja la obra y se marcha, así tenga entre manos y á medio hacer el camarín de una Vírgen" (López Tuero, *Estudios de Economía Rural*, 9–10).

6. "Cuando el campesino se decide á prestar sus servicios, lo hace con buena voluntad; pero en honor de la verdad no se impone la obligación de ser estricto cumplidor de lo convenido, ni se afana por los objetos confiados á su custodia; trabaja y lo hace como pocos obreros, si se tiene en cuenta su insuficiente alimentación, pero mantiene una cierta independencia que á veces se traduce en falta de asistencia al trabajo á que se comprometió, y esto sin más razón que los impulsos de su voluntad" (del Valle Atiles, *El campesino puertorriqueño*, 137–38).

In 1917 a Redemptorist priest complained about the attitude of one employee, stating, "Roque Borges, the janitor, employed only 9 days ago, took his bundle of clothes on his shoulders and marched off in the direction of Borinquen. Too much work with the Padres, he said. It seems he came here to take life easy, sleep, eat and grow fat. It's hardly a calumny to say that he is minus some buttons" (*Crónicos de los Padres Redentoristas*, vol. 1, January 25, 1917).

7. "Reformemos, pues, nuestras leyes, evitando el desmembramiento de las propiedades rurales, la subdivisión sin término de las fincas, y según vaya extendiéndose el área de la propiedad, irá tomando mayor vuelo el de su labor, sustituyendo los grandes á los pequeños cultivos, yendo estos últimos a refugiarse á las huertas en los contornos de las poblaciones. Estimulemos el uso de las maquinarias agrícolas, que simplificando las faenas de la agricultura, arrojará al campesino de sus soledades, buscando en las poblaciones el empleo de sus brazos. . . . El pequeño propietario venderá su finca al que tenga mejores medios para explotarla, colocando su modesto capital en negocios más productivos; el desvalido marchará detrás del que pueda saciar sus necesidades. (P. Morales Cabrera, "La población rural, IV," *La Correspondencia*, March 17, 1897).

8. "Las clases proletarias en Puerto Rico," *El Buscapié*, October 1, 1882, 1; "Crisis obrera en Puerto Rico," *El Buscapié*, April 5, 1885, 1. In a letter to the U.S. governor of Puerto Rico requesting mercy for a well-to-do man, prominent Cagüeños stated: "Entendemos que las represiones de la ley acaban cuando se consigue la regeneración del responsable de un hecho punible, así como cesan los tratamientos de la medicina cuando triunfa la ciencia porque estirpa el cáncer y devuelve al paciente con la salud su vida" ("Indulto para un desgraciado: La sociedad de Caguas implora su perdón," *La Democracia*, June 19, 1901, 2 [letters and signatures follow the report]). When implementing moral and repressive measures, the upper classes did not necessarily practice their own propaganda but targeted the working population as the social infection. After all, only the working classes were considered to be part of the social problem.

9. Martínez-Vergne, *Shaping the Discourse on Space*, 135–44.

10. In San Juan, authorities' main objective was to train individuals for domestic labor (Félix Matos Rodríguez, "Gender and the Abolition of Slavery in Puerto Rico," April 7, 2003, lecture at the University of Connecticut Visiting Scholars in Gender and History).

11. Román, *Estado y criminalidad en Puerto Rico*, 2. New discoveries of criminal behavior were frequently published by the local press in Puerto Rico. The use of scientific methods to define the "criminal" was popular in the late nineteenth and early twentieth centuries. For example, head measurements represented a breakthrough technology in the early twentieth century ("El cerebro del criminal: Curiosas investigaciones," *La Democracia*, February 10, 1904, 2).

12. Acosta Lespier, "Poderes y resistencias," 144, 148.

13. In Ponce women represented 2.5 percent of criminal records in 1884, but after 1896, with the campaigns against prostitution, women constituted one-third of the records (Suárez Findlay, *Imposing Decency*, 91). In the rural barrios of Caguas, prostitution did not seem a concern for the authorities. The campaign against prostitution was launched mainly in the urban areas, but two women from the countryside were referred to as prostitutes (*vida licenciosa*) by authorities.

14. This is a perfect example of the relationship between scientific racism and colonialism. Trouillot argues that colonization provided the most potent impetus for the transformation of European ethnocentrism into scientific racism (*Silencing the Past*, 77).

15. Zeno Gandía, *La Charca*, 84–85. Although some intellectuals debated it, the mestizo theory was well accepted in the period. Manuel Fernández Juncos believed that the racial origin of peasants was white (Fernández Juncos, *Varias Cosas*, 92). In 1945 Ana Margarita Silva concluded, "Salvador Brau, Francisco del Valle Atiles, Agustín Navarrete y la mayoría de los autores extranjeros que no conocen bien nuestros campos, se inclinan hacia la mezcla de razas, mientras que Cayetano Coll y Toste, Angel Paniagua y Oller, Manuel Fernández Juncos, José Julián Acosta y varios escritores españoles, insisten en encontrar en nuestros campesinos los caracteres distintivos de la raza española" (see Silva, *El jíbaro en la literatura de Puerto Rico*, 18). In contrast to nineteenth-century intellectuals who emphasized that Puerto Rican peasants were white, most intellectuals today believe in the racially mixed nature of the Puerto Rican rural population (see Scarano, "The Jíbaro Masquerade," 1402, and Hernández, "Conquest Theory from the Puerto Rican Experience," 54).

16. "Las deficiencias de moralidad del negro han sido capaz de producir resultados dañosos en la índole moral del hombre de campo" (del Valle Atiles, *El campesino puertorriqueño*, 22–23 and 146).

17. Del Valle Atiles, *El campesino puertorriqueño*, 106.

18. Suárez Findlay, *Imposing Decency*, 56.

19. "Las razas débiles desaparecen ante las razas fuertes: es pues preciso para no ser aniquilados, alcanzar por el trabajo y la cultura intelectual y moral la fortaleza orgánica conveniente" (del Valle Atiles, *Cartilla de higiene*, 113–14). This text was used in the public schools of Puerto Rico in the late nineteenth century.

20. In Cuba, the census used the term *mestizo* (Fuente, *A Nation for All*, 31).

21. Duany, *The Puerto Rican Nation*, chapter 3. In 1905 *Chicago Inter Ocean* printed a cartoon representation comparing the skin color of Puerto Ricans and Cubans. Puerto Rico is represented as a dutiful, light skin child, while the image of a wild, black child embodies Cuba (the cartoon is reprinted in Johnson, *Latin America in Caricature*, 191).

22. "Conditions Existing in Porto Rico Upon the Assumption of Control by the U.S." in Headquarters Department of Porto Rico, "Report of Brig. Gen. Geo. W. Davis, V.S.V., on Civil Affairs of Puerto Rico. 1899," 56 Congress, 1 Session: House of Representatives, Document # 2, 784.

23. Miss Lilian D. Powers, "Report of the Twenty-Sixth Annual Meeting of the Lake

Mohonk Conference of Friends of the Indian and Other Dependent Peoples," 1908, 148. BKA Library, Ciencias Médicas, UPR Porto Rican Anemia Commission, Letters, Magazine Articles, C2.

24. Ashford and Gutierrez Igaravidez, *Uncinariasis (Hookworm Disease) in Porto Rico*, 8. See also George Adami, "The Conquest of Hookworm Disease," editorial in the *New York Medical Journal*, March 30, 1912. Porto Rico Anemia Commission. Discovery Uncinariasis, Founding of Commission, Newspaper Comment, Bailey K. Ashford Library, Ciencias Médicas, Box 1, Document 46; and Miss Lilian D. Powers, "Report of the Twenty-Sixth Annual Meeting," 148.

25. A. Huston to Dr. Bailey K. Ashford, Porto Rico Anemia Commission, Questionaire Physicians, Legislation, Reports Substations, Letters, Box 6, Expedient 5, p. 218. Some Puerto Rican doctors also supported the idea that Spanish colonial rule affected negatively Puerto Rican society but claimed that the lack of public health explained better the backwardness of the island (Dr. M. Quevedo Báez to Dr. Bailey K. Ashford, December 16, 1903, Porto Rico Anemia Commission, Questionaire Physicians, Legislation, Reports Substations, Letters, Box 6, Expedient 7, p. 306).

26. Duany, *The Puerto Rican Nation*, chapter 3.

27. Fuente, *A Nation for All*, 107.

28. Cooper, "Conditions Analogous to Slavery, 124–25."

29. See Acosta Lespier, "Poderes y resistencias."

30. Centro de Investigaciones Históricas, "Ley de abolición," documento 203, p. 144. Interestingly, the War of Independence in Cuba (1895–98) helped large landowners who increased their production in order to supply products to Cuba, such as tobacco and sugar (Mayor of Caguas to the alcalde of Barrio San Antonio, December 3, 1896, AHMC, SEC Secretaría, SSEC Seguridad Pública, SER Correspondencia, SSER Alcalde de Barrio, 1896, C17).

31. Cruz Monclova, *Historia de Puerto Rico*, vol. 2, part 2, 638 (ed. 1957).

32. Gómez Acevedo, *Organización y reglamentación del trabajo*, 279.

33. Fray Pepino, "Calderón y las cédulas de vecindad," *El Buscapié*, June 5, 1881, 2; "El recargo á las Cédulas de Vecindad," *El Buscapié*, September 27, 1892.

34. Centro de Investigaciones Históricas, "Proyecto de reglamento," documento 254, artículos 9, 10, 11, 14, and 18, pp. 344–50.

35. In Caguas the oldest existing cédulas date back to 1868.

36. José Martí, alcalde of Barrio Cañaboncito, to the mayor of Caguas, January 12, 1880, AHMC, SEC Gobierno, SSEC Alcalde, SER Correspondencia, 1880, C65.

37. Nistal Moret, *Esclavos, prófugos, y cimarrones*.

38. Centro de Investigaciones Históricas, "Proyecto de reglamento," documento 254, artículos 5 and 21, pp. 344–50. See also Picó, "Cafetal Adentro."

39. "Segun me escriben de Caguas, parece que allí hay empeño en atropellar á los pobres labradores, por pequeñas faltas que á otras personas se les toleran ó dispensan con facilidad. No hace muchos dias que fueron conducidos á la alcaldía dos honrados vecinos del barrio de Cañaboncito. El delito de que se les acusaba era el de no llevar la cédula en el bolsillo. El Alcalde, que bien pudo averiguar si la tenian ó no, por los talones que en aquella oficina se guardan, obligó á dichos vecinos á que fueran inmediatamente á sus respectivas casas, situadas á muchas distancia del pueblo, y le llevaran los documentos indicados. Hiciéronlo así los dos labradores, y despues de haber presentado sus cédulas en forma, fueron conde-

nados uno á seis dias de prision y otro á pagar seis duros de multa" (*El Buscapié*, August 15, 1880, 2).

40. Road patrol to the mayor of Caguas (and response), June 17, 1880, AHMC, SEC Gobierno, SSEC Alcalde de Barrio, SER Correspondencia, 1880, C66.

41. Mayor of Caguas to Eladio Caballero, alcalde of Barrio Culebras, (and response), April 13, 1881, AHMC, SEC Secretaría, SSEC Seguridad Pública, SER Correspondencia, SSER Alcalde de Barrio, 1880–1881, C8. In 1883 a policeman sent Manuel Soto to the mayor of Caguas for not having his cédula de vecindad (Mayor of Cayey to the mayor of Caguas, November 16, 1883, AHMC, SEC Gobierno, SSEC Alcalde, SER Correspondencia, 1884, C73). In 1884 Gil Ortiz and José Morales did not have identification when they were in Barrio Beatriz and were ordered to present themselves to the mayor of Caguas (Luis Báez to the mayor of Caguas, July 4, 1884, AHMC, SEC Gobierno, SSEC Alcalde de Barrio, SER Correspondencia, 1884, C75).

42. "Cédulas personales," *La Democracia*, May 5, 1897, 2.

43. Mayor of Caguas to the alcalde of Barrio Borinquen, April 27, 1882, AHMC, SEC Secretaría, SSEC Seguridad Pública, SER Correspondencia, SSER Alcalde de Barrio, 1881–82, C9.

44. Gómez Acevedo, *Organización y reglamentación del trabajo*, 39–40.

45. Mayor of Caguas to the alcaldes of Barrios Bairoa and Culebras, March 5, 1880, AHMC, SEC Secretaría, SSEC Seguridad Pública, SER Correspondencia, SSER Alcalde de Barrio, 1880–81, C5, 8; Mayor of Caguas to the alcaldes of Barrios Turabo and Culebras, July 1 and 8, 1881, AHMC, SEC Secretaría, SSEC Seguridad Pública, SER Correspondencia, SSER Alcalde de Barrio, 1880–82, C8, 9.

46. Rafael Polo, mayor of Caguas, to the alcaldes of Barrios Turabo, Río Cañas, and Bairoa, April 26, 1893, AHMC, SEC Secretaría, SSEC Seguridad Pública, SER Correspondencia, SSER Alcalde de Barrio, 1893, C14, 17.

47. Gómez Acevedo, *Organización y reglamentación del trabajo*. In the Dominican Republic, the Trujillo state charged the peasantry with the work of modernizing communication systems (San Miguel, *Los campesinos del Cibao*).

48. Vega to the juez municipal, October 5, 1883, AHMC, SEC Secretaría, SSEC Judicial, SER Libro Copiador, SSER Juzgados, 1883–89, C27.

49. Otero was a single man, born in Aguas Buenas, who had moved to Caguas seven years before with his widower father and four brothers. All of them were day laborers, and yet, only José Otero confronted problems with the legal authorities of Caguas. Otero also shared his home with Saturnino Rivera and Estefanía Pedraza, but this is not noted in the census (AHMC, SEC Secretaría, SSEC Archivo, SER Censos, SSER Habitantes, 1882–83, C26).

50. Vega to the juez municipal, October 29, 1883, AHMC, SEC Secretaría, SSEC Judicial, SER Libro Copiador, SSER Juzgados, 1883–89, C27.

51. Mayor of Caguas to Juan Santana, alcalde of Barrio Culebras (and response), March 24, 1881, AHMC, SEC Secretaría, SSEC Seguridad Pública, SER Correspondencia, SSER Alcalde de Barrio, 1880–81, C8.

52. Vega to the juez municipal, October 27, 1883, AHMC, SEC Secretaría, SSEC Judicial, SER Libro Copiador, SSER Juzgados, 1883–89, C27.

53. Mayor of Cayey to the mayor of Caguas, September 22, 1888, AHMC, SEC Gobierno, SSEC Alcalde de Barrio, SER Correspondencia, 1888, C86. In 1900 the municipal police of Caguas arrested Francisco Santiago because he was sleeping in one of the houses near the cemetery. Santiago claimed that he worked in the Hacienda San José, but the police did not

believe him (Ignacio Lizardi Delgado, Cabo Comandante, to the Tribunal de Policía, September 22, 1900, AHMC, SEC Secretaría, SSEC Seguridad Pública, SER Expedientes/Documentos, SSER Tribunal de Policía, 1900–1901, C60).

54. Matías Ledesmas, mayor of San Juan, to the mayor of Caguas, December 2, 1896, AHMC, SEC Gobierno, SSEC Alcalde de Barrio, SER Correspondencia, 1896, C111.

55. "Los jornaleros de una comarca emigran á otra, con detrimento de sus afecciones, de sus deberes domésticos, de los sagrados vínculos de la sociedad y de la familia; sin contar con que en este género de vida nómada y errante no hay medio de aprovechar eficazmente las ventajas de la instruccion, ni de los demás medios que actualmente se emplean ó que se empleen en lo sucesivo para mejorar las condiciones sociales de aquella clase infortunada" ("La contribución de los proletarios," *El Buscapié*, April 1, 1883, 1).

56. José María Rodríguez, alcalde of Barrio San Antonio, to the mayor of Caguas, November 11, 1897, AHMC, SEC Gobierno, SSEC Alcalde de Barrio, SER Correspondencia, 1897, C117.

57. José María Rodríguez to the mayor of Caguas, November 6 and 11, 1897, AHMC, SEC Gobierno, SSEC Alcalde de Barrio, SER Correspondencia, 1897, C117.

58. José María Rodríguez to the mayor of Caguas, December 4, 1897, AHMC, SEC Gobierno, SSEC Alcalde, SER Correspondencia, 1897, C117.

59. "Para el [Pedro Coto] no hay comisario pues el no hobedese cuando se nesesita que salga a dal un habiso" (José María Rodríguez to the mayor of Caguas, July 17, 1899, AHMC, SEC Gobierno, SSEC Alcalde de Barrio, SER Correspondencia, 1899 [in box to be organized]).

60. Juan Rodríguez to the mayor of Caguas, April 27, 1888, AHMC, SEC Secretaría, SSEC Seguridad Pública, SER Correspondencia, SSER Alcalde de Barrio, 1887–90, C12. Discontent with forced labor often translated into violence toward municipal officials or among workers. In 1881, for example, Juan Rodríguez, a resident of Barrio Beatriz, broke a tool while working on the road. The overseer reprimanded Rodríguez, who in response verbally assaulted him (Assistant of Public Work to the mayor of Caguas, January 14, 1881, AHMC, SEC Secretaría, SSEC Seguridad Pública, SER Expedientes/Documentos, SSER Tribunal de Policía, 1899–1900, C59).

61. Mayor of Caguas to the alcalde of Barrio Turabo, October 1, 1880, AHMC, SEC Secretaría, SSEC Seguridad Pública, SER Correspondencia, SSER Alcalde de Barrio, 1880, C5.

62. Picó, *El día menos pensado*, 28. Examples of prisoners who escaped having to work on the roads were Anselmo Cruz, originally from Barrio Tomás de Castro, and Juan Nepomuceno González (Vega to the juez municipal, November 5, 1883. AHMC, SEC Secretaría, SSEC Judicial, SER Libro Copiador, SSER Juzgados, 1883–89, C27; Mayor of Caguas to the alcaldes de barrio, July 20, 1880, AHMC, SEC Secretaría, SSEC Seguridad Pública, SER Correspondencia, SSER Alcalde de Barrio, 1880, C7). In 1903 laborers in Caguas condemned the use of prisoners' labor in the road by writing a protest letter to the mayor (Laborers of Caguas to the mayor of Caguas as published in *La Democracia*, May 5, 1903, 5).

63. Acting secretary of Puerto Rico to the mayor of Caguas, June 4, 1906, AHMC, SEC Gobierno, SSEC Alcalde de Barrio, SER Correspondencia, 1906, C136.

64. Guerra, *Popular Expression and National Identity*, 170–211.

65. "Gobierno General de la Isla de Puerto Rico." First published in *La Gaceta de Puerto Rico*, April 18, 1876, Centro de Investigaciones Históricas, *El proceso abolicionista en Puerto Rico*, documento #280, pp. 447–50.

66. Antonio Ramírez to the mayor of Caguas, January 29, 1880, AHMC, SEC Gobierno, SSEC Alcalde de Barrio, SER Correspondencia, 1880, C65.

67. Mayor of Caguas to the alcaldes de barrio, June 1, 1880, AHMC, SEC Secretaría, SSEC Seguridad Pública, SER Correspondencia, SSER Alcalde de Barrio, 1880, C5.

68. During the first three-quarters of the nineteenth century, comisarios, too, avoided denouncing people to the police to avoid confrontations and personal enemies (Gómez Acevedo, *Organización y reglamentación del trabajo*, 206).

69. "Se les impondrá la pena que hubiere lugar tratandoles como incubridores de individuos sin ocupacion lucrativa" (Mayor of Caguas to the alcaldes de barrio, January 30, 1880, AHMC, SEC Secretaría, SSEC Seguridad Pública, SER Correspondencia, SSER Alcalde de Barrio, 1880–81, C8).

70. "Gobierno General de la Isla de Puerto Rico." First published in *La Gaceta de Puerto Rico*. April 18, 1876. Centro de Investigaciones Históricas, *El proceso abolicionista en Puerto Rico*, Documento # 280, 447–50.

71. In 1888 the comisario of Barrio Beatriz reported some individuals who engaged in illegal games (Mayor of Caguas to the juez municipal, March 8, 1888, AHMC, SEC Secretaría, SSEC Judicial, SER Libro Copiador, SSER Juzgados, 1883–89, C27.

72. Mayor of Caguas to José Y. Esterás, alcalde of Barrio Cañabón, March 9, 1880, AHMC, SEC Secretaría, SSEC Seguridad Pública, SER Correspondencia, SSER Alcalde de Barrio, 1880–81, C8. In 1884 a municipal guard caught a rural laborer from the same hacienda playing prohibited games in Barrio Cañabón (Mayor of Caguas to the juez municipal, May 13, 1884, AHMC, SEC Secretaría, SSEC Judicial, SER Libro Copiador, SSER Juzgados, 1883–89, C27). In 1890 Vicente Díaz, comisario of Barrio Cañabón, solicited the assistance of the police through the mayor of Caguas in order to catch some individuals who were playing illegal games in the barrio (Vicente Díaz to the mayor of Caguas, October 11, 1890, AHMC, SEC Gobierno, SSEC Alcalde de Barrio, SER Correspondencia, 1890, C90). In 1898 the mayor of Caguas heard of cockfights in Barrio Cañabón and directed the alcalde de barrio to take legal action (Mayor of Caguas to Dionisio Martínez, December 9, 1898, AHMC, SEC Secretaría, SSEC Seguridad Pública, SER Correspondencia, SSER Alcalde de Barrio, 1898, C19).

73. In 1894 the mayor of Caguas wrote to the alcalde of Barrio Cañaboncito reminding him to report individuals who engaged in cockfights. The letter also stated that cockfights took place in this barrio quite commonly and the alcalde the barrio did not notice (F. Méndez to the alcalde of Barrio Cañaboncito, December 4, 1894. AHMC, SEC Secretaría, SSEC Seguridad Pública, SER Correspondencia, SSER Alcalde de Barrio, 1894, C15). In 1895 the mayor of Caguas wrote the alcaldes de barrio, stressing that cockfights were prohibited in the countryside (Arturo Más to the alcalde of Barrio Borinquen, October 16, 1895, AHMC, SEC Secretaría, SSEC Seguridad Pública, SER Correspondencia, SSER Alcalde de Barrio, 1895, C16).

74. In 1890 Juan Jiménez Saurí held thirty-two cuerdas of land (AHMC, SEC Finanzas, SSEC Contribuciones, SER Planillas de Riqueza, SSER Agrícola, 1890–91, C89).

75. Ildefonso Suarez, cabo of the civil guard, to the mayor of Caguas, December 15, 1890, AHMC, SEC Gobierno, SSEC Alcalde de Barrio, SER Correspondencia, 1890, C90.

76. Affidavits by Ignacio Lizardi Delgado and Regis Ramos, July 1, 1890 and July 1, 1891, AHMC, SEC Secretaría, SSEC Judicial, SER Expedientes/Documentos, SER Expedientes/Documentos, 1860–1917, C9.

77. After 1898 the U.S. government in the island also prohibited cockfights (Mayor of Caguas to the alcalde of Barrio Turabo, October 13, 1898, AHMC, SEC Secretaría, SSEC Seguridad Pública, SER Correspondencia, SSER Alcalde de Barrio, 1898, C19). In 1900 the

guards caught Isidoro Gotay and other individuals in Barrio Río Cañas playing prohibited games (Insular police to the president of the tribunal de policía, April 22, 1900, AHMC, SEC Secretaría, SSEC Seguridad Pública, SER Expedientes/Documentos, SSER Tribunal de Policía, 1899–1900, C59). In 1907 the newspaper reported that the police caught a group of people in a cockfight in Caguas ("Notas de Caguas," *La Democracia*, February 15, 1907, 2).

78. Bartolomé Borrás to the mayor of Caguas, February 10, 1900, AHMC, SEC Secretaría, SSEC Seguridad Pública, SER Expedientes/Documentos, SSER Tribunal de Policía, 1899–1900, C59; G. García, mayor of Caguas, to the alcalde of Barrio Cañabón, February 12, 1900, AHMC, SEC Secretaría, SSEC Seguridad Pública, SER Correspondencia, SSER Alcalde de Barrio, 1900–1909, C21; Michael A. Brook to the mayor of Caguas, October 2, 1900, AHMC, SEC Secretaría, SSEC Seguridad Pública, SER Expedientes/Documentos, SSER Tribunal de Policía, 1900–1901, C60.

79. S. López to the mayor of Caguas (and response), February 2, 1880, AHMC, SEC Gobierno, SSEC Alcalde de Barrio, SER Correspondencia, 1880, C65. Alcohol was tremendously popular during the Christmas holiday season. In 1889 Gavino Cazuela, alcalde of Barrio Borinquen, solicited the assistance of the police in order to avoid public scandal caused by a neighbor's drunkenness (Gavino Cazuela to the mayor of Caguas, December 24, 1889. AHMC, SEC Gobierno, SSEC Alcalde de Barrio, SER Correspondencia, 1889, C88).

80. Joaquín Aponte to the comisario of Barrio Borinquen (and responses from the comisario and the mayor of Caguas), January 4, 1880, AHMC, SEC Gobierno, SSEC Alcalde, SER Correspondencia, 1880, C65. Likewise, in 1881 Ruperto Caballero reported to the alcalde de barrio Felipe Colón's aggressive behavior resulting from his drunken status. Two years later municipal authorities arrested Colón again for drunkenness and violence. This time Colón wounded another man with a small sword (Ruperto Caballero to the alcalde of Barrio Borinquen [and response], April 3, 1881, AHMC, SEC Secretaría, SSEC Seguridad Pública, SER Correspondencia, SSER Alcalde de Barrio, 1881–82, C9; Vicente [?] to Juan Delgado [and responses from the comisario and the municipal judge], May 6, 1883, AHMC, SEC Secretaría, SSEC Seguridad Pública, SER Correspondencia, SSER Comisario de Barrio, 1880–1906, C24).

81. Trías Monge, *El sistema judicial de Puerto Rico*, 40.

82. Roniger and Herzog, *The Collective and the Public*, 8.

83. "Don Manuel Vélez, vecino de ese barrio, ha desobedecido abiertamente á mis órdenes, no concurriendo, en el día de hoy, ante mi Autoridad, á pesar de habérselo citado oportunamente" (Mayor of Caguas to the alcalde of Barrio Cañaboncito, April 2, 1880, AHMC, SEC Secretaría, SSEC Seguridad Pública, SER Correspondencia, SSER Alcalde de Barrio, 1880, C5).

84. "Para que mañana, sin falta, concurra a esta Alcaldía, apercibiendole *con mayor pena* caso de desobediencia" (Mayor of Caguas to the alcalde of Barrio Cañaboncito, April 2, 1880, AHMC, SEC Secretaría, SSEC Seguridad Pública, SER Correspondencia, SSER Alcalde de Barrio, 1880, C5).

85. Mayor of Caguas to the alcalde of Barrio Cañaboncito, April 9, 1881, AHMC, SEC Secretaría, SSEC Seguridad Pública, SER Correspondencia, SSER Alcalde de Barrio, 1880–81, C8.

86. Mayor of Caguas to the alcalde of Barrio Tomás de Castro, December 15, 1880. AHMC, SEC Secretaría, SSEC Seguridad Pública, SER Correspondencia, SSER Alcalde de Barrio, 1880, C5.

87. Mayor of Caguas to the alcalde of Barrio Tomás de Castro, December 16, 1880,

AHMC, SEC Secretaría, SSEC Seguridad Pública, SER Correspondencia, SSER Alcalde de Barrio, 1880, C5.

88. In 1880 Toribio Vázquez and Toribio Forastier from Barrio Tomás de Castro, Álvaro Medina and Felipe Rosa from Borinquen used distance as an excuse to avoid authorities (Mayor of Caguas to the alcalde of Barrio Tomás de Castro, February 14, 1880, and Mayor of Caguas to the alcaldes de barrio, October 1, 1880, both in AHMC, SEC Secretaría, SSEC Seguridad Pública, SER Correspondencia, SSER Alcalde de Barrio, 1880, C5).

89. For example, a man named Cirilo Cruz kept moving from barrio to barrio to avoid authorities. Authorities believed that his residence was officially in Barrio Tomás de Castro but were never able to confirm (Mayor of Caguas to the alcalde of Barrio Tomás de Castro, July 8, 1880. AHMC, SEC Secretaría, SSEC Seguridad Pública, SER Correspondencia, SSER Alcalde de Barrio, 1880, C5). Moving temporarily to another municipality often achieved the same effect. Ramón Maimí in 1881 moved from Barrio Turabo to Cayey (Mayor of Caguas to the alcalde of Barrio Turabo, May 5, 1881, AHMC, SEC Secretaría, SSEC Seguridad Pública, SER Correspondencia, SSER Alcalde de Barrio, 1881–82, C9). Likewise, Felipe Medina, resident of Barrio Borinquen, left to move to Hato Grande in 1884 (Mayor of Caguas to the alcalde of Barrio Borinquen, July 13, 1884, AHMC, SEC Secretaría, SSEC Seguridad Pública, SER Correspondencia, SSER Alcalde de Barrio, 1883–85, C11).

90. Luis Acosta to the mayor of Caguas, May 1, 1881, AHMC, SEC Secretaría, SSEC Seguridad Pública, SER Correspondencia, SSER Alcalde de Barrio, 1881–82, C9.

91. "El campesino piensa que las leyes son algo misterioso elaborado no con el propósito de protegerle, sino con el fin de oprimirle" (Luis Muñoz Rivera qtd. in Trías Monge, *El sistema judicial de Puerto Rico*, 44). Trías Monge agrees with Muñoz Rivera's assessment of peasants' attitude toward the law.

92. Camuñas, *Hacendados y comerciantes*, 157–58.

93. Nistal Moret, *Esclavos, prófugos, y cimarrones*, 67–70.

94. Kinsbruner, *Not of Pure Blood*, 25.

95. Although in general leaving the plantations represented a goal for most former slaves in the Caribbean, ex-slaves had different levels of success as far as their ability to acquire land, depending on the region where they lived. In the Dominican Republic, for example, former slaves were very successful abandoning plantation zones and forming peasant communities. Also, in eastern Cuba, former slaves had a good chance of obtaining land. In contrast, most ex-slaves in Matanzas, Cuba, remained in the plantation zones. See Ayala, *American Sugar Kingdom*, 20, 150, 158, and 185. In Cienfuego, Cuba, a group of former slaves formed a peasant community at the outskirts of the plantation where they used to work (see Sartorious, "Conucos y subsistencia," and Stein, *Vassouras*, 268.

96. AHMC, SEC Secretaría, SSEC Archivo, SER Censos, SSER Habitantes, 1882–83, C26.

97. Scott, *Slave Emancipation*, 50.

98. AHMC, SEC Secretaría, SSEC Archivo, SER Censos, SSER Esclavos, 1867–73, C19.

99. AHMC, SEC Secretaría, SSEC Archivo, SER Censos, SSER Habitantes, 1882–83, C26.

100. AHMC, SEC Secretaría, SSEC Archivo, SER Censos, SSER Esclavos, 1867–73, C19; AHMC, SEC Secretaría, SSEC Archivo, SER Censos, SSER Habitantes, 1882–83, C26.

101. Cabán, *Constructing a Colonial People*, 143.

102. "Sixteenth Annual Report of the Governor of Porto Rico." War Department Annual Report, 1916, 4; and War Department, "Education in Porto Rico. Letter from the Secretary of War in Response to Resolution of the Senate of April 12, 1900, A Letter from Brig.

Gen. George W. Davis, together with the Reports of Dr. Victor S. Clark, and Other Papers Accompanying the Same, Relative to Education in Porto Rico," 1900, 4–5, 8.

103. "First Annual Report of Charles H. Allen," Governor of Porto Rico, Covering the Period from May 1, 1900, to May 1, 1901," 1902, 98.

104. Marcus, "Labor Conditions in Porto Rico," 46–48.

105. "La anemia y la ignorancia," *La República Española*, March 19, 1905; Porto Rico Anemia Commission, Discovery Uncinariasis, Founding of Commission, Newspaper Comment, Bailey K. Ashford, Box 1, Document 151b; Geo. R. Colton, governor of Puerto Rico, "Tenth Annual Report of the Governor of Porto Rico," September 1, 1910, War Department Annual Reports, 1910, 61 Congress, 3 Session House of Representatives, Document # 1002, p. 39; Dr. A. Stahl, "Dr. Stahl sobre trabajo Ashford," Porto Rico Anemia Commission, Discovery Uncinariasis, Founding of Commission, Newspaper Comment, Bailey K. Ashford, Box 7, pp. 1–69, Document 231c; War Department, "Conditions in Porto Rico," document 615, p. 7.

106. "Cuestionario," from José M. Batista, Corozal, Sala Bailey K. Ashford, Letters to Dr. Ashford from José E. Morales, Aguas Buenas, July 27, and August 10, 1912, Sala Bailey K. Ashford, Document 56; Letter to Dr. Ashford from Ramón Muñoz, Aguas Buenas, August 14, 1912, Sala Bailey K. Ashford, Document 52; Letter to Dr. Ashford from Félix Muñoz Grillo, Caguas, August 17, 1912, Sala Bailey K. Ashford, Document 136; Letter to Dr. Ashford from Rafael Arce, Caguas, August 21, 1912, Sala Bailey K. Ashford, Document 134; "Cuestionario," signed by Ramón Muñoz, Nicolás Quiñonez Cabezudo, José E. Morales, Ramón Caballero, Marcelino Solá, Félix Muñoz Grillo, and Rafael Arce, Sala Bailey K. Ashford, Documents 54, 60, 130, 133, 135, and 141.

107. "Avaunt the Lazy Bug. That Tired Feeling Now on the Run in Porto Rico," Porto Rico Anemia Commission, Discovery Uncinariasis, Founding of Commission, Newspaper Comment, Bailey K. Ashford, Box 7, pp. 1–69, Document 176a-b.

108. "First Annual Report of Charles H. Allen, Governor of Porto Rico, Covering the Period from May 1, 1900, to May 1, 1901," 1902, 99.

109. Bird Carmona, *A Lima y Machete*, 127–34.

110. Bird Carmona, *A Lima y Machete*, 41–42.

111. Marcus, "Labor Conditions in Porto Rico," 18.

112. See Dávila Santiago, *El derribo de las murallas*.

113. Dávila Santiago, *El derribo de las murallas*, 84.

114. Cabán, *Constructing a Colonial People*, 242.

115. Bureau of Labor, Government of Porto Rico, "Special Bulletin," 30, 34.

116. Bureau of Labor, Government of Porto Rico, "Special Bulletin," 6, 11–12.

117. Bird Carmona, *A Lima y Machete*, 96–97; and Archivo General de Puerto Rico (AGPR), Libro de Novedades de la Policía de Puerto Rico, F Policía de Puerto Rico, SER Libro de Novedades, Caguas, February, 1932.

118. On November 15, 1931, for example, laborers of Barrio Río Cañas participated in a rally called by the Socialist Party (AGPR, Libro de Novedades de la Policía de Puerto Rico, F Policía de Puerto Rico, SER Libro de Novedades, Caguas, November 15, 1931).

5. Marginal but Not Equal

1. The phrase the "long nineteenth century" refers to the end of the eighteenth century through the 1920s. Traditionally, the history of nineteenth-century Latin America was informed by positivism and notions of progress and assumed that the position of women also

improved. However, concrete studies of the effects of government policies in women's lives demonstrate that, in fact, women's position in society often deteriorated throughout the nineteenth century (Dore, "One Step Forward, Two Steps Back," 5).

2. J. A. y M., "La oración en el hogar doméstico," *Boletín Eclesiástico*, Año XXXIV: Number 8. April 15, 1892, 89–96, 90, 92; and Juan Antonio Puig y Monserrat, Bishop of Puerto Rico, "Carta Pastoral," *Boletín Eclesiástico*, Año XXI, Number 5, March 1, 1879, 5–63, AHD.

3. Schmidt-Nowara, "The Problem of Slavery," 214, 220. The Catholic Church also proclaimed that women were guardians of home life, responsible for future generations (J. A. y M. "La oración en el hogar doméstico," *Boletín Eclesiástico*, Año XXXIV: Number 8. April 15, 1892, 89–96, 90, 93, AHD). Women also had the responsibility for maintaining healthy marriages through their beauty and sensibility ("Influencia de la mujer en el matrimonio," *El Buscapié*, November 25, 1883, 1).

4. Findlay, "Domination, Decency, and Desire," 90 and 113.

5. Suárez Findlay, *Imposing Decency*, 59. From the eighteenth century on in European countries, family life was a focus of reform. Jacques Donzelot explains that many philanthropic and religious associations aimed at helping and moralizing the poorer classes by concentrating their efforts toward the restoration of family life (understood as the first and the most economical means of mutual aid) (Donzelot, *The Policing of Families*, 32).

6. Schmidt-Nowara, "The Problem of Slavery," 232. See also Findlay, "Domination, Decency, and Desire" 117, 120.

7. The Catholic Church held the idea that sensuality reduced men and women to the mental and physical condition of bestiality (V.S. y M., "El sensualismo embrutece al hombre," *Boletín Eclesiástico*, Año XXVI: Number 14 [July 15, 1884], 163–67, AHD).

8. Findlay, "Domination, Decency, and Desire" 41, 52, and 120; Suárez-Findlay, *Imposing Decency*, 58.

9. Dore, "One Step Forward, Two Steps Back," 9.

10. Holt, "The Essence of the Contract," 40.

11. Francisco Báez was arrested in La Muda, Caguas (*La Correspondencia*, May 10, 1897). In 1900 Rodulfo Renta accused his son of lack of respect and going to the extreme of slapping his father's face (Manuel Muñoz, comisario of Barrio Borinquen, to the mayor of Caguas, October 1, 1900, AHMC, SEC Secretaría, SSEC Seguridad Pública, SER Expedientes/Documentos, SSER Tribunal de Policía, 1900–1901, C60). Sometimes women, too, used authorities to strengthen their own authority with rebellious children. For example, in 1880 Andrea García solicited the mayor's help when her seven-year-old son ran away from her house (Mayor of Caguas to the alcaldes of Barrio Cañabón, Cañaboncito, Tomás de Castro, and Cagüitas, September 15, 1880, AHMC, SEC Secretaría, SSEC Seguridad Pública, SER Correspondencia, SSER Alcalde de Barrio, 1880, C7). On December 5, 1908, Maximo Roja, a ten-year-old mulatto, ran away from his father's house in Barrio Turabo (AGPR, F Policía de Puerto Rico, SER Novedades, SSER Correspondencia, T57-P, C4, December 5, 1908).

12. Francisco Rivera, alcalde of Barrio Bairoa, to the mayor of Caguas, November 25, 1897, AHMC, SEC Gobierno, SSEC Alcalde de Barrio, SER Correspondencia, 1897, C117.

13. In the nineteenth century women asked for government assistance mainly to maintain male support. This trend continued in the twentieth century, becoming women's main reason for divorce (Suárez Findlay, *Imposing Decency*, 125).

14. "Tiene en éste barrio abandonada su familia, sin que en el periodo de seis meses que

desapareció le haya enviado ninguna clase de alimentos, ni medios de proporsionarselos . . . vive dicha familia á merced de la caridad pública, y sufriendo además desnudez y enfermedades" (J. Y. Esterás to the mayor of Caguas, March 29, 1880, AHMC, SEC Gobierno, SSEC Alcalde de Barrio, SER Correspondencia, 1880, C65).

15. Mayor of Hato Grande to the mayor of Caguas, January 16, 1892, AHMC, SEC Gobierno, SSEC Alcalde de Barrio, SER Correspondencia, 1892, C93.

16. Stern, *The Secret History of Gender*, 98–111.

17. Manuel Rodríguez to the mayor of Caguas, July 19, 1880, AHMC, SEC Gobierno, SSEC Alcalde de Barrio, SER Correspondencia, 1880, C66. Rodríguez owned a farm in Barrio Tomás de Castro of sixty cuerdas, while Don José Domingo López was the comisario and owned a store (*bodegón*) (AHMC, SEC Finanzas, SSEC Contribuciones, SER Planillas de Riqueza, SSER Agrícola, 1880–81, C81; José D. López to the mayor of Caguas, March 15, 1884, AHMC, SEC Gobierno, SSEC Alcalde de Barrio, SER Correspondencia, 1884, C74).

18. Manuel Rodríguez was born in the Canary Islands. In 1882 he was eighty years old and had lived in Caguas for forty years. Rodríguez lived with his wife, Clara Miranda, and their children: Berta, Juana, Miguel, and Juliana. His granddaughter was also living in the same house (AHMC, SEC Secretaría, SSEC Archivo, SER Censos, SSER Habitantes, 1882–1883, C26).

19. Mayor of Caguas to the juez municipal, February 26, 1884, AHMC, SEC Secretaría, SSEC Judicial, SER Libro Copiador, SSER Juzgados, 1883–89, C27.

20. Donzelot, *The Policing of Families*, 32.

21. Suárez Findlay, *Imposing Decency*, 111–12, 122; Nazario Velasco, *Discurso legal y orden poscolonial*, chapter 6.

22. "Juzgado de Paz de Caguas. Causa Criminal contra Pedro Cortés por lesiones," 1902, AHMC, SEC Secretaría, SSEC Judicial, SER Juicios, 1902, C21.

23. "Criminal. Sumario contra Ramona Nerí sobre lesiones á Anselma Bernal," June 1902, AHMC, SEC Secretaría, SSEC Judicial, SER Juicios, 1865–1902, C20.

24. Suárez Findlay, *Imposing Decency*, 48.

25. Ramón Grillo, comisario of Barrio Cañaboncito, to the mayor of Caguas, February 9, 1900, AHMC, SEC Secretaría, SSEC Seguridad Pública, SER Expedientes/Documentos, SSEC Tribunal de Policía, 1899–1900, C59.

26. G. García, mayor of Caguas, to the alcalde of Barrio Cañaboncito, February 10, 1900, AHMC, SEC Secretaría, SSEC Seguridad Pública, SER Expedientes/Documentos, SSEC Tribunal de Policía, 1899–1900, C59. In 1900 Julia Guzmán told people in Barrio Bairoa that Isabel Martínez was cheating on her husband with the farm owner, Don Benito Domínguez. Isabel responded by reporting Guzmán to the police because her husband had started to believe the gossip (Ignacio Lizardi Delgado, comandante del puesto, to the Tribunal de Policía, June 13, 1900, and G. García, mayor of Caguas, to the alcalde of Barrio Bairoa, June 14, 1900, both in AHMC, SEC Secretaría, SSEC Seguridad Pública, SER Expedientes/Documentos, SSER Tribunal de Policía, 1899–1900, C59).

Through her husband, Sebastiana González accused Nicolasa Ramos, a sharecropper in Barrio Cañabón, of slander (Manuel López to the tribunal, April 18, 1900, AHMC, SEC Secretaría, SSEC Seguridad Pública, SER Expedientes/Documentos, SSER Tribunal de Policía, 1899–1900, C59).

27. "No le tiene miedo a la justicia y tambien me han declarado que Anastasia se linpia el trasero con el comisario que el comisario no le hase ni letra. Señor Alcalde hay que determinar hargun deber con esta mujer y de no llo no esisto mas de comisario por que esta mujer puede

hatrael un compromiso como ha hido el hermano Casimiro Estrada con una hoja de sable a la casa de Miguel a desafiarlo" (José María Rodríguez to the mayor of Caguas, July 12, 1900, AHMC, SEC Secretaría, SSEC Seguridad Pública, SER Expedientes/Documentos, SSER Tribunal de Policía, 1900–1901, C60).

28. In 1901 the press reported a fire in Barrio Bairoa, where a house (*bohío*) was reduced to ashes. Two of the female residents were absent because they were working in the field ("Incendio en Bairoa," *La Democracia*, March 25, 1901). In 1924 the labor press published an article about the important role of women in agriculture ("La mujer en Puerto Rico," *Justicia*, January 21, 1924, 13).

29. Francisco del Valle Atiles compared legal marriage to consensual union and stressed the hygienic condition of the former as opposed to the latter (del Valle Atiles, *Cartilla de higiene*, 112–13; Nazario Velasco, *Discurso legal y orden postcolonial*, 265–69).

30. J. Rodríguez Castro, "El jornalero puertorriqueño," *El Buscapié*, June 18, 1882, 1.

31. Del Valle Atiles, *El campesino puertorriqueño*, 146.

32. Rosario, *The Development of the Puerto Rican Jíbaro*, 83. Francisco M. Zeno explained prevalence of consensual unions in the nineteenth century, stating that "los numerosos requisitos exigidos anteriormente por el rito católico, las 'proclamas,' el espediente de 'impedimentos, etc., etc., resultaban demasiado complicados para la atolondrada mentalidad del ignorante labriego; y recurrir por aquella época donde el Juez, dentro de aquel medioambiente de intolerancia religiosa, implicaba provocar el enojo de la superior autoridad del sacerdote, en la comisión de un vituperante sacrilegio" ("the multiple requirements of the Catholic ritual, the 'proclamation,' the 'impediment' file, etc., etc., were too complicated for the hare-brained mentality of the ignorant laborer; and in a period of religious intolerance, to resort to the Judge implied provoking the anger of the priest's superior authority, a sacrilege)" (Zeno, "El obrero agrícola o de los campos," 71–72).

33. Nazario Velasco, *Discurso legal y orden postcolonial*, 274–83; "Modificación de la ley de matrimonio," *La Democracia*, March 24, 1899; "Proyecto de ley presentado por Mr. Harlan y aprobado por ambas Cámaras: Definiendo el matrimonio natural y estableciendo un procedimiento para legitimar é inscribir dicha unión," *La Democracia*, March 14, 1903, 2.

34. "El concubinato, con sus secuelas de la basatardía y la bigamia, va siendo reemplazado por el matrimonio canónico y civil, y por tanto, el estado social del campesino puertorriqueño, en relación con este órgano vital e institucional de nuestra sociedad, es francamente, evolutivo en evolución ascendente" (Meléndez Muñoz, *Estado social del campesinado*, 351).

35. Suárez Findlay, *Imposing Decency*, 121.

36. AHMC, SEC Secretaría, SSEC Archivo, SER Expedientes/Documentos, SSER Matrimonios, 1866–1933, C145–50.

37. Rosario, *The Development of the Puerto Rican Jíbaro*, 84.

38. According to U.S. records, in Caguas in 1888 there were thirty-one marriages, fifteen in 1889, sixty-four in 1890, sixty-nine in 1891, eighty-one in 1892, seventy-five in 1893, seventy in 1894, seventy-seven in 1895, sixty-six in 1896, eighty-three in 1897, and fifty-four in 1898 (Departamento de la Guerra, *Informe sobre el censo de Puerto Rico, 1899*, 352).

39. Nazario Velasco, *Discurso legal y orden postcolonial*, 283.

40. Nazario Velasco, *Discurso legal y orden postcolonial*, 280–81.

41. Kinsbruner, *Not of Pure Blood*, 21. See also Schwartz, *Sugar Plantation*, 248.

42. In nineteenth-century Cuba, young people also used elopement to curb parental opposition to their loved ones (see Martínez-Alier, *Marriage, Class, and Colour,* chapter 7).

43. Ruggiero, *The Boundaries of Eros,* 11.

44. "Declaración de Gumersindo Nieves y Alicea," AGPR, F Judicial de Guayama, SF Tribunal General de Justicia, SEC Tribunal Superior de Guayama, SER Expedientes Criminales, SSER Cidra, C724.

45. Marcelino Solá, alcalde of Barrio Borinquen, to the mayor of Caguas, January 26, 1880, AHMC, SEC Gobierno, SSEC Alcalde de Barrio, SER Correspondencia, 1880, C65.

46. Gabriel Dalmau to the mayor of Caguas, February 28, 1880 AHMC, SEC Gobierno, SSEC Alcalde de Barrio, SER Correspondencia, 1880, C65.

47. Luis Acosta, alcalde of Barrio Turabo, to the mayor of Caguas, October 27, 1880, AHMC, SEC Gobierno, SSEC Alcalde, SER Correspondencia, 1880, C67. In 1881 Carmen Tirado of Barrio Beatriz solicited the help of Ignacio Martínez, her brother-in-law, because her fifteen-year-old daughter had left the house with a man. Martínez appealed to a powerful man in his barrio, Don Vicente R. Muñoz Barros, for help. Muñoz wrote to the mayor, specifying the laws that would apply (Ignacio Martínez [written by Vicente Muñoz Barros] to the mayor of Caguas, July 30, 1881, AHMC, SEC Gobierno, SSEC Alcalde, SER Correspondencia, 1881, C69).

48. Twinam, "The Negotiation of Honor," 83.

49. "[Su hija] fue llevada por Simeon Estrella que reside en este pueblo ó en el barrio de Turabo; dejándola abandonada despues de haber tenido actos carnales con ella, á orillas del rio habiendo tenido que refujiarse en casa Juana Mercado de aquel barrio" (Micaela Rosado [written by José A. (?)] to the mayor of Caguas, June 19, 1880, AHMC, SEC Gobierno, SSEC Alcalde de Barrio, SER Correspondencia, 1880, C66).

Another example of a parent seeking intervention by the municipal authorities is the case of Eufemia Rodríguez, a resident of Barrio Toita in Cayey, who in 1915 accused Virgilio Vega of seducing her daughter. Rodríguez stated to the police that her daughter was single and her reputation was pure in the community ("estaba reputada por pura en la comunidad") ("El pueblo contra Virgilio Vega por seducción," AGPR, F Judicial de Guayama, SF Tribunal General de Justicia, SEC Tribunal Superior de Guayama, SER Expedientes Criminales, SSER Cayey, C757).

50. Suárez Findlay, *Imposing Decency,* 35.

51. At the turn of the century, the Hermanos Cheo developed as a millenarian movement in the interior highlands of Puerto Rico. It was coined after the nickname of one of the most important leaders, Cheo (José de los Santos Morales). The teachings were simple interpretations of Catholic doctrines and were very appealing to the poor.

52. Santaella Rivera, *Historia de los Hermanos Cheos*; Reyes, *La Santa Montaña.*

53. Seminario Evangélico, *Actas de la Asociación de Iglesias Bautistas de Puerto Rico,* September 1910, 13–15; September 1912, 6; September 1913, 13–14. See also Riggs, *Baptists in Puerto Rico,* 4.

54. Taylor, "A Visit to Baptist Missionaries in Porto Rico," 583.

55. Letter to the Bishop of Puerto Rico, author unknown, and response, October 27, 1911, AHD, F Diocesano, SEC Gobierno, SER Correspondencia, SSER Obispo, 1910–1911, C G-10.

56. *Crónicos de los Padres Redentoristas,* Annals from January 1922 to December 31, 1928. Vol. III, May 20–26, 1923, ARPR.

57. See appendix E. "Todo en usted es atractivo e inspira tanta atención que yo he

caído rendido a sus plantas para implorar ese santo amor, esas palabras tan dulces que solo pueden salir de un corazón de mujer que encanta y sublimiza todo cuanto su boca dice y su corazón siente" (AGPR, F Judicial, SF Tribunal General de Justicia, SEC Tribunal Superior de Guayama, SER Exp. Civiles, SSER Cayey, C45).

58. Ignacio Lizardi Delgado, comandante del puesto, to the tribunal de policía, April 25, 1900, AHMC, SEC Secretaría, SSEC Seguridad Pública, SER Expedientes/Documentos, SSEC Tribunal de Policía, 1899–1900, C59.

59. See appendix F. "Amas papa me dijo que habia hablado con el [Alonso] para que no me diera mas trabajo y si asi resultare yo me mato antes de moril asufrimentos por que papa lo hace por que yo no hable con tigo fuera de casa y amas supo hablabamos to dos los dias en el almacen. el se lo dijo á mama y yo le dije que si por causa de el dejaria yo de ir á trabajar [sic] a al pueblo y hablaba siempre con tigo que si por eso lo hacia lo haria peor por que yo á ti siempre te quiero e obligarian á dejarte matandome de lo contrario no pueden" (AGPR, F Judicial de Guayama, SF Tribunal General de Justicia, SEC Tribunal Superior de Guayama, SER Expedientes Criminales, SSER Cayey, C757 [November 30, 1915]).

60. "Noticias de Caguas," *La Democracia*, September 13, 1897, 3.

61. The names are pseudonyms to protect the women's identities.

62. Interview with Don Pablo Morales Díaz by Rosa E. Carrasquillo, April 2, 1997, Hartford, Connecticut.

63. AHMC, SEC Secretaría, SSEC Archivo, SER Censos, SSER Habitantes, 1882–83, C26.

64. See Suárez Findlay, *Imposing Decency*, 58, 125, 128.

65. AHMC, SEC Secretaría, SSEC Archivo, SER Censos, SSER Habitantes, 1882–83, C26.

66. The median family size in Puerto Rico was also 5.2 (Departamento de la Guerra, *Informe sobre el censo de Puerto Rico*, 1899, 339 and 341).

67. AHMC, SEC Secretaría, SSEC Archivo, SER Censos, SSER Habitantes, 1882–83, C26.

68. AHMC, SEC Secretaría, SSEC Archivo, SER Censos, SSER Habitantes, 1882–83, C26.

69. Suárez Findlay, *Imposing Decency*, 40.

70. Merino Falú, *Raza, género y clase social*, 119–25, 137–43.

71. Alternative coding attempts to count families, single males or females living together, domestic workers, day laborers, and clerks who lived with other people but made a living on their own. For more information on alternative and co-residential coding, see Kinsbruner, *Not of Pure Blood*, 147–49.

72. Suárez Findlay, *Imposing Decency*, 80; Kinsbruner, *Not of Pure Blood*, 108–9.

73. AHMC, SEC Secretaría, SSEC Archivo, SER Censos, SSER Habitantes, 1882–83, C26.

74. AHMC, SEC Secretaría, SSEC Archivo, SER Censos, SSER Habitantes, 1882–83, C26.

75. AHMC, SEC Secretaría, SSEC Archivo, SER Censos, SSER Habitantes, 1882–83, C26.

76. Azize Vargas, *Luchas de la mujer en Puerto Rico*, 85.

77. Nazario Velasco, *Discurso legal y orden postcolonial*, 291–93.

78. Teresa Guerra to the Ilustre Ayuntamiento, September 13, 1884, AHMC, SEC Gobierno, SSEC Asamblea Municipal, SER Correspondencia, 1884–86, C82. Dolores Arroyo inherited twenty-five cuerdas de land in Barrio Río Cañas (Dolores Arroyo to the mayor of Caguas, March 26, 1896, AHMC, SEC Gobierno, SSEC Asamblea Municipal, SER Correspondencia, 1894–98, C87). María López inherited land from her father in Barrio Beatriz (Salvador Caballero to the ayuntamiento, March 28, 1901, AHMC, SEC Gobierno, SSEC Asamblea Municipal, SER Correspondencia, 1901–5, C89).

79. Marcos Ríos to the Ilustre Ayuntamiento, July 5, 1887 AHMC, SEC Gobierno, SSEC Asamblea Municipal, SER Correspondencia, 1886–87, C83; Marcos Ríos to the Ilustre Ayun-

tamiento, June 27, 1888, AHMC, SEC Gobierno, SSEC Asamblea Municipal, SER Correspondencia, 1888–89, C85.

80. Picó Vidal, "Derecho de familia y cambio social," 538–44.

81. AHMC, SEC Secretaría, SSEC Archivo, SER Censos, SSER Habitantes, 1882–83, C26.

82. Suárez Findlay, *Imposing Decency*, 144.

83. AHMC, SEC Secretaría, SSEC Archivo, SER Censos, SSER Habitantes, 1882–83, C26.

84. U.S. Bureau of the Census, *Thirteenth Census of Population, 1910. Porto Rico* and *Fourteenth Census of Population, 1920. Porto Rico.*

85. Manning, "The Employment of Women's in Puerto Rico," 27–28.

86. Rivera Quintero, "El femenismo obrero," 9; Silvestrini, "Women as Workers," 63–64, 69.

87. Bureau of Labor, Government of Porto Rico, *Special Bulletin of the Bureau of Labor*, 30.

88. "Notas de Caguas, Movimiento Obrero," *El Mundo*, June 27, 1919, 4.

89. "Juicios or infracción a la Ley del Salario Mínimo en Caguas," *El Mundo*, November 1, 1919, 3.

90. The board was presided over by the mayor and comprised the parish priest, three parents, and a municipal official (López Yustos, *Historia documental de la educación*, 68). The municipality reserved some funds for education, but well-to-do parents paid for the education of their children. Caguas municipality paid for the benches in the school of Barrio Borinquen (AHMC, Actas, August 20, 1884). Teachers received their pay from the municipality (AHMC, Actas, July 16, 1883).

For parents' contributions to educational funds, see interview with Carmen Bauzá Medina by Manuel Silva Torres, Centro de Historia Oral, Universidad Interamericana de Puerto Rico, File 882; interview with Antonio Pérez by Ada Álvarez Sánchez, Centro de Historia Oral, Universidad Interamericana de Puerto Rico, File 839.

91. Salvador Brau, "La campesina" (1886), in Brau, *Ensayos*, 93–122. See also, Sabas Marín, "Maestros auxiliares y rurales," *La Correspondencia*, May 31, 1897; "La educación popular. Escuelas Rurales. II," *El Buscapié*, October 3, 1886, 1; Angel Julián, "Las escuelas en los campos. III," *El Buscapié*, March 27, 1888, 1; and Rivera Nieves, *El tema de la mujer*, 25 and 46.

92. "Un factor importantísimo para el desarrollo de los pueblos y para su progreso moral y material" ("Libro de Actas de la Junta Local de Instrucción Pública," October 26, 1896, AHMC, SEC Secretaría, SSEC Instrucción Pública, SER Actas, SSER Junta Local de Instrucción, 1890–97, C3).

93. "Report of the President and Officers of the Insular Board of Education Upon the Public Schools of Porto Rico for the Year Ending December 31, 1899. Rendered to Brig. Gen. George W. Davis, Military Governor of the Island," in War Department, "Education in Porto Rico. Letter from the Secretary of War, Transmitting in Response to Resolution of the Senate of April 12, 1900, A Letter from Brig. Gen. George W. Davis, Together with The Report of Dr. Victor S. Clark, and Other Papers Accompanying the Same, Relative to Education in Porto Rico," 1900, 56 Congress, 1 Session: Senate, Document: 363, p.151. Student absenteeism was very high in Caguas. In 1883, 169 students were enrolled but only 120 attended, and the figures were similar year after year (AHMC, SEC Secretaría, SSEC Instrucción Pública, SER Expedientes/Documentos, SSER Visita Escolar, 1883–99, C17–20; AHMC, SEC Secretaría, SSEC Instrucción Pública, SER Actas, SSER Junta Local de Instrucción, 1881–88, 1890–1911, C2–5; AHMC, Actas, June 27, 1891; Department of Education of Porto

Rico, "Report of the Commissioner of Education for Porto Rico." September 21, 1903. 58 Congress, 2 Session: House of Representatives, Document: 5, p. 776; The School Board of Caguas, "Informe anual al pueblo de Caguas," Caguas, 1902).

94. Ángel Julián, "Las escuelas en los campos," *El Buscapié*, April 8, 1888, 1.

95. Secretary of the Gobierno General de la Isla de Puerto-Rico to the mayor of Caguas, September 20, 1884, AHMC, SEC Gobierno, SSEC Alcalde, SER Correspondencia, 1884, C76.

96. AHMC, SEC Gobierno, SSEC Asamblea Municipal, SER Actas del Cabildo, 1884–85, C17, September 2, 1884.

97. "Le apena tener que informar á S.E. que no existiendo en este término municipal ningún centro de población, no cree de resultados positivos . . . pues teniendo las niñas que recorrer largos trayectos de caminos y atravesar ríos y quebradas, entorpece esto, como es consiguiente, la concurrencia de éllas á dichos planteles de enseñanza" ("Libro de Actas de la Junta Local de Instrucción Pública," October 26, 1896, AHMC, SEC Secretaría, SSEC Instrucción Pública, SER Actas, SSER Junta Local de Instrucción, 1890–1897, C3). Two months later, the board again discussed the possibility of establishing a rural school for girls in Barrio Cañaboncito ("Libro de Actas de la Junta Local de Instrucción Pública," December 23, 1896, AHMC, SEC Secretaría, SSEC Instrucción Pública, SER Actas, SSER Junta Local de Instrucción, 1890–97, C3).

98. "Libro de Actas de la Junta Local de Instrucción Pública," November 28, 1898, AHMC, SEC Secretaría, SSEC Instrucción Pública, SER Actas, SSER Junta Local de Instrucción, 1898, C4; "Minuta. Sr. D. Antonio E. Grillo," June 3, 1899, AHMC, SEC Secretaría, SSEC Instrucción Pública, SER Expedientes/Documentos, SSER Visita Escolar, 1898–99, C20.

99. "Pertenecemos á una nación tan progresista, que ha llegado á educar á la mujer de un modo tan perfecto, que para los demás países es todavía un ideal" (Mariano Abril, "Educación Americana," *La Democracia*, January 12, 1899). Marcia Rivera Quintero analyzes how educational policies had the double effect of reaffirming women's subordinate position in society through their emphasis on domestic education and preparing women to engage in cheap labor activities, which were extensions of women's work at home (Rivera Quintero, "Educational Policy and Female Labor," 351.

100. "Mira Lino, las muchachas mujeres no se mandan a la escuela que aprenden a escribir y lo que hacen es escribirles cartas a los novios. Manda a los muchachos" (Interview with Conrado Carrasquillo by Rosa Carrasquillo, August 27, 1997, Caguas, Puerto Rico).

101. The School Board of Caguas, "Informe anual al pueblo de Caguas," 1902. Sala de la Colección Puertorriqueña, UPR, 2.

102. War Department, "Report of the Commissioner of Education for Porto Rico to the Secretary of the Interior, U.S.A., for the Fiscal Year Ended June 30, 1906," Washington: Government Printing Office, 1907, 59 Congress, 2 Session: Senate, Document 17 and 75.

103. Colón Ramírez, "Educación y sociedad," 163. These teachers had from one month to eleven years of experience in their profession, but most of them had three years' or less experience (AHMC, SEC Secretaría, SSEC Instrucción Pública, SER Expedientes/Documentos, SSER Maestros, 1882–1951, C 15–16). See also AHMC, SER Gobierno, SSER Asamblea Municipal, SER Actas del Cabildo, 1880, 1882, 1888, 1892, 1898, and 1899, C13, 15, 21, 24, and 29, February 5 and April 22, 1880; September 7, 1882; April 13 and 20, 1888; March 2, 1892; December 21, 1898, July 14, 1899.

104. Cabán, *Constructing a Colonial People*, 64.

105. Mayor of Humacao to the mayor of Caguas, May 10, 1898, AHMC, SEC Gobierno, SSEC Alcalde de Barrio, SER Correspondencia, 1898, C118. In June, Doña María del Carmen

Segué de Cordero applied for the same position and was not hired either (Vicente Muñoz Barros to the mayor of Caguas, June 10, 1898, AHMC, SEC Gobierno, SSEC Alcalde de Barrio, SER Correspondencia, 1898, C119; AHMC, SER Gobierno, SSER Asamblea Municipal, SER Actas del Cabildo, 1898–99, C29, October 21, 1898; November 18, 1898; December 2, 1898.

106. In 1906 María Santiago López taught in a rural school ("Para desempeñar escuelas rurales," July 17, 1906, and September 25, 1907, AHMC, SEC Secretaría, SSEC Instrucción Pública, SER Actas, SSER Junta Local de Instrucción, 1901–11, C5).

107. "Report of the Commissioner of Education," August 10, 1910, in Geo R. Colton, "Tenth Annual Report of the Governor of Porto Rico," September 1, 1910, War Department, 61 Congress, 3 Session: House of Representatives, Document 1002, p. 156.

108. There were 8,638 inhabitants in the rural barrios of Caguas in 1882 (AHMC, SEC Secretaría, SSEC Archivo, SER Censos, SSER Habitantes, 1882–83, C26).

109. AHMC, SEC Secretaría, SSEC Archivo, SER Censos, SSER Habitantes, 1882–83, C26.

110. U.S. Bureau of the Census, *Thirteenth Census of the United States*, 3:1211.

111. Jelin, "Women, Gender, and Human Rights," 179.

6. Conclusion

1. As used by Duany, *The Puerto Rican Nation*.

2. Galvin, *The Organized Labor Movement*, 53.

3. Cabán, *Constructing a Colonial People*, 241–45.

4. See Dávila Santiago, *El derribo de las murallas*.

5. Dávila Santiago, *El derribo de las murallas*, 84.

Bibliography

Archives and Special Collections

Archivo General de Puerto Rico (AGPR), San Juan, Puerto Rico

Archivo Histórico Diócesano (AHD), San Juan, Puerto Rico

Archivo Histórico Municipal de Caguas (AHMC), Caguas, Puerto Rico

Archivo Redentorista de Puerto Rico (ARPR), San Juan, Puerto Rico

Bailey K. Ashford Library, Ciencias Médicas, Universidad de Puerto Rico, San Juan, Puerto Rico

Centro de Historia Oral de la Universidad Interamericana (CHO), San Juan, Puerto Rico

Centro de Investigaciones Históricas, Universidad de Puerto Rico, Río Piedras, Puerto Rico

Colección Puertorriqueña, Universidad de Puerto Rico, Río Piedras, Puerto Rico

Puerto Rican Collection, University of Connecticut, Storrs, Connecticut

Redemptorist Archives, San Juan, Puerto Rico

Seminario Evangélico, Río Piedras, Puerto Rico

Interviews conducted by author

Cecilia Carrasquillo, March 24, 1993, Caguas, Puerto Rico.

Conrado Carrasquillo, April 6 and 18, 1992, May 4, 1992, March 26, 1993, August 27, 1997, Caguas, Puerto Rico.

José Carrasquillo, July 2, 1992, Caguas, Puerto Rico.

Luz María Carrasquillo. June 23, 1992. Caguas, Puerto Rico.

Flora Lebrón, April 9, 1997, Hartford, Connecticut.

Juan Martínez Martínez, April 9, 1997, Hartford, Connecticut.

Pablo Morales Díaz, April 2 and 25, 1997, May 27, 1997, Hartford, Connecticut.

Gladys Ramos, May 20, 1997, Hartford, Connecticut.

Antonia Resinos, April 30, 1997, Hartford, Connecticut.

Ramón Luis Rivera, April 30, 1997, Hartford, Connecticut.

Gregoria Rodríguez, May 20, 1997, Hartford, Connecticut.

Juana Rodríguez, March 17, 1993, Caguas, Puerto Rico.

Nicolás Rodríguez, March 9 and 23, 1997, Hartford, Connecticut.

María Santiago, March 29, 1997, Hartford, Connecticut.

Salvadora Torres, May 12, 1997, Hartford, Connecticut.

Juan Vázquez, May 8, 1997, Hartford, Connecticut.

Books and Articles

Acosta Lespier, Ivonne. "Poderes y resistencias en la vida cotidiana de Caguas, 1897–1900." In Álvarez Curbelo, Gallart, and Rafucci, *Los arcos de la memoria*, 142–57.

———. *Santa Juana y Mano Manca: Auge y decencia del azúcar en el valle del Turabo en el siglo XX*. San Juan: Editorial Cultural, 1995.

Adas, Michael. "From Avoidance to Confrontation: Peasant Protest in Precolonial and Colonial Southeast Asia." In Dirks, *Colonialism and Culture*, 89–126.

Allen, Charles H. "Porto Rico." In *The New America and the Far East: A Picturesque and Historic Description of These Lands and People*, by G. Waldo Browne. Boston: Marshall Jones Company, 1899.

Alonso, Ana María. " 'Progress' as Disorder and Dishonor: Discourses of Serrano Resistance." *Critique of Anthropology* 7, no. 3 (1987): 93–112.

———. "The Politics of Space, Time, and Substance: State Formation, Nationalism and Ethnicity." *Annual Review of Anthropology* (1994): 379–405.

———. *Thread of Blood: Colonialism, Revolution, and Gender on Mexico's Northern Frontier.* Tucson: University of Arizona Press, 1995.

Álvarez Curbelo, Silvia. "El afán de la modernidad: La constitución de la discursividad moderna en Puerto Rico (Siglo XIX)." PhD diss., University of Puerto Rico, 1998.

———. "La patria agrícola: La ideología de los agricultores, Puerto Rico, 1924–1928." MA thesis, University of Puerto Rico, 1986.

———. "Un discurso ideológico olvidado: Los agricultores puertorriqueños (1924–1928)." *Op.Cit: Boletín del Centro de Investigaciones Históricas* 2 (1986–87): 141–60.

Álvarez Curbelo, Silvia, Mary Francis Gallart, and Carmen I. Rafucci, eds. *Los arcos de la memoria: el '98 de los pueblos puertorriqueños.* San Juan: Postdata, 1998.

Angelli, John P. "San Lorenzo: A Case Study of Recent Migrations in Interior Puerto Rico." *American Journal of Economics and Sociology* 11, no. 2 (1952): 155–60.

Appelbaum, Nancy P. "Whitening the Region: Caucano Mediation and 'Antioqueño Colonization' in Nineteenth-Century Columbia," *Hispanic American Historical Review* 79, no. 4 (1999): 631–67.

———. *Muddied Waters: Race, Region, and Local History in Colombia, 1846–1948.* Durham: Duke University Press, 2003.

Appelbaum, Nancy P., Anne S. Macpherson, and Karin Alejandra Rosemblatt, eds. *Race and Nation in Modern Latin America.* Chapel Hill: University of North Carolina Press, 2003.

Arnold, David. *Colonizing the Body: State Medicine and Epidemic Disease in Nineteenth-Century India.* Berkeley: University of California Press, 1993.

Arrom, Sylvia M. *Containing the Poor: The Mexico City Poor House, 1774–1871.* Durham: Duke University Press, 2000.

Ashford, Bailey K. *Problemas Higiénicos en Puerto Rico.* New York: World Book Editores, 1916.

———. *A Soldier in Science: The Autobiography of Bailey K. Ashford, Colonel MC., U.S.A.* San Juan: Editorial de la Universidad de Puerto Rico, 1998.

Ashford, Bailey K., and Pedro Gutierrez Igaravidez. *Uncinariasis (Hookworm Disease) in Porto Rico. A Medical and Economic Problem.* Porto Rico Anemia Commission. 61st Cong. 3rd sess. Senate, 1911.

Ayala, César. *American Sugar Kingdom: The Plantation Economy of the Spanish Caribbean, 1898–1934.* Chapel Hill: University of North Carolina Press, 1999.

Azize Vargas, Yamila. *Luchas de la mujer en Puerto Rico, 1898–1919.* San Juan: Tipografía Metropolitana, 1979.

———, ed. *La mujer en Puerto Rico: Ensayos de investigación.* Río Piedras: Ediciones Huracán, 1987.

Baldrich, Juan José. *Sembraron la no siembra: Los cosecheros de tabaco puertorriqueños frente a las corporaciones tabacaleras.* Río Piedras: Ediciones Huracán, 1988.

Barbalet, J. M. "Citizenship, Class Inequality, and Resentment." In Turner, *Citizenship and Social Theory,* 36–56.

Barbosa de Rosario, Pilar. *Historia del autonomismo puertorriqueño: El ensayo de la autonomía, 1897–1898.* San Juan: Model Offset Printing, 1986.

Barceló Miller, María de F. *Política ultramarina y gobierno municipal: Isabela, 1873–1887.* Río Piedras: Ediciones Huracán, 1984.

Baud, Michael. *Peasants and Tobacco in the Dominican Republic, 1870–1930.* Knoxville: University of Tennessee Press, 1995.

Baver, Sherrie L. *The Political Economy of Colonialism: The State and Industrialization in Puerto Rico.* Westport: Praeger, 1993.

Becker, Marjorie. *Setting the Virgin on Fire: Lázaro Cárdenas, Michoacán Peasants, and the Redemption of the Mexican Revolution.* Berkeley: University of California Press, 1995.

Beckford, George, and Michael Witter. *Small Garden . . . Bitter Weed: The Political Economy of Struggle and Change in Jamaica.* Morant Bay: Maroon Publishing House, 1982.

Beiner, Ronald, ed. *Theorizing Citizenship.* New York: State University of New York Press, 1995.

Benítez-Rojo, Antonio. *The Repeating Island: The Caribbean and the Postmodern Perspective.* Durham: Duke University Press, 1992.

Bergard, Laird W. "Agrarian History of Puerto Rico, 1870–1930." *Latin American Research Review* 13, no. 3 (1978): 63–94.

————. *Coffee and the Growth of Agrarian Capitalism in Nineteenth-Century Puerto Rico.* Princeton: Rutdgers University Press, 1983.

Berkowitz, Edward, and Kim McQuaid. *Creating the Welfare State: The Political Economy of Twentieth-Century Reform.* New York: Praeger, 1980.

Bird Carmona, Arturo. *A Lima y Machete: La huelga cañera de 1915 y la fundación del Partido Socialista.* Río Piedras: Ediciones Huracán, 2001.

Bird-Piñero, Enrique. "The Politics of Puerto Rican Land Reform: A Study in the Dynamics of Legislation." MA thesis, University of Chicago, 1950.

Black, M. L. "My Mother Never Father Me: Rethinking Kinship and the Governing of Families." *Social and Economic Studies,* 44, no. 1 (1995): 49–71.

Blackburn, Robin. *The Overthrow of Colonial Slavery, 1776–1848.* New York: Verso, 1988.

Bolland, O. Nigel. "Systems of Domination after Slavery: The Control of Land and Labor in the British West Indies after 1838." *Comparative Studies in Society and History* 23, no. 4 (1981).

Bonilla, Zobeida E. "Kinship and Household in a Puerto Rican Rural Community." MA thesis, Colorado State University, 1994.

Bothwell, Reece B. *Orígenes y desarrollo de los partidos políticos de Puerto Rico, 1869–1980.* Río Piedras: Editorial Edil, 1988.

Bourdieu, Pierre. *Distinction: A Social Critique of the Judgement of Taste.* Cambridge: Harvard University Press, 1984.

————. *In Other Words: Essays Towards a Reflexive Sociology.* Stanford: Stanford University Press, 1990.

————. *The State Nobility: Elite Schools in the Field of Power.* Stanford: Stanford University Press, 1996.

Brau, Salvador. *Ensayos: Disquisiones sociológicas.* Río Piedras: Editorial Edil, 1972.

Brockmann, Vernon C. "Land Types and Land Utilization in the Caguas-San Lorenzo Region." In *Symposium on the Geography of Puerto Rico,* edited by Clarence F. Jones and Rafael Picó, 297–323. Río Piedras: University of Puerto Rico Press, 1955.

Bunker, Oscar L. *Historia de Caguas,* vol 2. Barcelona: I.G. Manuel Pareja, 1975.

Bureau of Labor, Government of Porto Rico, "Special Bulletin of the Bureau of Labor on Strikes in Porto Rico During Fiscal Year 1917–1918 and Appendix of Labor Laws

Approved from 1916 to March, 1918." San Juan: Bureau of Supplies, Printing, and Transportation, 1918.

Cabán, Pedro A. *Constructing a Colonial People: Puerto Rico and the United States, 1898–1932*. Boulder: Westview Press, 1999.

Cabrera Collazo, Rafael L. "Los peninsulares y la transición hacia el siglo XX en la zona central no-cafetalera de Puerto Rico: El caso de Corozal, 1890–1905." MA thesis, University of Puerto Rico, 1988.

Camuñas, Ricardo. *Hacendados y comerciantes en Puerto Rico en torno a la década revolucionaria de 1860*, second ed. Mayagüez: N.p., 1994.

Caro Costas, Aida R. *Legislación municipal puertorriaqueña del siglo XVIII*. San Juan: Instituto de Cultura Puertorriqueña, 1971.

Carroll, Henry K. *Report on the Island of Puerto Rico: Its Population, Civil Government, Commerce, etc*. Washington DC: Submitted to the President of U.S. William McKinley, 1899.

Casanova, Carlos R. "Propiedad agrícola y poder en el municipio de Manatí: 1885 a 1898." MA thesis, University of Puerto Rico, 1985.

Castillo Bueno, María de los Reyes. *Reyita: The Life of a Black Cuban Woman in the Twentieth Century as Told to Her Daughter Daisy Rubiera Castillo*. Durham: Duke University Press, 2000.

Centro de Investigaciones Históricas, "Ley de abolición. 22 marzo 1873," in *El proceso abolicionista en Puerto Rico: Documentos para su estudio* (San Juan: Instituto de Cultura Puertorriqueña, 1978).

———. "Proyecto de reglamento sobre las relaciones entre el capital y el trabajo destinados a la industria agrícola," in *El proceso abolicionista en Puerto Rico: Documentos para su estudio* (San Juan: Instituto de Cultura Puertorriqueña, 1978).

Chambers, Sarah C. *From Subjects to Citizens: Honor, Culture, and Politics in Arequipa, Peru, 1780–1854*. University Park: Pennsylvania State University Press, 1999.

Clark, Edith. *My Mother Who Fathered Me: A Study of the Family in Three Selected Communities in Jamaica*. London: George Allen and Unwen, 1975.

Coll y Toste, Cayetano. *Reseña del estado social, económico e industrial de la isla de Puerto-Rico al tomar posesión de ella los Estados-Unidos*. Puerto Rico: Imprenta de la "Correspondencia," 1899.

Conklin, Alice L. "Colonialism and Human Rights, A Contradiction in Terms? The Case of France and West Africa, 1895–1914." *The American Historical Review* 103, no. 2 (1998): 419–42.

Cooper, Frederick. "Conditions Analogous to Slavery: Imperialism and Free Labor Ideology in Africa." In Cooper, Holt, and Scott, *Beyond Slavery*, 107–49.

Cooper, Frederick, et. al., *Confronting Historical Paradigms: Peasant, Labor, and the Capitalist World System in Africa and Latin America*. Madison: University of Wisconsin Press, 1993.

Cooper, Frederick, Thomas C. Holt, and Rebecca J. Scott. *Beyond Slavery: Explorations of Race, Labor, and Citizenship in Postemancipation Societies*. Chapel Hill: University of North Carolina Press, 2000.

Córdova, Gonzalo F. *Santiago Iglesias: Creador del movimiento obrero de Puerto Rico*. Río Piedras: Editorial Universitaria, 1980.

Corrigan, Peter, and Derek Sayer. *The Great Arch: English State Formation as Cultural Revolution*. New York: Blackwell, 1985.

Cruz Monclova, Lydio. *Historia de Puerto Rico (Siglo XIX)*. Vols. 2 and 3, 1875–98. Río Piedras: Editorial Universitaria, 1979.

Cubano-Iguina, Astrid. "El autonomismo en Puerto Rico, 1887–1898: notas para la definición de un modelo de política radical." In *La Nación Soñada: Cuba, Puerto Rico y Filipinas ante el 98*, edited by Consuelo Naranjo Orovio, Miguel Ángel Puig-Samper, and Luis Miguel García Mora, 405–15. Madrid: Ediciones Doce Calles, 1996.

———. "Political Culture and Male Mass-Party Formation in Late-Nineteenth-Century Puerto Rico." *Hispanic American Historical Review* 78, no. 4 (1998): 631–62.

Cutter, Charles. "The Legal System as a Touchstone of Identity in Colonial New Mexico." In Roniger and Herzog, *The Collective and the Public*, 57–70.

Dapena, José A. *Trayectoria del pensamiento liberal puertorriqueño en el siglo XIX*. San Juan: Instituto de Cultura Puertorriqueña, 1963.

Dávila Santiago, Rubén. *El derribo de las murallas: Orígenes intelectuales del socialismo en Puerto Rico*. Río Piedras: Editorial Cultural, 1988.

Davis, Brig. Gen. Geo. W. *Report of Brig. Gen. Geo. W. Davis, U.S.U., on Civil Affairs of Puerto Rico. 1899*, Reports of the War Department: 56th Congres-1st Session: House Documents, Vol. 7, 1899.

Deere, Carmen D. *The Peasantry in Political Economy: Trends of the 1980s*. Amherst: Program of Latin American Studies Occasional Papers no. 19, 1987.

Del Valle Atiles, Francisco. *Cartilla de higiene*. San Juan: Imprenta de José González Font, 1886.

———. *El campesino puertorriqueño: sus condiciones físicas, intelectuales y morales, causas que las determinan y medios para mejorarlas*. San Juan: Tipografía de José González Font, 1887.

Departamento de la Guerra, Dirección del Censo de Puerto Rico, *Informe sobre el censo de Puerto Rico, 1899*. Washington DC: Imprenta del Gobierno, 1900.

Diacon, Todd A. *Millenarian Vision, Capitalist Reality: Brazil's Contestado Rebellion, 1912–1916*. Durham: Duke University Press, 1991.

Díaz, Arlene J. *Female Citizens, Patriarchs, and the Law in Venezuela, 1786–1904*. Lincoln: University of Nebraska Press, 2004.

Díaz Soler, Luis M. *Puerto Rico: Desde sus orígenes hasta el cese de la dominación española*. Río Piedras: Editorial de la Universidad de Puerto Rico, 1994.

Dietz, James L. *Economic History of Puerto Rico: Institutional Change and Capitalist Development*. Princeton: Princeton University Press, 1986.

Dirks, Nicholas B., ed. *Colonialism and Culture*. Ann Arbor: University of Michigan Press, 1995.

Donzelot, Jacques. *The Policing of Families*. Baltimore: John Hopkins University Press, 1979.

Dore, Elizabeth. "One Step Forward, Two Steps Back." In Molyneux and Dore, *Hidden Histories*, 3–32.

Duany, Jorge. "Ethnicity in the Spanish Caribbean: Notes on the Consolidation of Creole Identity in Cuba and Puerto Rico, 1762–1868." In *Caribbean Ethnicity Revisited*, edited by Stephen Glazier, 15–39. New York: Gordon and Breach Science Publishers, 1985.

———. *The Puerto Rican Nation on the Move: Identities on the Island and in the United States*. Chapel Hill: University of North Carolina Press, 2002.

Duby, George. *The Knight the Lady and the Priest: The Making of Modern Marriage in Medieval France*. Chicago: University of Chicago Press, 1981.

Dumond, Don E. *The Machete and the Cross: Campesino Rebellion in Yucatan*. Lincoln: University of Nebraska Press, 1997.

Duncan, Kenneth, Ian Rutledge, and Colin Harding, eds. *Land and Labour in Latin America: Essays on the Development of Agrarian Capitalism in the Nineteenth and Tweintieth Centuries*. New York: Cambridge University Press, 1977.

Escobar, Cristina. "Bullfighting Fiestas, Clientelism, and Political Identities in Northern Colombia." In Roniger and Herzog, *The Collective*, 174–91.

Falcón, Romana. "Force and the Search for Consent: The Role of the Jefaturas Políticas of Cohauila in National State Formation." In Joseph and Nugent, *Everyday Forms of State Formation*, 107–34.

Feinberg, Richard E., and Robin L. Rosenberg, eds. *Civil Society and the Summit of the Americas: The 1998 Santiago Summit*. Miami: North-South Center Press, 1999.

Fernández de Encinas, Serapio. *Sociología rural de Cayey*. Río Piedras: Editorial Universitaria, 1971.

Fernández Juncos, Manuel. *Tipos y caracteres*. Puerto Rico: Biblioteca "El Buscapié," 1882.

———. *Varias Cosas, Colección de artículos, narraciones, sátiras y juicios literarios*. Puerto Rico: Tipografía de las Bellas Letras, 1884.

Ferré, Rosario. *Maldito Amor*. New York: Vintage Books, 1998.

Ferrer, Ada. *Insurgent Cuba: Race, Nation, and Revolution, 1868–1898*. Chapel Hill: University of North Carolina Press, 1999.

Findlay, Eileen J. "Domination, Decency, and Desire: The Politics of Sexuality in Ponce, Puerto Rico, 1870–1920." PhD Dissertation, University of Wisconsin–Madison, 1995.

Fitzsimmons, Tracy. *Beyond the Barricades: Women, Civil Society, and Participation after Democratization in Latin America*. New York: Garland Publishing, 2000.

Flathman, Richard E. "Citizenship and Authority: A Chastened View of Citizenship." In Beiner, *Theorizing Citizenship*, 105–51.

Flores, William V., and Rina Benmayor, eds. *Latino Cultural Citizenship: Claiming Identity, Space, and Rights*. Boston: Beacon Press, 1997.

Fonval, Françoise. "Ethnocide and Acculturation," in *Minority Peoples in the Age of Nation-States*, edited by Gérard Chaliand, 149–52. London: Pluto, 1989.

Foucault, Michael. *Discipline and Punishment: The Birth of the Prison*. New York: Vintage Books, 1979.

———. *The Care of the Self: The History of Sexuality, Volume 3*. New York: Vintage Books, 1988.

———. *History of Sexuality: An Introduction, Volume 1*. New York: Vintage Books, 1990.

———. *The Use of Pleasure: The History of Sexuality, Volume 2*. New York: Vintage Books, 1990.

Fuente, Alejandro de la. *A Nation for All: Race, Inequality, and Politics in Twentieth-Century Cuba*. Chapel Hill: University of North Carolina Press, 2001.

Galvin, Miles. "The Early Development of the Organized Labor Movement in Puerto Rico," *Latin American Perspectives* 3, no. 3 (1976): 17–35.

———. *The Organized Labor Movement in Puerto Rico*. New Jersey: Associated University Presses, 1979.

García Ochoa, María Asunción. *La política española en Puerto Rico durante el siglo XIX.* Río Piedras: Editorial de la Universidad de Puerto Rico, 1982.

Gavillán Rivera, Manuel. "Gobierno y justicia en Juncos: 1850–1880." MA thesis, University of Puerto Rico, 1993.

Giddens, Anthony. *The Constitution of Society: Outline of the Theory of Structuration.* Berkeley: University of California Press, 1984.

Glasser, Ruth. *Aquí me quedo: Puerto Ricans in Connecticut.* Middletown CT: Humanities Council, 1991.

Godreau, Michael J., and Juan A. Giusti. "Las concesiones de la Corona y propiedad de la tierra en Puerto Rico, siglos XVI–XX." *Revista Jurídica. Universidad de Puerto Rico* 62, no. 3 (1993): 351–579.

Gómes, P. I., ed. *Rural Development in the Caribbean.* New York: Saint Martin's Press, 1985.

Gómez Acevedo, Labor. *Organización y reglamentación del trabajo en el Puerto Rico del siglo XIX (propietarios y jornaleros).* San Juan: Instituto de Cultura Puertorriqueña, 1970.

Góngora, Mario, and Jean Borde. *Evolución de la propiedad rural en el Valle del Puangue.* Santiago de Chile: Editorial Universitaria, 1956.

González, José Luis. *La luna no era de queso: Memorias de infancia.* San Juan: Editorial Cultural, 1988.

González Díaz, Emilio. "El Estado y las clases dominantes en la situación colonial." *Revista Mexicana de Sociología* 40, no. 3 (1978): 1141–52.

González Libra, Manuel. "Agricultores y comerciantes en la última frontera del café: Ciales, 1885–1898." MA thesis, University of Puerto Rico, 1988.

González Velez, Pedro A. "Tenencia de tierra y producción agraria en Bayamón, 1890–1910." MA thesis, University of Puerto Rico, 1986.

Gould, Jeffrey L. *To Lead as Equals: Rural Protest and Political Consciousness in Chinandega, Nicaragua, 1912–1979.* Chapel Hill: University of North Carolina Press, 1990.

Greenfeld, Liah. "Nationalism and Modernity." *Social Research* 63, no. 1 (1996): 3–40.

Guardino, Peter. *Peasants, Politics, and the Formation of Mexico's National State: Guerrero, 1800–1857.* Stanford: Stanford University Press, 1996.

Guerra, Lillian. *Popular Expression and National Identity in Puerto Rico: The Struggle for Self, Community, and Nation.* Gainesville: University Press of Florida, 1998.

Guha, Ranjit. *Dominance without Hegemony: History and Power in Colonial India.* Cambridge: Harvard University Press, 1997.

Haber, Stephen. "Anything Goes: Mexico's 'New' Cultural History." *Hispanic American Historical Review* 79, no. 2 (1999): 309–30.

———. "The Worst of Both Worlds: The New Cultural History of Mexico," *Mexican Studies/Estudios Mexicanos* 13 (1997).

Hernández, José. "Conquest Theory from the Puerto Rican Experience." *Latino Studies Journal* 7, no. 2 (1996): 51–68.

Hernández, Juan David. "Reflexiones sobre Caguax," *Historia y arqueología del Valle del Turabo* 4, no. 1 (2000): 68–89.

———. "Orígenes y fundamentos del criollo con especial atención en Caguas," manuscript in progress.

Herr, Richard. *Rural Change and Royal Finances in Spain at the End of the Old Regime.* Berkeley: University of California Press, 1989.

Hill, Christopher. *The World Turned Upside Down: Radical Ideas During the English Revolution.* New York: Penguin Books, 1987.

Hobsbawn, Eric J. *Primitive Rebels: Studies in Archaic Forms of Social Movement in the Nineteenth and Twentieth Centuries.* New York: Frederick A. Praeger Publisher, 1959.

Holt, Thomas C. "The Essence of the Contract: The Articulation of Race, Gender, and Political Economy in British Emancipation Policy, 1838–1866." In Cooper, Holt, and Scott, *Beyond Slavery,* 33–59.

Horowitz, Michael M., ed. *Peoples and Cultures of the Caribbean: An Anthropological Reader.* New York: Natural History Press, 1971.

Hunt, William H. *Second Annual Report of the Governor of Porto Rico, Covering the Period From May 1, 1901, to July 1, 1902.* 57th Cong., 2nd Session. Senate, 1902.

Jelin, Elizabeth, "Citizenship Revisited: Solidarity, Responsibility, and Rights." In Jelin and Hershberg, *Constructing Democracy,* 101–19.

———. "Women, Gender, and Human Rights." In Jelin and Hershberg, *Constructing Democracy,* 177–96.

Jelin, Elizabeth, and Eric Hershberg, eds. *Constructing Democracy: Human Rights, Citizenship, and Society in Latin America.* Boulder: Westview Press, 1996.

Jiménez-Muñoz, Glayds. "'A Storm Dressed in Skirt': Ambivalence in the Debate on Women's Suffrage in Puerto Rico, 1927–1929." PhD diss., State University of New York, 1993.

Johnson, John J. *Latin America in Caricature.* Austin: University of Texas Press, 1980.

Johnson, Paul R. *The Economics of the Tobacco Industry.* New York: Praeger, 1984.

Justiniano, Carmen Luisa. *Con valor y a como dé lugar: Memorias de una jíbara puertorriqueña.* Río Piedras: Editorial de la Universidad de Puerto Rico, 1996.

Kearns, Thomas R., and Austin Sarat, eds. *Law in the Domains of Culture.* Ann Arbor: University of Michigan Press, 1998.

Kearny, Michael. *Reconceptualizing the Peasantry: Anthropology in Global Perspective.* Boulder: Westview Press, 1996.

Kinsbruner, Jay. *Not of Pure Blood: The Free People of Color and Racial Prejudice in Nineteenth-Century Puerto Rico.* Durham: Duke University Press, 1996.

Lalinde Abadía, Jesús. *La administración española en el siglo XIX puertorriqueño (Pervivencia de la variante indiana del decisionismo castellano en Puerto Rico).* Sevilla: Publicaciones de la Escuela de Estudios Hispano-Americanos de Sevilla, 1980.

Lauria, Aldo J. "'Respeto,' 'Relajo,' and Inter-personal Relations in Puerto Rico." *Anthropological Quarterly* 37, no. 2 (1964): 53–67.

Lauria-Santiago, Aldo, Jr., and Aviva Chomsky, eds. *Identity and Struggle at the Margins of the Nation-State: The Laboring Peoples of Central America and the Hispanic Caribbean.* Durham: Duke University Press, 1998.

León, Magdalena, and Carmen D. Deere. *Debate sobre la mujer en América Latina y el Caribe.* Bogotá: ACEP, 1982.

Leonard Reyes, Harold E. "El impacto de la campaña contra la uncinariasis y la política de salud pública norteamericana en Puerto Rico, 1898–1918." MA thesis, University of Puerto Rico, 1991.

Lewin, Linda. *Politics and Parentela: A Case Study of Family-Based Oligarchy in Brazil.* Princeton: Princeton University Press, 1987.

Lewis, Gordon K. *Puerto Rico: Freedom and Power in the Caribbean.* New York: Monthly Review Press, 1963

Ley electoral de 20 de agosto de 1870. Puerto-Rico: Establecimiento Tipográfico de Acosta, 1881.

Leyes provincial y municipal de 24 de mayo de 1878, mandadas á cumplir en Puerto-Rico, en 17 de junio último. Puerto Rico: Imprenta del Boletín Mercantil, 1878.

Lipsett-Rivera, Sonya, and Lyman L. Johnson, eds. *The Faces of Honor: Sex, Shame, and Violence in Colonial Latin America.* Albuquerque: University of New Mexico Press, 1998.

Liu, Tessie P. *The Weaver's Knot: The Contradictions of Class Struggle and Family Solidarity in Western France, 1750–1914.* Ithaca NY: Cornell University Press, 1994.

López Garrido, Diego. *La Guardia Civil y los orígenes del Estado centralista.* Barcelona: Editorial Crítica, 1982.

López Tuero, Fernando. *Estudios de Economía Rural.* San Juan: Imprenta del "Boletín Mercantil," 1893.

López Yustos, Alfonso. *Historia documental de la educación en Puerto Rico 1503–1970.* Puerto Rico: Sandeman, 1985.

Lovejoy, Paul E. *Transformations in Slavery: A History of Salvery in Africa, Second Edition.* Cambridge: Cambridge University Press, 2000.

Luque, María Dolores. *La ocupación y la Ley Foraker (La opinión pública puertorriqueña) 1898–1904.* Río Piedras: Editorial Universitaria, 1980.

Lustig, R. Jeffrey. *Corporate Liberalism: The Origins of Modern American Political Theory, 1890–1920.* Berkeley: University of California Press, 1982.

Maclean, Gerald, Donna Landry, and Joseph P. Ward, eds. *The Country and the City Revisited: England and the Politics of Culture, 1550–1850.* Cambridge: Cambridge University Press, 1999.

Mallon, Florencia E. *The Defense of Community in Peru's Central Highlands: Peasant Struggle and Capitalist Transition, 1860–1940.* Princeton: Princeton University Press, 1983.

———. "Gender and Class in the Transition to Capitalism: Household and Mode of Production in Central Peru." *Latin American Perspectives* 13, no. 1 (1986): 147–74.

———. "Patriarchy in the Transition to Capitalism: Central Peru, 1830–1950." *Feminist Studies* 13, no. 2 (1987): 379–407.

———. *Peasant and Nation: The Making of Postcolonial Mexico and Peru.* Berkeley: University of California Press, 1995.

Mandle, Jay R. *The Plantation Economy: Population and Economic Change in Guyana, 1838–1960.* Philadelphia: Temple University Press, 1973.

Manning, Caroline. "The Employment of Women's in Puerto Rico." *Bulletin of the Women's Bureau*, no. 118. Washington DC: U.S. Department of Labor, 1934.

Marcus, Joseph (special agent of U.S. Employment Service). "Labor Conditions in Porto Rico." Washington DC: Government Printing Office, 1919.

Martí, José. *Nuestra América.* La Habana: Casa Editorial Abril, 2001. (Orig. December 19, 1889.)

Martínez-Alier, Verenna. *Marriage, Class, and Colour in Nineteenth-Century Cuba: A Study of Racial Attitudes and Sexual Values in a Slave Society.* Ann Arbor: University of Michigan Press, 1989.

Martínez Heredia, Fernando, Rebecca J. Scott, and Orlando F. García Martínez, *Espacios, silencios y los sentidos de la liberated: Cuba entre 1878 y 1912.* Havana: Ediciones Unión, 2001.

Martínez-Vergne, Teresita. *Shaping the Discourse on Space: Charity and Its Wards in Nineteenth-Century San Juan, Puerto Rico.* Austin: University of Texas Press 1999.

Matos Rodríguez, Félix V. *Women and Urban Change in San Juan, Puerto Rico, 1820–1868.* Gainesville: University Press of Florida, 1999.

Matos Rodríguez, Félix V., and Linda C. Delgado, eds. *Puerto Rican Women's History: New Perspectives.* Armonk NY: M. E. Sharpe, 1998.

Mawson, Harry P., and James W. Buel, *Leslie's Official History of the Spanish-American War: A Pictorial and Descriptive Record of the Cuban Rebellion, the Causes that Involved the United States, and Complete Narrative of Our Conflict with Spain on Land and Sea.* Washington DC: Marcus J. Wright, 1899.

McConville, Brendan. *These Daring Disturbers of the Public Peace: The Struggle for Property and Power in Early New Jersey.* Ithaca NY: Cornell University Press, 1999.

McCurdy, Charles. *The Anti-Rent Era in New York Law and Politics, 1839–1865.* Chapel Hill: University of North Carolina Press, 2001.

McGlynn, Frank, and Seymour Drescher, eds. *The Meaning of Freedom: Economics, Politics, and Culture After Slavery.* Pittsburgh: University of Pittsburgh Press, 1992.

Meléndez, Edwin, and Edgardo Meléndez, eds. *Colonial Dilemma: Critical Perspectives on Contemporary Puerto Rico.* Boston: South End Press, 1993.

Meléndez Muñoz, Miguel. *Obras Completas.* San Juan: Instituto de Cultura Puertorriqueño. 1, 1963.

Merino Falú, Aixa. *Raza, género y clase social: El discrimen contra las mujeres afropuertorriqueñas.* San Juan: Ofician de la Procuradora de las Mujeres, 2004.

Mintz, Sidney W. "The Caribbean as a Socio-cultural Area." In Horowitz, *Peoples and Cultures of the Caribbean,* 17–46.

———. "The Rural Proletariat and the Problem of Rural Proletariat Consciousness." *Journal of Peasant Studies* 1 (1974): 291–325.

Mintz, Sidney, and Eric Wolf. "An Analysis of Ritual Co-Parenthood," *Southwestern Journal of Anthropology* 6, no. 4 (1950): 341–68.

Molyneux, Maxine, and Elizabeth Dore, eds. *Hidden Histories of Gender and the State in Latin America.* Durham: Duke University Press, 2000.

Momsen, Janet, and Jean Besson, eds. *Land and Development in the Caribbean.* London: Warwick University Caribbean Studies, 1987.

Montgomery, David. *Citizen Worker: The Experience of Workers in the United States with Democracy and the Free Market during the Nineteenth Century.* Cambridge: Cambridge University Press, 1993.

Morales Carrión, Arturo. *Puerto Rico: A Political and Cultural History.* New York: W. W. Norton and Co, 1983.

Morelli, Frederica. "Territorial Hierarchies and Collective Identities." In Roniger and Herzog, *The Collective and the Public,* 37–56.

Muñoz Rivera, Luis. *Obras Completas, seleccionadas y recopiladas por Luis Muñoz Marín.* Madrid: Editorial Puerto Rico, 1925.

Nash, June. *We Eat the Mines and the Mines Eat Us: Dependency and Exploitation in Bolivian Tine Mines*. New York: Columbia University Press, 1993.

Navarro Azcue, Concepción. *La abolición de la esclavitud negra en la legislación española, 1870–1886*. Madrid: Ediciones Cultura Hispánica, 1987.

Nazario Velasco, Rubén. "Negociación en la tradición legal: Los abogados y el estado colonial de Puerto Rico, 1898–1905." PhD Dissertation, University of Puerto Rico, 1996.

———. *Discurso legal y orden poscolonial: Los abogados de Puerto Rico ante el 1898*. Hato Rey: Publicaciones Puertorriqueñas, 1999.

Negrón de Montilla, Ada. *La americanización de Puerto Rico y el sistema de instrucción pública, 1900–1930*. Río Piedras: Editorial Universitaria, 1977.

Negrón Portillo, Mariano. *Cuadrillas anexionistas y revueltas campesinas en Puerto Rico, 1898–1899*. Río Piedras: Centro de Investigaciones Sociales, 1987.

Negrón Sanjurjo, Quintín. *Los primeros treinta años de Luis Muñoz Rivera. Terminada en San Juan de Puerto Rico en 1919*. República Dominicana: Editora Corripio, 1993.

Nistal Moret, Benjamín. *Esclavos, prófugos, y cimarrones: Puerto Rico, 1770–1870*. Río Piedras: Editorial de la Universidad de Puerto Rico, 1984.

Nugent, Daniel. *Spent Cartridges of Revolution: An Anthropological History of Namiquipa, Chihuahua*. Chicago: University of Chicago Press, 1993.

Nugent, Daniel, and Gilbert M. Joseph, eds. *Everyday Forms of State Formation: Revolution and the Negotiation of Rule in Modern Mexico*. Durham: Duke University Press, 1994.

Padilla, Elena. "Contemporary Social-Rural Types in the Caribbean Region," in *Caribbean Studies: A Symposium. Institute of Social and Economic Research*. V. Rubin. Jamaica: University College of the West Indies, 1957: 22–29.

Paquette, Robert L. *Sugar Is Made with Blood: The Conspiracy of La Escalera and the Conflict Between Empires over Slavery in Cuba*. Middletown CT: Wesleyan University Press, 1988.

Pateman, Carol. *The Sexual Contract*. Stanford: Stanford University Press, 1988.

Pedreira, Antonio S. *Tres ensayos*. Río Piedras: Editorial Edil, 1969.

Peloso, Vincent C., and Barbara A. Tenenbaum, eds. *Liberals, Politics, and Power: State Formation in Nineteenth-Century Latin America*. Athens: University of Georgia Press, 1996.

Picó, Fernando. *1898: La guerra después de la guerra*. Río Piedras: Ediciones Huracán, 1987.

———. *Amargo cafe: los pequeños y medianos caficultores de Utuado en la mitad del siglo XIX*. Río Piedras: Ediciones Huracán, 1985.

———. "Cafetal Adentro: Una historia de los trabajadores agrícolas en el Puerto Rico del siglo 19." *El Sol: Revista Oficial de la Asociación de Maestros de Puerto Rico* 30, no. 1 (1986): 1–36.

———. *El día menos pensado: historia de los presidarios en Puerto Rico (1793–1993)*. Río Piedras: Ediciones Huracán, 1994.

———. "Fuentes para la historia de las comunidades rurales en Puerto Rico durante los siglos 19 y 20." *Op. Cit: Boletin del Centro de Investigaciones Historicas* 1, no. 1 (1985): 1–14.

———. *Los gallos peleados*. Río Piedras: Ediciones Huracán, 1988.

———. *Libertad y servidumbre en el Puerto Rico del Siglo XIX*. Río Piedras: Ediciones Huracán, 1983.

————. "Las trabajadoras del tabaco en Utuado, Puerto Rico, segun el censo de 1910." *Homines* 9, nos. 1–2 (1985): 268–82.

Picó Vidal, Isabel. "Derecho de familia y cambio social: Una interpretación historico-social de la reforma de la administración de los bienes gananciales," *Revista Jurídica de la Universidad de Puerto Rico* 55 (1986): 537–85.

Pocock, J. G. A. "The Ideal of Citizenship since Classical Times." In Beiner, *Theorizing Citizenship*, 29–52.

Puerto Rico Reconstruction Administration. *Puerto Rico: A Guide to The Island of Boriquén.* New York: The University Society, 1940.

Quiles, Inés M. *Memoria oral de la ciudad de Caguas.* Caguas: Gobierno Municipal de Caguas, 1994.

Quiñones Calderón, Antonio. *Trayectoria política de Puerto Rico.* San Juan: Ediciones Nuevas de Puerto Rico, 1988.

Quintero Rivera, Angel G. "La clase obrera y el proceso politico en Puerto Rico." *Revista de Ciencias Sociales* 18, nos. 3–4 (1974): 61–107.

————. "La dominación imperialista del Estado en Puerto Rico y la política obrera (1900–1934)." *Revista Mexicana de Sociología* 40, no. 3 (1978): 1119–39.

————. "La ideología populista y la institucionalización universitaria de las ciencias socials." In Álvarez Curbelo and Rodríguez Castro, *Del nacionalismo al populismo*, 107–45.

————. *Patricios y plebeyos, burgueses, hacendados, artesanos y obreros: las relaciones de clase en el Puerto Rico de cambio de siglo.* Río Piedras: Ediciones Huracán, 1988.

Raldiris, J. P. *Higiene, puericultura, bacteriología, patología médica y terapéutica clínica: Libro consagrado a la conservación de la salud y a la vulgarización científica.* Barcelona: Imprenta de la viuda de Luis Tasso, 1925.

Rama, Angel. *The Lettered City.* Durham: Duke University Press, 1996.

Ramírez de Arellano, Annette B. "La escuela de medicina tropical: Raíces ideológicas e imperativos políticos." *Revista de Historia* 2, no. 4 (1986): 102–20.

Reyes, Jaime M. F. *La Santa Montaña de San Lorenzo, Puerto Rico, y el misterio de Elenita de Jesús (1899–1909).* San Lorenzo: Librería Santuario de la Virgen del Carmen, 1991.

Riesenberg, Peter. *Citizenship in the Western Tradition: Plato to Rousseau.* Chapel Hill: University of North Carolina Press, 1992.

Rigau-Pérez, José G. "The Introduction of Smallpox Vaccine in 1803 and the Adoption of Immunization as a Government Function in Puerto Rico." *Hispanic American Historical Review* 69, no. 3 (1989): 393–423.

Riggs, George A. *Baptists in Puerto Rico: Brief Historical Notes of Forty Years of Baptist Work in Puerto Rico, 1899–1939.* Ponce: Puerto Rico Evangélico, [1939].

Rivera Nieves, Irma N. *El tema de la mujer en el pensamiento social de Hostos,* Río Piedras: Editorial de la Universidad de Puerto Rico, 1992.

Rivera Quintero, Marcia, "Educational Policy and Female Labor, 1898–1930." In Zavala and Rodríguez, *The Intellectual Roots of Independence*, 349–53.

————. "El femenismo obrero en la lucha de clases en Puerto Rico, 1900–1920," Colegio de Abogados, Segunda Conferencia de la Mujer Trabajadora, 1981.

Rivera Ramos, Efrén. *The Legal Construction of Identity: The Judicial and Social Legacy of American Colonialism in Puerto Rico.* Washington DC: America Psychological Association, 2001.

Rodríguez Nieves, Héctor. "Las fluctuaciones en la población de Cayey, 1815–1861." MA thesis, University of Puerto Rico, 1980.

Rogler, Charles C. *Comerío: A Study of a Puerto Rican Town.* Lawrence: University of Kansas, 1940.

Román, Madeline. *Estado y criminalidad en Puerto Rico: un abordaje criminológico alternativo.* San Juan: Publicaciones Puertorriqueñas, 1993.

Romero Cantero, Calixto. "Agentes Higiénicos." *El EcoMédico Farmacéutico de Puerto Rico* 1, no. 6 (1882): 107.

Roniger, Luis, and Tamar Herzog, eds. *The Collective and the Public in Latin America: Cultural Identities and Political Order.* Portland: Sussex Academic Press, 2000.

Rosario, José Colombán. *Implicaciones educativas de los problemas socio-económicos de Puerto Rico.* Río Piedras: U.P.R. Sala de la Colección Puertorriqueña.

———. *The Development of the Puerto Rican Jíbaro and His Present Attitude Towards Society.* New York: Arno Press, 1975.

Rosario Rivera, Raquel. *La Real Cédula de Gracias de 1815 y sus primeros efectos en Puerto Rico.* San Juan: First Book Publishing of P.R., 1995.

Roseberry, William. *Coffee and Capitalism in the Venezuelan Andes.* Austin: University of Texas Press, 1983.

Ruggiero, Guido. *The Boundaries of Eros: Sex Crime and Sexuality in Renaissance Venice.* New York: Oxford University Press, 1995.

Ruiz Arnau, Dr. R. *Influencia en la medicina del carácter de los pueblos,* Conferencia dada en el Ateneo Puertorriqueño el 25 de abril, Boletín Mercantil, 1904.

Ryan, Mary P. *Civic Wars: Democracy and Public Life in the American City during the Nineteenth Century.* Berkeley: University of California Press, 1997.

Salvatore, Ricardo D. "The Enterprise of Knowledge: Representational Machines of Informal Empire." In *Close Encounters of Empire: Writing the Cultural History of U.S.–Latin American Relations,* edited by Gilbert M. Joseph, Catherine C. LeGrand, and Ricardo D. Salvatore, 69–104. Durham: Duke University Press, 1998.

San Miguel, Pedro L. *Los campesinos del Cibao: Economía agraria en la República Dominicana, 1880–1960.* San Juan: Editorial de la Universidad de Puerto Rico, 1997.

———. "Peasant Resistance to State Demands in the Cibao during the U.S. Occupation." *Latin American Perspectives* 22, no. 3 (1995): 41–62.

Sanders, James E. " 'Citizens of a Free People': Popular Liberalism and Race in Nineteenth-Century Southwestern Columbia," *Hispanic American Historical Review* 84, no. 2 (2004): 275–313.

———. *Contentious Republicans: Popular Politics, Race, and Class in Nineteenth-Century Columbia.* Durham: Duke University Press, 2004.

Santaella Rivera, Rev. P. Esteban. *Historia de los Hermanos Cheos: Recopilación de escritos y relatos.* Santo Domingo: Editora Alfa y Omega, 1979.

Santiago González, Joaquín. "El régimen de la propiedad rural en Puerto Rico: patrones de tenencia de tierra en Aibonito, 1750–1898." MA thesis, University of Puerto Rico, 1989.

Santiago-Valle, Kelvin A. *"Subject People" and Colonial Discourses: Economic Transformation and Social Disorder in Puerto Rico, 1898–1947.* Albany: State University of New York Press, 1994.

Sartorius, David. "Conucos y subsistencia: el caso del ingenio Santa Rosalía," in Martínez Heredia, Scott, and García Martínez, *Espacios, silencios, y los sentidos,* 108–27.

Scarano, Francisco A. *Sugar and Slavery in Puerto Rico: The Plantation Economy of Ponce, 1800–1850.* Madison: University of Wisconsin Press, 1984.

———. *Inmigración y clases sociales en el Puerto Rico del siglo XIX.* Río Piedras: Ediciones Huracán, 1985.

———. "The Jíbaro Masquerade and the Subaltern Politics of Creole Identity Formation in Puerto Rico, 1745–1823." *American Historical Review,* 101, no. 5 (1996): 1398–1431.

Scheper-Hughes, Nancy. *Death without Weeping: The Violence of Everyday Life in Brazil.* Berkeley: University of California Press, 1992.

Schmidt-Nowara, Christopher Ebert. "The Problem of Slavery in the Age of Capital: Abolitionism, Liberalism, and Counter-Hegemony in Spain, Cuba, and Puerto Rico, 1833–1886." PhD Dissertation, University of Michigan, 1995.

Schudson, Michael. *The Good Citizen: A History of American Civic Life.* New York: The Free Press, 1998.

Schwartz, Stuart B. *Sugar Plantation in the Formation of Brazilian Society, Bahia, 1550–1835.* Cambridge: Cambridge University Press, 1985.

Scott, Rebecca J. *Slave Emancipation in Cuba: The Transition to Free Labor, 1860–1899.* Princeton: Princeton University Press, 1985.

Seda, Carmen L. "Participación gubernamental en el desarrollo del cooperativismo agrícola en Puerto Rico." MA thesis, University of Puerto Rico, 1985.

Seda Prado, Jorge. *El campesinado en Puerto Rico a fines del siglo XIX y principios del XX: El caso de Toa Alta 1894–1910.* Río Piedras: Ediciones Huracán, 1996.

Seipp, Conrad, and Annete B. Ramírez. *Colonialism, Catholicism, and Contraception: A History of Birth Control in Puerto Rico.* Chapel Hill: University of North Carolina Press, 1983.

Sharpe, Keneth Evan. *Peasant Politics: Struggle in a Dominican Village.* Baltimore: Johns Hopkins University Press, 1977.

Silva, Ana Margarita. *El jíbaro en la literatura de Puerto Rico (Comparado con el campesino de España e Hispanoamérica).* San Juan: N.p., 1957.

Silva Gotay, Samuel. *Protestantismo y política en Puerto Rico. 1898–1930: Hacia una historia del protestantismo evangélico en Puerto Rico.* Río Piedras: Editorial de la Universidad de Puerto Rico, 1997.

Silvestrini, Blanca G. "Women as Workers: The Experience of the Puerto Rican Woman in the 1930s." In *The Puerto Rican Woman: Perspectives on Culture, History, and Society,* edited by Edna Acosta-Belén, 59–74. New York: Praeger, 1986.

Silvestrini de Pacheco, Blanca. *Violencia y criminalidad en Puerto Rico (1898–1973): Apuntes para un estudio de historia social.* Río Piedras: Editorial Universitaria, 1980.

———, ed. *Politics, Society and Culture in the Caribbean.* San Juan: Universidad de Puerto Rico, 1983.

Sklar, Martin. *The Corporate Reconstruction of American Capitalism, 1890–1916: The Market, the Law, and Politics.* Cambridge: Cambridge University Press, 1988.

Smith, Raymond T. *The Negro Family in British Guiana: Family Structure and Social Status in the Villages.* New York: Routledge, 1956.

———. "Race, Class, and Gender in the Transition to Freedom." In McGlynn and Drescher, *The Meaning of Freedom,* 257–90.

Socolow, Susan Migden. "Putting the 'Cult' in Culture." *Hispanic American Historical Review* 79, no. 2 (1999): 355–65.

Stavig, Ward. *The World of Túpac Amaru: Conflict, Community, and Identity in Colonial Peru*. Lincoln: University of Nebraska Press, 1999.

Stein, Stanley J. *Vassouras: A Brazilian Coffee County, 1850–1900: The Roles of Planter and Slave in a Plantation Society*. Princeton: Princeton University Press, 1985.

Stern, Steve J. "The Struggle for Solidarity: Class, Culture, and Community in Highland Indian America." *Radical History Review* 27 (1983): 21–45.

———. *The Secret History of Gender: Women, Men, and Power in Late Colonial Mexico*. Chapel Hill: University of North Carolina Press, 1995.

Steward, Julian H. et. al. *The People of Puerto Rico*. Urbana: University of Illinois Press, 1972.

Stinson Fernández, John. "Hacia una antropología de la emigración planificada: El Negociado de Empleo y Migración y el caso de Filadelfia." *Revista de Ciencias Sociales: Nueva Época* 1 (1996): 112–55.

Stolcke, Verena. *Coffee Planters, Workers and Wives: Class Conflict and Gender Relations on Sao Paulo Plantations, 1850–1980*. New York: San Martin's Press, 1988.

Stoler, Ann Laura. *Race and the Education of Desire: Foucault's History of Sexuality and the Colonial Order of Things*. Durham: Duke University Press, 1995.

Suárez Findlay, Eileen J. *Imposing Decency: The Politics of Sexuality and Race in Puerto Rico, 1870–1920*. Durham: Duke University Press, 1999.

Taylor, Solatia M. "A Visit to Baptist Missionaries in Porto Rico." *Missions* 5, no. 7 (1914): 582–84.

Taylor, William B. *Drinking, Homicide and Rebellion in Colonial Mexican Villages*. Stanford: Stanford University Press, 1979.

Thomas, Clive Y. *Plantations, Peasants, and State: A Study of the Mode of Sugar Production in Guyana*. Los Angeles: Center for Afro-American Studies, University of California, 1984.

Thompson, E. P. *Customs in Common*. New York: New Press, 1991.

Thurner, Mark. *From Two Republics to One Divided: Contradictions of Postcolonial Nationmaking in Andean Peru*. Durham: Duke University Press, 1997.

Tilly, Charles, ed. *Citizenship, Identity and Social History*. New York: Press Syndicate of he University of Cambridge, 1995.

Torrech San Inocencio, Rafael A. "Los Barrios de Caguas," *Historia y arqueología del Valle del Turabo* 4, no. 1 (2000): 96–114.

Trías Monge, José. *El sistema judicial de Puerto Rico*. Santo Domingo: Editorial de la Universidad de Puerto Rico, 1988.

———. *Historia constitucional de Puerto Rico*, vol. 1. Río Piedras: Editorial Universitaria, 1980.

Trouillot, Michel-Ralph. "Discourses of Rule and the Acknowledgment of the Peasantry in Dominica, W.I., 1838–1928." *American Ethnologist* 16, no. 4 (1989): 704–15.

———. "The Inconvenience of Freedom: Free People of Color and the Political Aftermath of Slavery in Dominica and Saint-Domingue/Haiti." In McGlynn and Drescher, *The Meaning of Freedom*, 147–82.

———. *Peasants and Capital: Dominica in the World Economy*. Baltimore: Johns Hopkins University Press, 1988.

———. *Silencing the Past: Power and the Production of History.* Boston: Beacon Press, 1995.

Turner, Bryan S., ed. *Citizenship and Social Theory.* London: Sage Publications, 1993.

Twinam, Ann. "The Negotiation of Honor: Elites, Sexuality, and Illegitimacy in Eighteenth-Century Spanish America." In Johnson and Lipsett-Rivera, *The Faces of Honor,* 68–102.

U.S. Bureau of the Census. *Fourteenth Census of Population, 1920. Porto Rico.* Washington DC: National Archives and Records Administration, 1920.

———. *Thirteenth Census of Population, 1910. Porto Rico,* Washington DC: National Archives and Records Administration, 1910.

———. *Thirteenth Census of the United States Taken in the Year 1910.* Vol. VII: Agriculture 1909 and 1910. Washington DC: Government Printing Office, 1913.

Vales, Pedro A. *Patrones de criminalidad en Puerto Rico: Apreciación socio-histórica, 1898–1980.* Puerto Rico: Wanseslao Serra Deliz, 1982.

Varela Ortega, José. *Los amigos políticos: Partidos, elecciones y caciquismo en la Restauración (1875–1900).* Madrid: Alianza Editorial, 1977.

Vassberg, David E. *Land and Society in Golden Age Castile.* New York: Cambridge University Press, 1984.

Vaughan, Mary Kay. "Cultural Approaches to Peasant Politics in the Mexican Revolution." *Hispanic American Historical Review* 79, no. 2 (1999): 269–305.

Verbrugge, Martha H. *Able-Bodied Womanhood: Personal Health and Social Change in Nineteenth-Century Boston.* New York: Oxford University Press, 1988.

War Department, "Annual Reports of the War Department for the Fiscal Year Ended June 30, 1900." Washington DC: Government Printing Office, 1902, 116.

———. "Conditions in Porto Rico. Message from the President of the United States, Transmitting a Report by the Secretary of War Upon Conditions Existing in Porto Rico." 61st Cong., 2nd sess., House of Representatives, 1910.

Walby, Sylvia. *Theorizing Patriarchy.* Cambridge: Basil Blackwell, 1990.

Weinreb, Lloyd L. *Natural Law and Justice.* Cambridge: Harvard University Press, 1987.

Williams, Eric. *From Columbus to Castro: The History of the Caribbean, 1492–1969.* New York: Vintage Books, 1970.

Williams, Raymond. *The Country and the City.* New York: Oxford University Press, 1973.

———. *Marxism and Literature.* Oxford: Oxford University Press 1977.

Williams, Robert G. *States and Social Evolution: Coffee and the Rise of National Governments in Central America.* Chapel Hill: University of North Carolina Press, 1994.

Wilson, Peter J. *Crab Antics: The Social Anthropology of English-Speaking Negro Societies of the Catibbea.* New Haven: Yale University Press, 1973.

Wolf, Eric R. "Closed Corporate Peasant Communities in Mesoamerica and Central Java." *Southwestern Journal of Anthropology* 13, no. 1 (1957): 1–18.

———. "The Vicissitudes of the Closed Corporate Peasant Community." *American Ethnologist* 13 (1986): 325–29.

Zavala, Iris M., and Rafael Rodríguez, eds. *The Intellectual Roots of Independence: An Anthology of Puerto Rican Political Essays.* New York: Monthly Review Press, 1980.

Zeno, Francisco M. *El obrero agrícola o de los campos.* San Juan: Imprenta y Librería "La Correspondencia de Puerto Rico," 1922?

Zeno Gandía, Manuel. *La Charca.* Mexico: Editorial Orion, 1965.

Index

Abbad, Fray Iñigo, 2
Abril, Mariano, 111
Acosta, Luis, 30, 56
Acosta, Serafín, 36
agriculture, 3–5; diversity of, products, 12–13; economic structure of Caguas and, 7–15, 136–37n15; farm sizes and, 13–15, 32, 63–65, 119–21, 140n37; people of color working in, 63–65; sharecroppers involved in, 13–15, 44, 46–47, 59, 67–68; taxation of farm laborers working in, 43; taxation of farms and, 43–44, 46–47. *See also* barrios of Caguas; land
Aguayo, Nicolás, 27, 38, 151–52n90
Álamo, Victorio, 56
alcaldes and comisarios de barrio, 146 n49, 150–51n82; ordinance for the comisarios of, 129–30; powers and duties of, 29–37, 81–82, 113–14; structure of comisarios de, 29–36
Allen, Charles H., 86
Almelia, Ramona, 99–100
Álvarez, Carmen, 100
Álvarez, Ramón, 27, 32
Álvarez Curbelo, Silvia, 17
American Federation of Labor, 88
Aponte, Joaquín, 31, 82
Aponte, Landelino, 27, 48, 50, 63, 143n22
Arroyo, Gregorio, 35–36, 58
Ashford, Bailey K., 71–72, 87
ayuntamientos, 29, 33, 34
Azuaga, Claudia, 103

Báez, Francisco, 92
barrios of Caguas: alcaldes of, 29–36; economic structure of, 8–15; farm sizes within different, 13–15, 119–20; illegal games and cockfights in, 81–82; occupations of people in, 9–10; urban *versus* rural, 138n11. *See also* peasantry of Caguas
Benítez, Tomás, 79
Bernal, Anselma, 94

Bobo, Juan, 60
Borrás, Bartolomé, 50
Borrás, Pascual, 3

Caballero, Ruperto, 34
Caraballo, Rosa, 84
Carattini, Gerardo, 100
Caribbean, the: civil rights in, 85; former slaves in, 63, 85, 170n95; landed elite of, 67; plantations of, 20; privatization of land in, 67, 159n74; racial tensions in, 60, 61, 65; settlement of, by Spain, 1, 2; urbanization of, 5
Carrasco y Sosa, Jesús, 104
Carrasquillo, Lino, 111
Castro, Tomás de, 1
Catholic Church, the: consensual unions and, 96–97; on family life and righteous sexuality, 90–92; marriage in, 101
cattle theft, 56–57, 155n30
cédulas de Gracias, 40–41
cédulas de vecindad, 74–77, 79, 115, 117
chicken thievery, 57–58
children, 104–5, 175n49; of consensual unions, 97–98; inheritance laws affecting, 107–8
citizenship: of colonial Puerto Ricans, 15–21; concept of marginal, 116–17; of Creoles, 16
Civil Code of 1890, 42
Civil Code of 1902, 43
Civil disobedience in Caguas: restriction of laborers' mobility to prevent, 74–76
Claudio, Petrona, 104
Clavijo, Juan, 103
cockfights, 81–82, 168n73
coffee production in Puerto Rico, 8
Colombán Rosario, José, 97
comisarios. *See* Alcaldes and comisarios de barrio
Concepción Rivera, Celia, 111
consensual unions, 174n32; children of, 97–98; defined, 96; elopements and, 99–100; legitimacy of, 96–97; rates of, 100–101. *See also* marriage

LaVergne, TN USA
20 August 2010
194026LV00003B/61/P